Physical Distribution Systems

Physical distribution is a major growth area in the economy and subject to a rapid rate of technological and managerial change. The efficient distribution of goods from factories to shops is now recognised as a major determinant of company profitability and general economic well-being.

The book provides a detailed insight into the planning and operation of distribution systems. It concentrates on the movement and storage of finished goods, examining how these activities have evolved, how they can be optimised and how firms actually organise them in practice. The general principles of physical distribution are clearly explained with the aid of numerous examples and illustrations. Particular emphasis is placed on the relationship between physical distribution and marketing and on the spatial structure of distribution systems.

The text will be of interest to students of business studies, marketing, economics, geography, operations research and transport. For those engaged in the planning and management of distribution, it offers a general overview of the subject and a full discussion of key strategic issues.

Dr Alan McKinnon is a lecturer in the Department of Business Organisation at Heriot-Watt University, Edinburgh. He has lectured and researched on physical distribution for over 10 years and published widely on the subject.

PHYSICAL DISTRIBUTION SYSTEMS

Alan. C. McKinnon

Routledge
London and New York

First published in 1989 by
Routledge
11 New Fetter Lane, London EC4P 4EE
29 West 35th Street, New York NY 10001

©1989 Alan C. McKinnon

Typeset by LaserScript Limited, Mitcham, Surrey

Printed in Great Britain by Billing & Sons Ltd, Worcester

British Library Cataloguing in Publication Data

McKinnon, Alan C., 1953-
  Physical distribution systems.
  1. Goods. Physical distribution.
  Management
  I. Title
  658.7'88

  ISBN 0-415-00438-1
  ISBN 0-415-03028-5 Pbk

Library of Congress Cataloging in Publication Data

McKinnon, Alan C., 1953-
  Physical distribution systems/by Alan C. McKinnon.
       p.   cm.
  Bibliography: p.
  Includes index.
  ISBN 0-415-00438-1.   ISBN 0-415-03028-5 (pbk.)
  1. Physical distribution of goods.   I. Title.
HF5415.6.M37 1989   88-25963
658.7'88—dc 19   CIP

To Sabine, Philip and Christopher

Contents

Figures

Tables

Preface

Authors of early books and articles on physical distribution had the problem of convincing people of the subject's importance. Now that it has gained wide recognition, a new set of problems has arisen. First, there is the need to address a larger and more varied readership, ranging from the manager with day-to-day involvement in distribution to the undergraduate student with no prior knowledge or experience in this area. Another problem is that of reviewing the extensive literature on the subject that has accumulated in recent years. This task is made all the more difficult by the fact that relevant work has been done in a variety of disciplines. This poses a further problem in that specialists often have different perspectives on the subject. For example, with my background in geography, I felt that many previous works devoted too little attention to the spatial organisation of physical distribution, a deficiency I have tried to correct in this book. In so doing, however, I may have diverted attention from other aspects of the subject that, in the opinion of some readers, deserve fuller treatment.

One problem which afflicted early writing on physical distribution remains acute today. This is the lack of general information about existing distribution systems. Over the past quarter century, researchers have been much more interested in optimising individual firms' distribution systems than in undertaking comparative studies of actual distribution operations. In the absence of an official 'census of physical distribution', comparable to the Census of Production, we have had to rely on case study material and the results of small sample surveys. It has, therefore, been difficult to judge the extent to which distribution systems exhibit particular characteristics and to monitor trends, such as the centralisation of inventory or consolidation of flows. Only in the case of the food and drink sector, has sufficient information been compiled in the UK to permit a reasonable degree of generalisation. The distribution of food and drink is thus given greater prominence in this book than that of other products. While this sector serves as a useful model, it would be wrong to infer that physical distribution is organised in an identical manner in other industries. To be able to build up a more comprehensive picture of how firms actually distribute their products, we shall require much more extensive surveys than have so far been attempted.

I am particularly indebted to the many people who have helped me at various stages in the planning and preparation of this book: particularly to the numerous distribution directors and managers who have painstakingly described their firms' operations and to fellow academics and students with whom I have had long and stimulating discussions on the subject. Special thanks must go to Jim Cooper, John Fernie and Alasdair Macleod for reading the original manuscript and suggesting many improvements. I, however, must accept responsibility for any errors and omissions in the final version. I am also grateful to Kate Moore, Ruth Pollington and Graeme Lewis for drawing the illustrations. Finally I must record a great debt to my wife, Sabine and son, Philip who have had to compete with this book for my attention for far too long.

Acknowledgements

The author and publishers gratefully acknowledge permission to reproduce, either in original or amended form, the following copyright material:

Figure 4.6 from Williams (1975), with the permission of the National Materials Handling Centre; Figure 5.3 from McKinnon (1986a), with permission from The Planner, Journal of the Royal Town Planning Institute; Figure 5.4 from McKinnon (1983) with the permission of Pergamon Press; Figure 7.7 from Slater (1980) with the permission of MCB Press; Figure 9.1 from McKinnon (1986b) with the permission of the Centre for Transportation Studies, University of British Columbia; Tables 7.2 and 9.2 from, respectively, Margason and Corcoran (1978) and Baugham et al. (1983) with the permission of the Transport and Road Research Laboratory; Table 7.3 from McDermott (1975) with the permission of the American Society of Transportation and Logistics.

Abbreviations

ANA	Article Number Association
AS/RS	Automated Storage/Retrieval Systems
AVI	Automatic Vehicle Guidance
BR	British Rail
C and F	Cost and Freight
CIF	Cost, Insurance, Freight
CPA	Customer Profitability Analysis
CPDM	Centre for Physical Distribution Management
DIY	Do-it-yourself
DPP	Direct Product Profitability
DRP	Distribution Requirements Planning
DSS	Decision Support System
DTp	Department of Transport (UK)
EC	European Community
EDI	Electronic Data Interchange
EMC	Export Management Company
EOQ	Economic Order Quantity
EPOS	Electronic Point of Sale
FAS	Free alongside Ship
FOB	Free on Board
FRC	Free Carrier
GDP	Gross Domestic Product
GLC	Greater London Council
GNP	Gross National Product
GVW	Gross Vehicle Weight
HCV	Heavy Commercial Vehicle
ICD	Inland Container Depot
IGD	Institute of Grocery Distribution
ILDM	Institute of Logistics and Distribution Management (1986-)
IPDM	Institute of Physical Distribution Management (1981-6)
ISO	International Standards Organisation

JIT	Just-in-Time
LDI	Logistics Data Interchange
LIS	Logistical Information System
LoLo	Lift-on, Lift-off
LRP	Logistics Requirements Planning
MRP	Materials Requirements Planning
NEDO	National Economic Development Office
OECD	Organisation for Economic Co-operation and Development
PDET	Portable Data Entry Terminal
PDM	Physical Distribution Management
PSERC	Public Sector Economics Research Centre
QHV	Quiet Heavy Vehicle
RDC	Regional Distribution Centre
RDSS	Radio Determination Satellite Service
RoRo	Roll-on, Roll-off
RPM	Resale Price Maintenance
SKU	Stock-keeping Unit
TDC	Total Distribution Cost
TRRL	Transport and Road Research Laboratory
ULW	Unladen Weight

Chapter one

Introduction

Rising status of physical distribution

People today place enormous faith in the system of distribution that supplies them with material goods. Consumers are confident that shops will be replenished and seldom enquire how goods find their way onto the retailers' shelves. Only when the supply of goods is interrupted by, for example, bad weather or industrial disputes, does distribution attract much public attention. Most people, therefore, have little appreciation of the scale and complexity of the distributive system. Even fewer are familiar with the expression *physical distribution*.

Physical distribution is the collective term for the series of inter-related functions (principally transport, stockholding, storage, goods handling and order processing) involved in the physical transfer of finished goods from producer to consumer, directly or via intermediaries. Some definitions of physical distribution include the movement and storage of raw materials and semi-finished goods, but the term *logistics* is more commonly used to describe the complete product flow from raw material source to final point of sale (Gattorna, 1983). In this book, attention will focus on the distribution of finished products, though on some topics, such as modal choice, it will be necessary to take a broader logistical perspective.

It is only recently that the full importance of physical distribution has been recognised in industrial and business circles. In 1958, for example, Stacey and Wilson noted that 'preoccupation with planning production, purchasing and sales often tends to relegate consideration of the actual movement of finished goods to a secondary role' (p.278). Distributive functions were commonly regarded as 'low grade nuisances' (Drucker, 1962), accorded little managerial status and assigned less able staff. Warehousing was often considered to be a 'necessary evil' (Warman, 1971) and freight transport 'a dismal calculus of rates and routes' (Alexander, 1969). Neither activity was felt to make a significant contribution to profitability nor to be worthy of much capital investment.

Over the past 30 years, however, managerial attitudes to distribution have been transformed. Today, distribution is generally considered to be a major cost centre, an important marketing tool and a critical determinant of profitability. There is much greater acceptance of the fact that the 'processes of manufacturing and distribution are complementary' and that 'an unsold product, however efficiently produced, represents a waste of resources' (Edwards, 1982, p.11). As a consequence, distribution now ranks highly in corporate affairs. In many firms, distribution managers are on equal terms with their counterparts in production, marketing and finance, while in some distribution has separate representation at board level. Through the introduction of specialist training programmes and the establishment of bodies such as the Institute of Logistics and Distribution Management in the UK and the Council of Logistics Management in the US, distribution has gained professional status and become a focus of academic and business research. Managerial and conceptual reforms have been accompanied by sweeping changes in the physical structure of firms' distribution systems. The application of new distribution principles, over a period of rapid economic, technological and infrastructural change, has radically altered patterns of stockholding and freight movement throughout the developed world.

Several attempts have been made to identify the factors that triggered the revolution in physical distribution in the late 1950s (Stewart, 1965; Bowersox, 1978; Ballou, 1978). This revolution should be seen within the context of long-term economic development. Kotler (1967) divides this development into three stages: the first characterised by a shortage of goods, the second a transitional period during which supply and demand come into balance and a third age of mass production when sales are constrained more by limited demand than by the amount of industrial capacity available. In the first two stages, industry's prime concern is to enhance the level of production. In the third stage, increasing emphasis is placed on marketing in an effort to generate additional sales. In the US, UK and other countries that became industrialised in the nineteenth century, many firms entered the third stage during the inter-war period, and since then have been forced to intensify their marketing effort by increasing competition.

Some of the early authorities on marketing regarded physical distribution as a key element in marketing strategy (La Londe and Dawson, 1969). Until the late 1950s, however, most firms were much more concerned about the promotion and merchandising of their products than about their distribution. In the early post-war years, most firms had little cause to upgrade their distribution systems as sales of industrial and consumer goods were buoyant and profits high. During this period, 'a certain amount of inefficiency in distribution could be tolerated' (Ballou, 1978, p.15). Periods of recession in the late 1950s and 1960s, coupled with mounting competition, awakened firms to the need to control costs and raise efficiency. By this time, other spheres of company business, such as production and marketing, had been overhauled, leaving distribution as 'the frontier of cost reduction' (Stewart, 1965). Prior to 1960, though, few firms possessed enough cost data to know how they might economise on distribution. One exception was Unilever, which in its 1955 Annual Report (quoted in Stacey and Wilson, 1958) demonstrated the importance of its physical distribution activities with a few startling statistics. The firm estimated, for example, that a delay of a single day in the flow of its products would absorb an additional £5 million of working capital. It also compared the 13 man hours of labour input that went into producing a ton of washing powder with the 19 man hours it required to transport this load 200 miles from the factory. In the following decade, many other firms subjected their distribution systems to detailed costing for the first time, exposing numerous inefficiencies and wide scope for rationalisation.

Distribution was also becoming a more important item in company accounts as the costs of transport, warehousing and stockholding were rising relative to the costs of other industrial inputs. Marketing initiatives, such as the extension of product lines and the penetration of new marketing channels, were imposing increasing strains on distribution systems, making them more difficult to manage and more costly to operate (Bowersox, Smykay and La Londe, 1968). Manufacturers were also having to modify their distribution operations in response to structural changes in wholesaling and retailing. The concentration of buying power at the retail level, for example, enabled large multiples to set more exacting standards for the delivery of supplies to their shops and warehouses (Johnson and Wood, 1982). Firms also reorganised their distribution systems to take advantage of the major improvements that were being made to transport infrastructure, particularly to the road network, vehicle performance and goods handling equipment. The advent of the computer greatly eased the collection and analysis of distribution cost data and promoted the use of operations research techniques in distribution planning. Many of these techniques had been developed in the context of military logistics during the Second World War (Smykay, 1964/5), but only found wide commercial application from the late 1950s onwards. More money also became available at this time to restructure and re-equip distribution operations. In European countries, the rebuilding of the manufacturing base, which had absorbed most of the scarce capital in the early post-war years, was, by the late 1950s, well underway, allowing firms to divert more of their resources into distribution (Hill, 1966).

A large number of factors, therefore, combined to create the necessary conditions for a major reassessment of the role of physical distribution in the modern industrial economy.

An integrated approach

Underlying the sweeping changes that have occurred in physical distribution over the past 30 years has been the simple principle that inter-related distribution functions should be planned, managed and costed integrally. Until the late 1950s, all but a few manufacturing firms divided responsibility for distribution between different branches of management. The delivery of goods to customers was usually under the control of the production or sales departments, stockholding administered by the marketing, production or finance departments and order processing handled by sales staff (Ballou, 1978). This fragmentation of managerial responsibility for distribution was disadvantageous in several respects. It gave distributive activities a subordinate role and allowed the main objectives of other branches of management to dictate how they were organised. The desire of production managers to maintain a stable level of processing, for example, led to the accumulation of large volumes of stock at both ends of the production line, while marketing and sales staff typically gave the rapid delivery of customers' orders priority over the efficient operation of delivery vehicles. The costs of individual distribution functions were generally concealed in the budgets of the controlling departments with the result that the impact of production and marketing policies on distribution costs was not properly appraised. Accounting conventions at the time prevented firms from measuring the efficiency of each distribution function separately and, more seriously, obscured the important cost trade-offs that could be made between these functions. Stockholding and storage costs, for instance, could be reduced at the expense of increasing the speed and frequency of freight deliveries, while improvements in packaging could permit higher levels of vehicle and warehouse utilisation. Traditional management structures neither recognised nor exploited the close links between the various distributive activities and provided no means of ensuring that distribution as a whole was organised in an economical and effective manner.

Advocates of the integrated approach to physical distribution found that systems theory provided an ideal conceptual framework for the new management and cost structure they were proposing (e.g. Magee, 1960). By treating distribution as an integrated system, one could examine the interactions between its constituent parts, principally transport, stockholding, storage and order processing, and discover how they should be co-ordinated to optimise the system as a whole (Christopher, 1971). In the early stages, this optimisation exercise was motivated by a desire to minimise the cost of providing a level of distribution service consistent with marketing and sales objectives. Schary (1984, p.5) asserts that 'costs were the initial focus because they provided a tangible measure for improving the system'. As the cost of many of the elements in the distribution system was inversely proportional, the aim was to find the cost trade-off that yielded the lowest total cost. Cost trade-off analysis of this kind was originally proposed by Dupuit (1844) in his work on the economic benefits of transport improvement and first applied in the context of distribution accounting by Heckert and Miner (1953). It was not until the late 1950s, however, that the practice of balancing distribution cost elements began to gain wide recognition. This approach to distribution costing, widely known as the total distribution cost (TDC) approach, was first publicised by airlines in an effort to expand their air-freight business. They argued that, in the case of the expensive cargoes they typically carried, high air-freight rates could be more than offset by the savings in inventory costs that resulted from the use of such a fast and reliable transport service (Lewis, Culliton and Steele, 1956).

All systems are optimised within a series of external constraints. In the case of distribution, a distinction can be made between constraints over which the firm has little control, such as general economic circumstances, government regulations and the prevailing level of technology, and those imposed by other branches of management within the firm. Of the latter, the requirements of the marketing and sales departments bear most heavily on the way in which distribution is organised. Until the mid-1960s, it was generally accepted that these departments should have the right to specify the level of customer service provided by the distribution system. The prime objective of distribution management was then to meet this specification at minimum cost. The goals of minimising distribution costs and maximising revenue were divorced and the latter invariably given priority. No attempt was made to measure the sensitivity of sales revenue to variations in the quality of the distribution service. It was possible, for example, that the standard of the delivery operation could be reduced with little loss of sales, permitting an increase in overall profitability. As Heskett (1966, p.40) noted, 'Unless demand is assumed constant regardless of system design, cost minimisation has little to do with profit maximisation in the physical distribution system'. Poist (1974) suggested that the total cost approach ought to be superseded by a total profit approach and presented a framework within which costs could be balanced against sales with a view to maximising profit. The maximisation of profitability is clearly a preferable goal to minimising distribution costs in isolation, but it requires a redefinition of the traditional relationship between physical distribution and marketing. Such a redefinition was proposed by Stewart (1965) and endorsed by the American Marketing Association (1967). Stewart cast physical distribution in a more positive role by showing how it could be used as a powerful marketing tool, capable of generating additional sales. In contrast to earlier writers on the subject, he stressed the importance of balancing the cost of distribution against the quality of service provided. The American Marketing Association went on to explore the effects of variations in the standard of distribution service on the level of sales and concluded that firms could significantly increase their profits by co-ordinating marketing and distribution more closely. The Association acknowledged, however, that the relationship between distribution service level and sales volumes could not be easily quantified. The effects of physical distribution on revenue generation were, therefore, much less 'tangible' than distribution costs, making it difficult in practice to decide what was an optimal balance between the cost and quality of service. This problem was compounded in many firms by differences in the negotiating strength of marketing, sales and distribution departments. Being longer established and occupying higher positions in the corporate hierarchy, marketing and sales departments have continued to dominate service level decisions. Lynagh and Poist (1984, p.35) observe that:

> very often the marketing department looks upon the physical
> distribution department as cost minimisers with no grasp of
> customers' needs. On the other hand, physical distribution
> managers often see marketing as being only interested in making
> sales with a philosophy of service at any cost.

Attempts have been made to establish closer working relationships between physical distribution and other branches of management, particularly those concerned with the procurement of supplies and the production process. It has been suggested that all the movement, storage and handling of goods within a firm should be considered to belong to a single logistical system. Bowersox (1978, p.11) argues that, 'The perspective of a total movement/storage system provides a higher order of trade-off and greater synergistic potential'. The integration of 'physical supply' and physical distribution can ensure much higher utilisation of vehicles, warehouse space and handling equipment. It can also lead to more co-ordinated efforts to reduce stock levels and accelerate product flows across the broad span of a manufacturer's operations.

It is difficult to generalise about the extent to which the new approach to the management and costing of distribution has been adopted in practice. Several case studies have been presented to show how individual firms have reorganised the management of their distribution operations (e.g. Brouwer, 1971), while La Londe (1974) has given a more general account of the emergence and growth of specialist distribution departments within corporate structures. Many of the case studies reported in the literature, however, are based on the experience of those firms that have been especially innovative in this field and are, therefore, unrepresentative of industry as a whole.

A survey of British manufacturers in 1974 found that only 22% had set up a separate physical distribution department (Whitehead Consulting Group, 1974). The firms consulted also differed markedly in what they considered to be the responsibilities of *physical distribution management* (PDM). Only transport was regarded unanimously as a physical distribution function. A later survey showed some broadening of the scope of PDM, but still found that a large proportion of firms excluded key functions like order processing and inventory control (Kearney, 1980). Even among a group of British firms that were 'active members of the Centre for Physical Distribution Management and others known to have a specific interest in distribution' (p.8) only 45% were able to make quantitative assessments of trade-offs in the physical distribution field. Ray and Gattorna (1980) considered that, although the total cost approach to distribution had been 'widely accepted in principle', many firms were taking a while to put it into practice.

The importance of physical distribution

Availability and customer service

The principal task of physical distribution is to ensure that products are available at the right places at the right time and in the right quantities to satisfy customer demand. Christopher, Schary and Skjøtt-Larsen (1979, p.180) contend that 'Availability should be viewed as the output of the physical distribution system'. Only when products are made available for purchase do they acquire a sales value and can the costs of producing and marketing them be recovered.

Customers generally define 'availability' in terms of the speed with which they can physically obtain supplies. This is principally determined by the adequacy of stocks held at the supply point and the order lead time:

1. Adequacy of supplier's stocks (or 'Product Availability')

Ideally a supplier should have sufficient stock at his factory or distribution depot to meet all customers' demands in full at the time their orders arrive. It is very expensive, however, for firms to hold enough stock to accommodate all possible fluctuations in the level of demand and rate of production. To economise on stockholding, they accept that, on occasion, stocks may prove inadequate and a *stock-out* occurs. The cost of holding stock is then balanced against the risk of losing sales as the result of stock deficiencies. Where stocks of a particular product are exhausted, a firm may be unable to supply a complete order within the specified lead time. The proportion of orders supplied in full within this time constraint is known as the *order fill rate*. Incomplete orders would be topped-up with *back-orders* at a later stage.

2. Order lead (or cycle) time

This is usually defined as the period between a customer ordering goods and their delivery to his premises. Where adequate stocks of the requested products are available at the supply point, the time taken to supply the order depends on the speed of four operations:

1. transmission of the order to the supplier;
2. order processing;
3. physically assembling the goods;
4. transporting them to the customer.

Most firms aim to supply a certain proportion of their orders within a specified lead time. Delivery targets are often poorly defined, though, and sales representatives prone to quote delivery times that distribution departments find it difficult, if not impossible, to meet. The latter practice can be counter-productive because customers are often more concerned about the reliability of order lead times than their average or advertised length (Shipley, 1985).

Although availability is mainly discussed with respect to lead times, it also has an important spatial dimension. Order lead times can vary geographically, with deliveries to more remote customers taking significantly longer than average. Manufacturers can confine the distribution of their products to particular market areas and to certain types of outlet. Small shops, for example, may not generate enough sales to qualify for a delivery. Availability can, therefore, be measured by a series of indices: frequency of stock-outs, order fill rate, back-order rate, average (or target) order lead time, variations in lead times, extent of the market area, numbers and types of delivery points and minimum order size. Thus defined, availability is only one of a series of factors determining the overall quality of a physical distribution service. Several authors (e.g. Perreault and Russ, 1976; La Londe and Zinszer, 1976) have defined physical distribution service more broadly to include other factors such as the following:

1. Convenience of the ordering process.
2. Provision of information about the status of an order (i.e. Progress Information).
3. Adherence to a delivery timetable at the customer's premises.
4. Compatibility of handling equipment and packaging.
5. Condition of the goods on arrival.
6. Order accuracy (i.e. extent to which the items received conform to the order specification).
7. Policy on returned goods.
8. Complaints and claims procedure.

The overall standard of distribution service can have as strong a bearing on customers' purchasing behaviour as prices, promotional activity and the quality of the product. It is difficult, however, to quantify the effect of customer service on sales and profitability. As Willett and Stephenson (1969) observe, there are 'substantial methodological problems in linking manipulable physical distribution variables and buyer response'.

Expenditure

Expenditure on physical distribution has been estimated at the level of individual firms (micro-level) and for the economy as a whole (macro-level):

1. Micro-level

Recent surveys have indicated that physical distribution costs account on average for approximately 8% of the net sales revenue of British and American firms (IPDM, 1986; O'Brien, 1987). One must exercise caution, however, in interpreting these average figures. There have been no comprehensive official surveys of distribution practices and costs in either of these countries. Most of the available cost data have been compiled by private consultancy firms, such as A.T. Kearney and P.W. International in the UK and Davis Database in the US, on the basis of small-sample surveys. Recent British surveys, for example, collected data from around 60-70 firms. The corresponding Data Audit

Table 1.1 Variations in physical distribution costs among industrial sectors

	Distribution costs as % of sales revenue (1984)		
Sector	*Sample Size*	*Mean*	*Range*
Food, drink and tobacco	22	13.4	0.9 – 20.4
Chemicals and allied products	13	6.2	1.9 – 15.7
Electrical engineering	2	14.5	5.5 – 23.5
Textiles, clothing	3	8.2	1.2 – 18.4
Distributive trades	7	11.4	0.5 – 32.3

Source: CPDM, 1984a.

surveys in the US covered only 53 companies in 1982 and 1983 (CPDM, 1984a). Such small samples provide weak bases upon which to generalise for industry as a whole, particularly as they are not stratified by industrial sector. It is common for major industrial sectors to be represented by a single firm. Furthermore, as the samples are not generated randomly, they are likely to be biased, mainly in favour of those firms that have a more positive attitude towards physical distribution and fewer qualms about divulging distribution cost data. In surveys of distribution costs, the composition of the sample is critical, because these costs have been shown to vary greatly within and between industrial sectors (Table 1.1). These variations can be attributed to the following factors:

1. nature of the firm;
2. level of involvement in physical distribution;
3. type of product(s);
4. functions included in physical distribution cost calculation;
5. methods of calculating distribution costs;
6. efficiency of the physical distribution operation.

The available data, nevertheless, indicate that the majority of firms spend a significant proportion of their sales revenue on physical distribution.

Table 1.2 Functional disaggregation of physical distribution costs

	% of total physical distribution costs	
	UK *(1986)*	*US* *(1984)*
Transport	48	46
Inventory	20	22
Storage	25	22
Administration/other	7	10
	100	100

Source: CPDM, 1984a; IPDM, 1986.

Table 1.3   Trends in physical distribution costs in the UK, 1981-6/7

(a) Total cost:				(b) Functional costs:		
	Sample				% of sales	
Survey	Date	Size	% of sales		1981	1986/7
McKibbin	1981	57	12.8	Transport	3.8	3.6
CPDM	1983	66	12.3	Inventory	2.6	1.1
CPDM	1984	67	11.6	Storage	3.5	1.7
IPDM	1985	—	8.3	Administration/other	2.9	1.2
ILDM	1986/7	—	7.6			
				Total	12.8	7.6

Sources: McKibbin, 1982; CPDM, 1983, 1984a; IPDM, 1986; O'Brien, 1987.

Table 1.2 shows the disaggregation of total distribution costs between the primary activities of transport, storage, inventory and administration/order processing/packaging for a sample of British firms. Transport receives slightly more expenditure than stockholding/storage, and together these functions account for roughly 90% of the total distribution budget.

Survey results suggest that distribution costs have declined as a percentage of net sales revenue in recent years (Table 1.3), mainly as a result of reduced expenditure on inventory and storage. This seems to have brought British firms' distribution costs steadily into line with those of their American counterparts (O'Brien, 1986). The available distribution cost data, however, provide a very poor basis upon which to observe general trends. The validity of time series analysis can easily be undermined by changes in the composition of the samples.

Table 1.4   Comparison of distribution cost trends 1984-5: Full and Core[a] Samples

	1984	1985	%
Full Sample			
Storage	2.9	2.5	−0.4
Inventory	1.5	1.0	−0.5
Transport	4.8	3.8	−1.0
Administration etc	2.4	1.1	−1.3
Total	11.6	8.3	−3.3
Core Sample			
Storage	2.1	2.6	+0.5
Inventory	1.0	1.0	0.0
Transport	4.3	4.1	−0.2
Administration etc	1.6	1.2	−0.4
Total	9.0	8.9	−0.1

Note: a. Firms participating in both 1984 and 1985 surveys.

Source: IPDM, 1986.

11

Table 1.5 Main sources of productivity improvement in logistics

Transport:	consolidation of flows
	use of specialist vehicles
	nominated day delivery schemes
	improved vehicle scheduling/routeing
	use of larger vehicles
	unitisation of loads
	improved intermodal transfer
	upgrading of road and rail networks
Warehousing:	increased mechanisation
	use of higher and denser racking
	centralisation of inventory
	improved internal communication
Administration:	management training/education
	installation of computerised information systems

Source: Partly based on A.T. Kearney, 1981.

Recent British and American surveys of distribution costs have experienced a high turnover of participants from year to year. The proportional representation of industrial sectors has also varied through time. Given the wide inter and intrasectoral differences in distribution cost level noted earlier, one would need a reasonably constant statistical base to obtain a reliable indication of changes in average distribution costs through time. Simply comparing sample averages from one year to the next can be misleading as illustrated with reference to the CPDM/IPDM surveys of 1984 and 1985 (Table 1.4). When one compares figures for the complete samples, one finds that, on average, distribution costs fell by 28% relative to sales revenue. Confining the comparison to the subsample of firms that participated in both surveys, one obtains an average figure of only 1% for the reduction in distribution costs. The disparities are even greater when the data are disaggregated by function. Average cost values can, therefore, reflect changes in the composition of the sample much more strongly than actual trends in distribution costs.

Having allowed for these statistical shortcomings, one can still say with some confidence that the costs of physical distribution have declined as a percentage of sales revenue over the past 20 years, despite increases over much of this period in the real cost of distribution inputs. Much of this cost reduction has been achieved by improvements in productivity stemming from the reorganisation of physical distribution over this period (Kearney, 1978, 1980). Table 1.5 lists numerous ways in which productivity has been enhanced. Some cost savings are attributable to factors outside firms' immediate control, such as road improvements.

Table 1.6 UK national expenditure[a] on logistics, 1976 and 1986

	1976 £m	1986 £m	% change
Inventory[b] (excluding appreciation)	9,955	21,896	+120.0
Storage/Materials Handling[c]	11,448	25,179	
Transport	9,940	25,478	+156.3
Total Logistics Expenditure	31,343	72,553	+131.5
Appreciation in the value of inventory	6,557	2,331	−64.5
Net Total	24,786	70,222	+183.3
Gross Domestic Product (at factor cost, expenditure-based)	113,790	319,089	+180.4
Total Logistics Expenditure as % of GDP	27.5	22.7	
Net Logistics Expenditure as % of GDP	21.8	22.0	

Notes: a. At current prices.
  b. Based on average interest rates of 15% in 1976 and 14% in 1986.
  c. Assumes (as in the calculation by Childerley, 1980) that the ratio of storage/materials handling costs to inventory costs was 1.15:1 in both years. As the cost of financing inventory was lower in 1986 than 1976, this allows for some improvement in the productivity of warehousing and materials handling. Productivity gains accruing from the installation of new handling systems, computerisation and better management may have been partly offset by a reduction in the utilisation of warehousing facilities following destocking. The cost estimate for this logistical component is, therefore, highly approximate.

Sources: Central Statistical Office, 1977, 1987a; Childerley, 1980; Department of Transport, 1987.

The true importance of physical distribution to a firm cannot be measured simply in terms of the ratio of distribution costs to sales revenue. The sales revenue figure, after all, gives no indication of how much the firm has contributed to the final value of the product. It would be preferable, therefore, to express distribution costs as a percentage of value added.

The ratio of distribution costs to profit can highlight the sensitivity of profit margins to variations in the efficiency of the distribution operation. Christopher (1981) shows that distribution can offer considerable 'profit leverage' by using the hypothetical example of a firm operating on a net profit margin of 10% with distribution costs accounting for 20% of total costs. A reduction of 10% in this firm's distribution costs would, *ceteris paribus*, yield a 20% increase in profit. Full account should also be taken of the heavy capital costs firms incur in setting up a distribution system and the large amounts of working capital they tie up in inventory. It is not unusual for stocks alone to absorb 20% or more of a company's total financial assets. Firms must, therefore, ensure that capital invested in physical distribution earns an adequate return.

13

2. Macro-level

Official estimates of national expenditure on freight transport and stockholding do not differentiate the distribution of finished goods from the movement and storage of raw materials and semi-finished products. Instead, they relate to the complete logistical system, extending from raw material source to final point of sale.

It was estimated that logistics accounted for 26% of GNP in the US in 1971 (Heskett, Glaskowsky and Ivie, 1973), 22.5% of GDP in the UK in 1976 (Childerley, 1980) and 24.5% of GNP in Canada in 1981 (Schell and Heuer, 1983). Childerley's estimate excluded stockholding by electricity and gas utilities and was based on a method of calculating GDP that was revised in 1978. If one incorporates the electricity and gas industries in the calculation and uses the revised GDP figure for 1976, the estimate of logistics expenditure in that year falls slightly to 21.8% (Table 1.6). In 1986, logistics' share of GDP was marginally higher at 22.0%, despite the fact that the relative amount of stock in the UK economy declined quite sharply during the intervening period. The average book value of stock declined as a percentage of GDP from 34.6% in 1976 to 28.3% in 1986. To explain this apparent anomaly, we must examine the stockholding component in more detail.

While goods are in storage or transit, they represent an investment of working capital. In the UK in 1986 approximately £91 billion was invested in physical stocks. Manufacturers, wholesalers and retailers owned roughly 80% of this stock, around half of it in the form of finished goods. If a firm finances stockholding with borrowed capital, it must pay interest on the loan. If, on the other hand, it chooses to tie up its own assets in stockholding, it still incurs a minimum financial cost at least equivalent to the interest they could have earned if invested elsewhere at prevailing market rates. The financial cost of stockholding is thus largely a function of interest rates. Allowance should also be made for the deterioration of goods while in storage, their gradual obsolescence, insurance charges and the cost of physically storing and handling them. Against all these stockholding costs must be set any increase in the monetary value of stocks resulting from inflation. In 1976, during a period of high inflation, increases in the book value of inventory offset 30.6% of total stockholding costs. The return to lower levels of inflation in the 1980s has reduced the cushioning effect of stock appreciation over a period when interest rates have remained relatively high. As a result, in 1986, price rises offset only 5.0% of stockholding costs. This largely explains why the sharp reduction in stock levels relative to GDP has had little net impact on total logistics' costs.

Logistics therefore accounts for a substantial proportion of national expenditure. As it is essentially a support function, however, embracing a diverse range of activities and widely diffused throughout the economy, its importance can easily be overlooked. Moreover, as the above calculation excludes packaging, order processing and most of the associated communication, it underestimates total logistical expenditure.

Contribution to industrial competitiveness

The performance of a nation's economy is critically dependent on the quality and cost of its logistical support. The cost of distribution affects the total volume of demand in the home market through its influence on the price at which goods are sold. Fast and reliable distribution can also help a country's manufacturers to secure a large share of this market. Christopher (1981) suggests that poor delivery by British producers is partly to blame for the high level of import penetration in the UK. In the case of industries subject to large economies of scale, substantial sales in the home market can reduce unit costs and improve competitiveness in foreign markets. Success in foreign markets can be more directly influenced by the way in which goods are exported. It is more difficult, and yet usually more critical, to distribute goods quickly and cost effectively to foreign customers. The relatively poor performance of some British exporters in foreign markets has been partly attributed to slow, costly and uncertain delivery (Turnbull, 1985).

Another determinant of the competitiveness of manufacturing industry is the amount of stock that it holds. If expenditure on stockholding varied in fixed proportion to manufacturing output, it would have little bearing on relative industrial performance. There are, however, wide international variations in the ratio of manufacturing output to stocks (known as the *rate of stockturn*). These variations have not been fully explained, though they are likely to reflect differences in the composition of national output, interest rates, systems of taxation, stability of the economic system, marketing practices, management traditions and the structure of the distributive trades. The rate of stockturn serves as the standard measure of the speed at which products flow through a logistical system. A slow rate weakens a country's competitive position in two respects. It burdens industry at any given time with large amounts of stock, which is expensive to finance, insure, store and handle. These higher inventory costs are translated into higher prices and lower profits. Inventory also absorbs capital that could be invested more productively in other economic activities.

Ray (1981) found that over the period 1969-77 the British economy, and in particular its manufacturing sector, was heavily overburdened with stock relative to other industrialised economies. Using mainly 1980-1 data, Waters (1984) calculated that British manufacturers' stock levels were slightly higher than the international average, but not 'markedly' so. He, nevertheless, conceded that even small increases in stockholding can be costly and warned against complacency in inventory management. A more recent study compared stock levels in British and American industry and found that in thirteen out of nineteen sectors, stock levels were lower in the US (relative to turnover); in sectors such as publishing, furniture manufacturing and vehicle assembly more than 60% lower (*Financial Times*, 28 February 1986). According to this research, British industry could release roughly £4 billion of working capital by matching American stock levels!

Japanese industry gains a major logistical advantage from operating on low stock levels. Many manufacturers there employ the *just-in-time* (JIT) system of procurement, only reordering supplies of components when they are actually required (Hall, 1983). This system not only enables firms to economise on stock, but also helps to uncover defects in the production process. The exposure of manufacturers in Western countries to Japanese competition has forced firms in several industrial sectors, particularly vehicle assembly and electrical engineering, to adopt a similar approach to inventory management. It has been estimated that the full application of JIT principles by British manufacturers could reduce the amount of capital tied up in stocks by a third (*Financial Times*, 10 January 1986). A survey of the application of the JIT principle in British manufacturing by Voss and Robinson (1987) found that around 57% of the 132 respondents were either implementing or planning to implement some aspects of it. Further analysis revealed, though, that many firms were attempting only a partial implementation and often neglecting those aspects which posed most difficulty yet could potentially offer the greatest benefit. In the UK, government agencies have published reports giving firms advice on how to improve the efficiency of their stockholding and materials handling operations (NEDO, 1967; Department of Industry, 1982). The government's main influence on stock levels has, however, been through the imposition of tight monetary policy in 1979-80 and the withdrawal of tax relief on stock appreciation in 1981. These measures induced massive destocking in the short term and helped to drive the economy into recession (Pratten, 1985). Contrary to Ray's (1981) pessimistic forecast that after the recession 'gradually but surely stocks will creep back up to their former level' (p.11), stock levels have since remained relatively low to the longer-term benefit of the economy.

Employment.

The sharp increase in unemployment levels in the 1980s has stimulated interest in the employment-generating characteristics of different sectors of the economy. In most developed countries, manufacturing has been shedding labour, causing central and local government to regard service industries as the most promising sources of new employment. This has prompted several assessments of employment creation in logistical activities (Childerley, 1980; McKinnon, 1988). Childerley estimated that in 1976 logistics employed approximately 29% of the total workforce in the UK. This estimate was based on the assumption that the logistics element accounted for 20% of employment in production/manufacturing and 95% of that in the distributive trades. Occupational data collected in the 1981 Population Census indicates that only around 5% of employees in production/manufacturing industries worked in transport, storage and materials handling, suggesting that Childerley based her calculations on a very wide definition of logistics. Moreover, to obtain such a high percentage for the distributive trade, she clearly included shop assistants in the calculation. If one adopts a narrower definition of logistics, excludes all shop staff and updates the calculation using 1981 data, the proportion of the total workforce engaged in logistical activities falls to around 10%, but this still makes logistics a major source of employment. Rajan and Pearson (1986) predict that 'wholesale distribution' (broadly defined to include distribution contractors as well as wholesale traders) will be a sector of rapid employment growth over the next few years, though some of this growth will be offset by job losses in manufacturers' and retailers' in-house distribution operations.

Although, quantitatively, logistics makes a large contribution to total employment, it is sometimes argued that it creates only low-skilled, poorly paid, blue-collar jobs. Recent evidence suggests, however, that the quality of employment in logistics compares quite favourably with that in manufacturing and other branches of the distributive trades. In 1981, for example, only about a quarter of those employed in wholesaling and dealing in the UK had blue-collar transport and materials handling jobs. A study of warehousing commissioned by the Department of the Environment concluded that, 'Warehousing employment on balance is probably more skilled than manufacturing, manufacturing having about twice the proportion of unskilled labour and fewer managerial staff than warehousing' (Buchanan and Partners, 1986, p.35). The same study also found that average earnings for male manual workers were appreciably higher in warehousing than in retailing.

General concepts

In essence, distribution is the dispersal of goods from producers to consumers. This dispersal can be construed either in organisational terms as the successive transfer of ownership along a marketing channel composed of producers, wholesalers and retailers, or in terms of the physical movement of these goods from factories through warehouses to shops (Aspinwall, 1958). This is an important distinction because the organisational structure of a distribution system is generally much simpler than its physical manifestation as a network of nodes and linkages. Only if each agency in the marketing channel were based at a single location would there be a direct correspondence between changes of ownership and freight movements. In practice, many producers and retailers operate premises at different levels in the distributive channel and control the movement of goods between them.

The system of physical distribution can be conceptualised as 'bridging the gap' between production and consumption by fulfilling five basic and essential functions (Buxton, 1975):

1. Transport: the spatial separation of producers and consumers creates the need for movement.
2. Storage: the production of goods in advance of demand makes it necessary to store them until they are required.
3. Breaking of bulk: most goods are produced in large batches but consumed in small quantities, necessitating the disaggregation of loads. (Note. In this book the term 'bulk' will relate to the size of a load rather than the mode of handling.)
4. Mixing: to satisfy diverse consumer demands and facilitate consumer choice, there must be a convergence of goods produced at different locations.
5. Communication: there must be a two way transmission of information between producers and consumers to regulate the flow of goods between them.

These functions are not mutually exclusive; while goods are in transit, for instance, they are effectively being stored for future use. Two or more functions can share the same facilities; storage, the breaking of bulk and the mixing of product ranges can all be carried out at the same depot.

The integration of transport and storage in a single system is founded on the concept of goods gaining *place and time utility* by moving through space (transport) and time (storage). This dynamic view of storage replaces the previous notion of stocks being essentially static and attaches much greater importance to the speed with which stock rotates. Warehouses which in the past would have been regarded as repositories are today considered to be distribution centres, where greater emphasis is placed on the sorting and through-flow of goods than on their storage.

One must resist taking a mechanistic view of the movement of goods through space and time, however, imagining that they are drawn through the distributive system by the force of consumer demand. In very few sectors of the modern economy does the outward flow of goods from point of production await the expression of a consumer demand. Goods are produced and, in most cases, begin their distribution ahead of demand. The volume and speed of flow through the system must, therefore, be determined on the basis of forecasts of future sales. Variations in the level of sales are difficult to predict accurately, introducing an element of uncertainty into the management of the distribution operation.

For firms engaged in distribution, the ownership of goods confers a risk. For example, as a result of unforeseen circumstances, demand for a particular item may slump, leaving the wholesaler or retailer with excess stock which can only be sold off at a loss. The way in which firms marshal their stocks also involves risks. For example, a manufacturer faced with a choice of centralising stocks at the factory or dispersing them to local depots may decide to hold too little stock locally and as a result prove unable to respond quickly enough to temporary fluctuations in demand, thus risking a loss of sales. Most risk stems from variations in consumer demand and uncertainties about how potential customers will respond to the desired products being unavailable. The scale of these risks can be reduced by improvements in the collection, communication and processing of sales data and by the development of accurate forecasting models. Schary (1970) judges the risk element to be so important that he considers physical distribution to be 'essentially a process of risk management'.

Distance, time and risk can be considered to form the three dimensions of physical distribution. Of these time serves as the 'unifying dimension' (Heskett, 1966), because distance and risk can both be expressed as functions of time. Transit time can act as a surrogate for distance and, in the context of distribution, the level of risk is often assumed to be directly proportional to time (Schary, 1970). It is not possible to standardise all three dimensions with respect to either distance or risk. General models of the internal operation of distribution systems have tended, therefore, to be time-based. Heskett presented an idealised model of a distribution system, composed of time-dependent 'inventory cells' representing goods in storage and transit. Schary incorporated a risk element into this framework to produce a general theoretical model of a physical distribution system.

In the 1970s, several time-based models were operationalised to allow firms to simulate the flows of goods and information through their distribution systems and, thereby, assess the impact of possible changes in system design (e.g. Connors *et al.*, 1972; Bowersox, 1972). Logistics system models have since been refined in various ways. They are now able to accommodate a large number of variables, employ more complex cost functions and, in some cases, incorporate optimising procedures. They can assist both in the long-range strategic planning of a distribution system and in the management of its day-to-day operation. Many firms have, nevertheless, lacked the necessary distribution data, computing facilities and management expertise to take advantage of these models (House and Karrenbauer, 1978).

Many strategic decisions relate to aspects of the spatial organisation of physical distribution that cannot be subsumed within an exclusively time-based model. Transport costs, for example, are not simply a function of transit times and many of the costs incurred in establishing and operating a depot are locationally specific. The spatial dimension of physical distribution is also of great interest to those not directly involved in its management, but concerned with its numerous external effects. Property developers and land use planners, for instance, wish to know where firms will require sites for warehousing. The pattern of freight movement at national and local levels is a major concern of transport planning authorities. Private firms providing distribution services, such as haulage, storage and freight forwarding, must be sensitive to geographical variations in the demand for these services.

In this book special emphasis will be placed on the spatial organisation of physical distribution and consideration given to the wider economic and environmental frameworks within which it operates.

Spatial organisation

Classical theories of agricultural and industrial location, such as those of Von Thünen (Hall, 1966) and Weber (1909), attached great importance to the attraction of the market, but were based upon a highly idealised view of the distribution of products throughout the market area. They assumed that goods travelled directly from point of production to point of sale in single, uninterrupted journeys. Such an assumption could reasonably be made in the early stages of economic development when production was locally based and the market areas of most products tightly constrained by poor transport. Then, most deliveries to markets or individual consumers were direct, short distance movements. Over the past 150 years, however, the regional specialisation of agriculture, the centralisation of manufacturing and the expansion of market areas have greatly increased the average distance goods travel to consumers and given rise to a complex system of distribution.

Few attempts have been made to examine the spatial structure of this system as a whole. Much research has focused on its interface with the consuming population, considering such topics as store location, retail catchment areas and shopping behaviour (Dawson, 1980). In the UK this research has displayed a 'distinct spatial bias', reflecting the fact that 'retailing has received relatively little research outside of the geographical and planning fields' (Davies and Kirby, 1983, p.85). There have been several localised studies of the spatial organisation of wholesaling (e.g. Rabiega and Lamoureux, 1973), though, like earlier research on retailing, they have tended to be preoccupied with the establishment of spatial hierarchies and the delimitation of trade areas. With the exception of Revzan's (1966) work on spatial variations in wholesale:retail sales ratios, geographical studies of wholesaling have generally examined the spatial organisation of wholesaling in isolation and given little consideration to the vertical linkages in the distributive channel that connect wholesalers with producers and retailers. They have also largely ignored the involvement of manufacturers and multiple retailers in the distribution of goods to retail outlets, despite the fact that these firms now undertake many of the functions previously handled by wholesalers, and, in some trades, are responsible for a much larger share of shop deliveries than wholesalers. Edwards (1982) ventures beyond the traditional confines of wholesaling to examine the changing locations of depots operated by manufacturers and retailers as well as wholesalers in Tyne and Wear. He uses the term 'intermediate distribution' to embrace 'the full range of commercial organisations engaged in the movement of goods from points of production to points of retail sale' (p.7). Only recently has the structure of this 'intermediate' system of distribution between factory and shop been subjected to detailed investigation.

Freight flows have been mapped, described and analysed for almost forty years, but this research has revealed surprisingly little about the spatial organisation of physical distribution. This is partly because it has employed highly aggregated flow data, usually relating to the movement of freight at the inter-regional level. Numerous attempts have been made to explain flow patterns with reference to regional interdependence, leading Hay (1979, p.10) to conclude that, 'The study of commodity flow is indissolubly linked to an explanation of regional specialisation'. At this level of analysis it is not possible to differentiate the types of premises between which freight is transported nor to trace the route that products follow in their distribution from factory to shop. The analysis of patterns of commodity flow has been based on a grossly oversimplified view of the routeing of freight traffic and this has effectively blocked consideration of the logistical framework within which freight transport is organised. In most commodity flow research, the unit of analysis has been the freight journey. This reflects the fact that the main data sources for this research have been official surveys of individual vehicle movements within and between specified traffic zones. The available statistics make no reference to the nature of the premises from which the vehicle originates or to which it travels, nor to the stage that a particular journey represents in the overall movement from point of production to point of sale. This led Chisholm and O'Sullivan (1973), in their study of freight flows in the UK, to admit that 'the freight flow data, while accurately representing the work done by the transport sector, do not faithfully reproduce the flows from first origin to final destination' (p.32). The Commodity Flow Studies commissioned by the British Department of Transport in 1975 were exceptional in examining patterns of flow between specific points of origin and destination, using data specially collected in a series of industrial surveys. This work was confined, however, to 'primary flows...from point of production to redistribution depots, ports or manufacturing plants' and ignored the distribution of finished products to final consumers (Pike and Gandham, 1981, p.4).

In the absence of information about the logistics of freight movement 'from first origin to final destination', it has been quite conveniently supposed that the plotting of journeys inter and intrazonally gives a representative picture of the pattern of flow from production to consumption (Chisholm and O'Sullivan, 1973; Benheddi and Pitfield, 1980). This supposition appears, however, to be based on an underestimation of the number of intermediate links in the logistical channel (McKinnon, 1981a). The manner in which freight flow data are officially compiled permits a crude assessment of the complexity of the logistical system. To estimate the total tonnage of freight lifted by goods vehicles, government statisticians record the weight of goods loaded onto a sample vehicle at the start of a journey. If the movement of a consignment from raw material source to point of final sale is broken into several discrete journeys, each requiring a reloading operation, then its weight would be recorded several times. This leads to much multiple counting and results in the tonnes-lifted statistic far exceeding the total weight of goods actually produced or consumed. The extent of this multiple counting is measured by the *handling factor*, which can be expressed as follows:

$$\text{handling factor} = \frac{\text{weight of goods lifted}}{\text{actual weight of goods consumed and exported}}$$

In 1980, the handling factor for food products in the UK was approximately five, suggesting that on average there were roughly five links in the food supply chain from raw material source to retail outlet (McKinnon, 1984). Many of the intermediate nodes in this chain would be stockholding, break-of-bulk or modal interchange points. Very seldom, however, does one find any reference to these activities in the literature on commodity flow analysis, despite the fact that their locations act as important 'hinge points' in the logistical channel, largely determining the route a product follows. In the course of their distribution from factory to shop, products often follow circuitous routes via one or more intervening depot. Conventional methods of freight flow analysis make no allowance for such devious routeing.

Research perspectives

The extensive reorganisation of the distribution function over the past thirty years has created a healthy demand for the services of operations researchers and stimulated a large amount of research in this field. Mercer, Cantley and Rand (1978, p.1) noted that distribution was 'proving a fruitful area for the application of operations research', while Ballou (1978) described the problem of depot location as 'an operations researcher's dream'. Most of the research effort has gone into the development of sophisticated optimisation techniques. Today, operations researchers have the necessary techniques at their disposal to furnish optimal or near optimal solutions to all the major problems distribution planners and managers encounter. Their technical armoury includes linear programming, vehicle scheduling algorithms, facility location models and queueing theory. The application of these techniques has been reported in numerous case studies of individual firms' distribution operations.

While the work of operations researchers has clearly been of enormous practical benefit to firms overhauling their distribution operations, it does not constitute a complete study of physical distribution. Most of their work has focused on the operations of individual firms and been concerned only with optimisation. There have been few attempts to explain in detail the rationale behind firms' actual distribution systems. Much of the case study material that has accumulated (e.g. Hemingway, 1979) has been fairly superficial and, as it does not adhere to a common format, cannot be easily compared.

Nor is there any guarantee that the firms whose distribution operations have been exposed in this way are representative of their industrial or trade sector. There have been a few general surveys in the UK of the distribution systems of samples of firms drawn from many industrial sectors (Industrial and Commercial Techniques Ltd, 1966; Whitehead Consulting Group, 1974; Kearney, 1980). These have been valuable sources of cross-sectional data, but have been lacking in two respects. First, they have not attempted to explain why firms differ in the way they organise their distribution and, second, they have largely ignored the spatial structure of distribution systems. Sectoral studies, undertaken by Smith (1979a, b) of distribution practices in the confectionery and record industries, provide a much deeper insight into the factors affecting the organisation of physical distribution. Explanatory studies of this kind have undoubtedly been inhibited, however, by the chronic lack of data, much of which are deemed to be confidential. The large number of relevant variables also poses a major problem as it is seldom possible to 'compare physical distribution systems parametrically, holding products and final markets constant, varying time and volume under different configurations' (Schary, 1970, p.14). In the absence of such controlled conditions and much of the hard quantitative data one would require to undertake rigorous statistical analysis, attempts to explain differences in distribution strategies must remain fairly tentative.

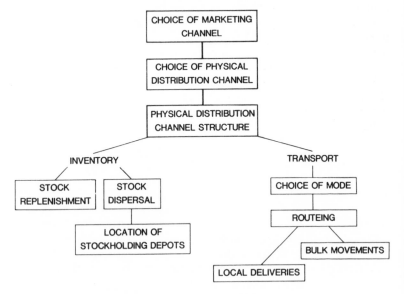

Figure 1.1 Analytical framework

The information presented in this book has been culled from case studies documented in specialist journals and the trade press, published reports of general surveys of firms' distribution operations and original surveys undertaken by the author. The aim has been to complement individual case studies, where possible, with a more general review of prevailing distribution practices and policies.

Figure 1.1 sets out the analytical framework that will be adopted in this book. At its highest level is the choice of marketing channel, which establishes the network of trading links through which the ownership of goods is transferred (Chapter 2). Individual agencies in the marketing channel, particularly manufacturers and multiple retailers, usually have a choice of physical distribution channel. Manufacturers can distribute output in bulk loads directly from the factory or send them via regional depots. Multiple retailers can channel goods through central warehouses or have suppliers deliver them directly to their branch stores. At the second level, we consider the allocation of product flow between direct and indirect physical distribution channels (Chapter 3). The following four chapters examine the structure of the physical distribution system in greater detail, concentrating on its two key elements of inventory and transport. Chapter 4 looks at the way in which firms control the movement of stock through the vertical channel and the factors influencing its geographical dispersal. Chapter 5 reviews the main methods of optimising depot location and analyses actual patterns of stock location. Having established the framework of intervening nodes through which products flow, we then examine the nature of this flow in terms of, first, the choice of transport mode (Chapter 6) and, second, the routeing of bulk movements from factories to depots and local deliveries from depots to customers (Chapter 7). The remaining chapters broaden the perspective to consider international distribution (Chapter 8), the environmental consequences of freight transport (Chapter 9) and future trends in physical distribution (Chapter 10).

Chapter two

Marketing channels

The relationship between marketing and physical distribution is not clearly defined. Some authors (e.g. Heskett, 1962; Kotler, 1967) incorporate physical distribution within a broad definition of marketing, while others (e.g. Stewart, 1965; Wentworth, 1976) consider marketing and physical distribution to be separate though inter-related activities. The former gain support from the traditional view of marketing as being concerned principally with the four 'Ps' of product, price, promotion and place. The 'placing' of goods at selling points clearly involves physical distribution. There is disagreement, however, over what can legitimately be regarded as physical distribution. Kotler distinguishes broad and narrow definitions of physical distribution. The broad definition embraces decisions on the number of outlets to be supplied and choice of intermediaries, as well as the physical organisation of transport and storage operations. The narrow definition assumes that the basic framework of outlets and intermediaries is already established and sees the role of physical distribution to be the efficient movement of goods through these predetermined channels. In theoretical discussions, the broad definition is generally favoured (Davis and Brown, 1972; Bartels, 1976). Marks and Taylor (1967) and Buxton (1975) adopt the expression 'marketing logistics' to describe this broader perspective. Buxton states that marketing logistics 'incorporates the selection and management of the institutional channel(s) of distribution for a company's products as well as the physical facilities required' (p.5). Schary and Becker (1973) explore the relationship between choice of marketing channel and physical distribution requirements in some detail. In practice, channel decisions are usually made independently of decisions on the structure of physical distribution systems. Partly for this reason, and partly for ease of explanation, we shall, in this chapter, consider the nature, choice and historical development of marketing channels separately from the physical structure of the distribution system.

Definitions

Very few products are sold by their producer directly to the final customer. The vast majority pass through the hands of one or more intermediaries, such as wholesalers, dealers, brokers or retailers. When trading links are established between these intermediaries, a marketing channel is formed. In attempting to define the term marketing channel more rigorously, one encounters several difficulties. First, one must distinguish the transfer of ownership (or *flow of title*) from the physical movement of goods (or *flow of product*). Some agencies, such as commodity dealers, assume ownership of goods without physically handling them in any way, while others distribute, on a third-party basis, goods they do not own. It is advisable, therefore, to consider the exchange of ownership separately from the logistics of the distribution operation. Second, if one then defines a marketing channel as a channel through which ownership is transferred, as widely recommended in the marketing literature (e.g. Gattorna, 1978, p.479), 'facilitating agencies' such as hauliers and public warehousing firms, which eschew ownership of the goods they handle, should be excluded (Kotler, 1967). This is not to deny, however, that these agencies interact closely with marketing channel members and can strongly influence their commercial behaviour (Dawson, 1979). Third, there has also been some disagreement over whether channel membership should be extended to producers or confined to intermediaries. As a producer can fulfil many of the functions of intermediaries, and as the sale of a producer's output to the first intermediary is a critical element in its marketing strategy, a strong case can be made for including the producer in channel analysis and discussion.

A marketing channel can, therefore, be defined as an organisational channel through which the ownership of goods flows from producer to final customer via one or more intermediaries.

The numerous approaches to the study of marketing channels are thoroughly reviewed by Gattorna (1978). Of these, the institutional and functional approaches have been the most widely adopted and influential. The institutional approach sees marketing channels as strings of agencies and makes heavy use of flow diagrams to depict their organisational structure. The functional approach emphasises the activities that are carried out in the course of a product's distribution and considers how these are allocated among channel members. The main activities are stockholding (I), transport (T), searching for suppliers (S_S) and customers (S_C) and promotion (P). Bucklin (1960) provides a symbolic representation of the 'mix' of functions undertaken by different types of agency in the marketing channel:

$$(Pr\ I\ T\ Sc\ P) \rightarrow (Ss\ I\ T\ Sc\ P) \rightarrow (Ss\ I\ Sc\ P) \rightarrow (Ss\ T\ I\ C)$$

Manufacturer   Wholesaler   Retailer   Consumer

where Pr is production and C consumption.

The institutional and functional approaches are essentially complementary. Ideally, agencies in the marketing channel should be distinguished not simply by institutional titles, such as wholesaler or retailer, but by the particular combination of activities they undertake. This greatly increases the number of channel permutations and gives a more realistic impression of the complexity of marketing systems. It also recognises that the institutional structure of a channel can remain constant while functions shift between channel members.

In building abstract models of marketing channels, marketing theorists have generally suppressed consideration of their geographical structure. Very few attempts have been made to map the linkages between channel members. The Runciman Committee (1958), for example, in its report on horticultural marketing in the UK showed how the passage of farm produce through several wholesale intermediaries could result in it following a long and circuitous route from farm to customer. Generally speaking, however, where the spatial structure of marketing systems has received explicit mention, it has been highly idealised and not subjected to detailed empirical investigation (e.g. Breyer, 1934). Plotting the transfer of ownership between the locations of channel members would not necessarily delineate the route products actually followed, but it would establish the spatial relationship between producers and the various levels of distributor.

The need for intermediaries

In theory, it would be possible for producers to sell their output directly to final customers, thereby obviating the need for intermediaries. The fact that so few products are sold in this way suggests that this method of trading is grossly inferior to the distribution of goods through intermediaries. As Bucklin (1972, p.14) has pointed out:

> since the middleman holds no monopoly on the performance of marketing functions...the viability of the middleman's position in the economic system depends on his ability to organise some portion (or all) of the flows in a manner that is superior to other alternatives.

The intervention of the 'middleman' is justified mainly on the grounds of transactional efficiency, product assortment and functional specialisation.

Transactional efficiency

The presence of an intermediary between producers and retailers can substantially reduce the number of trading links in the marketing system, streamlining the network of product and information flows (Artle and Berglund, 1959). As illustrated in Figure 2.1, in the absence of an intermediary, the number of direct trading links is calculated by multiplying the number of producers by the number of retailers. The presence of an intermediary can reduce the number of transactions to the sum of the numbers of producers and retailers. As one increases the numbers of producers and retailers to make the model more realistic, the sum of these two numbers grows at a much slower rate than their product, enhancing the relative advantage of trading through an intermediary. Where there are large numbers of final customers, many

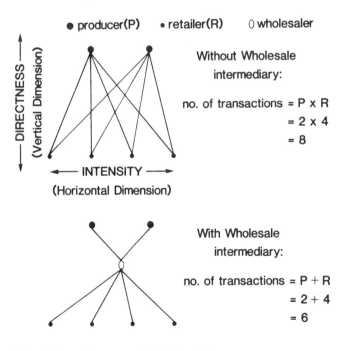

● producer(P)   • retailer(R)   ○ wholesaler

DIRECTNESS (Vertical Dimension)

Without Wholesale intermediary:

no. of transactions = P x R
= 2 x 4
= 8

◄— INTENSITY —►
(Horizontal Dimension)

With Wholesale intermediary:

no. of transactions = P + R
= 2 + 4
= 6

With 100 producers and 1,000 retailers:

without wholesaler:	100,000 transactions
with wholesaler:	1,100 transactions

Presence of wholesaler reduces the no. of transactions by 98.9%.

Figure 2.1 Marketing systems with and without intermediaries

intermediaries may be required to serve them efficiently. As the number of intermediaries grows, there is a proliferation of trading links between producers and intermediaries, creating the opportunity for a second tier of intermediaries to emerge and thus streamline the marketing system at a higher level. The insertion of additional intermediaries between any two levels in a marketing channel can improve its efficiency by reducing the number of transactions and consolidating flows of products and information on a smaller number of links.

Product assortment

Intermediaries assemble a wide variety of products drawn from many different producers and sort them into mixed orders for distribution to agencies or customers further down the channel. Alderson (1954) argues that sorting is fundamental to the distribution process and that the need for separate agencies to consolidate and sort diverse product ranges is the prime *raison d'être* for the development of marketing channels. Few individual producers would wish to assume responsibility for these activities as this would require them to market the products of competing firms alongside their own.

Functional specialisation

By specialising on distributive functions, intermediaries can develop greater expertise in this field than producers and provide a superior marketing service to that which producers themselves could mount. By relinquishing much of the responsibility for distribution to intermediaries, producers can concentrate management effort and financial resources on their main production activity. Mallen (1973) explains this process of 'functional spin-off' in terms of the relative efficiency with which producers and intermediaries can perform distribution activities. All but the very largest firms lack the resources to establish a comprehensive distribution network, and even if they had the available capital to do so, it is likely that many would find that investment in distributive facilities yielded a lower rate of return than investment in productive capacity (Kotler, 1967). Intermediaries can also relieve producers of much of the financial burden of stockholding and spread the risks of ownership.

Intermediaries can carry out physical distribution functions, such as the breaking of bulk, consolidation of mixed loads, decentralised storage and local delivery, more economically than individual producers, because they handle the output of numerous producers and can, therefore, secure larger economies of scale. Bucklin (1972) has shown that intermediaries' cost advantage increases as:

1. the number of producers and consumers increases;
2. the distance between producer and consumer increases;
3. average order size diminishes;
4. order lead times shorten;
5. the market area becomes more fragmented;
6. the product range expands.

Physical distribution functions do not in themselves, however, provide sufficient justification for the existence of full marketing intermediaries such as wholesalers and retailers. Hauliers, public warehousing firms and other contractors can, after all, perform these functions just as economically. What distinguishes marketing intermediaries from transport and storage contractors is their active participation in buying and selling.

The importance of marketing intermediaries is not always recognised. It is sometimes suggested that they do not earn the additional margin they impose on the final selling price. As shown on Table 2.1, the retailers' gross margin can represent a substantial proportion of the selling price. In the case of some products, distribution costs can exceed the cost of production. There is no reason, though, why it should cost more to make a product than to distribute it. High distribution costs are partly a consequence of the effort to reduce production costs by centralising the manufacturing process (Braithwaite and Dobbs, 1932). Baker (1985, p.296) considers it 'especially ironic that the pursuit of economies of scale in production - which is seen as laudable and to be encouraged - tends to lead to diseconomies in distribution'. Furthermore, when comparing distributors' margins with producers' charges, it must be remembered that the latter are artificially low because producers rely on outside agencies to handle much of their distribution (Kotler, 1967). The position of intermediaries is generally defended on the grounds that they 'appear in a channel when the incremental cost of their presence

Table 2.1 Retailers' gross margins in selected trades, 1984

Product Class	Gross margin as % of Total Turnover
Confectionery, tobacco and newspapers	15.4
Groceries	18.9
Chemist products	23.7
Fruit and vegetables	25.3
Electrical and music goods	31.8
Furniture	35.4
Women's, girls' and children's clothing	37.8
Men's and boys'. wear	41.9
Footwear	47.7

Source: Business Statistics Office. 1986.

is less than the savings they provide to other agencies in the system'
(Bucklin, 1972, p.14). Instead of inflating final selling prices, the use
of intermediaries can result in lower prices than would be attainable in
a system composed of direct producer-consumer linkages.

Types of marketing channel

Marketing channels can be distinguished on the basis of three major
criteria: organisational structure, the nature of the participating firms
and their trading relationships.

Organisational structure

Marketing channels have horizontal and vertical dimensions. The
horizontal dimension is represented by the number of separate
agencies at each level in the channel. The breadth of the channel,
particularly at its base, where it interfaces with final customers, is
generally referred to as its *intensity* (Guirdham, 1972). The length of
the channel, measured by the number of levels in the vertical
dimension, is usually described as its *directness*. Channels can be
differentiated in terms of both intensity and directness.

Table 2.2   Numbers of retail and wholesale businesses in selected trades,
1984

Product class	Businesses	Outlets
Retail:		
Groceries	32,230	45,918
Confectionery, tobacco, newspapers	37,602	47,115
Women's, girls', infants' clothing	15,246	25,233
Electrical/gas appliances, music goods	9,606	16,809
Furniture	9,447	13,263
Footwear	3,353	12,023
Chemist products	8,060	11,756
Hardware, china, fancy goods	8,368	10,586
Toys, hobby/cycle/sports goods	7,255	9,134
Men's and boys' clothing	3,443	8,094
Books and stationery	5,512	7,452
Jewelry	4,455	7,070
Wholesale:		
Food and drink	16,072	
Clothing, furs, textiles, footwear	9,626	
Petroleum products	978	
Coal and oil	4,050	
Other products	49,933	
(excludes builders' and agricultural merchants and industrial dealers)		

Sources: Central Statistical Office, 1987[a] ; *British Business*, 17 July 1987.

In considering the intensity variable, it is necessary to distinguish the total number of agencies available at each level of the channel from the number actually stocking a producer's goods. Table 2.2 shows the total number of wholesale and retail enterprises in the UK dealing in different classes of product. These figures are very approximate as overlapping product ranges make it difficult to classify intermediaries, particularly wholesalers, by commodity. So great is the overlap in the case of wholesalers that almost half of all wholesale businesses are not differentiated and simply assigned to a miscellaneous category. The available statistics do, nevertheless, reveal wide differences in the number of agencies specialising in particular types of product. These differences can be attributed mainly to three factors:

1. Volume of sales: the greater the total expenditure on a particular class of products, the more distributors it can support.
2. Cost structure: in trades where distributors must invest heavily in specialised facilities or acquire large amounts of expensive stock, the number of intermediaries is restricted by high start-up costs. In other trades, where initial capital outlays are small and economies of scale limited, intermediaries are likely to be more numerous.
3. Purchasing behaviour: the more frequently goods are purchased and the shorter distances people are prepared to travel to obtain them, the greater the need for decentralised distribution through large numbers of local intermediaries.

Producers seldom manage to sell their products through all the available channel intermediaries. Such market saturation is generally achieved only by the leading brands of a few consumer goods. Not all producers, of course, want to maximise the number of intermediaries stocking their products. They differ in the degree of market exposure they seek for their products and this is reflected in the structure of the channels they employ. Kotler (1967) differentiates three levels of market exposure:

1. Intensive distribution: where the producer aims to distribute his products through as many outlets as possible to maximise their availability to consumers. This is the preferred method of distribution for fast-moving inexpensive products, such as cigarettes and confectionery, that require little customer service and whose quality is not associated with the nature of the outlet.
2. Selective distribution: where the producer is more discerning in his choice of intermediary, confining the sale of his products to more specialist outlets capable of providing a specified level of customer service.

3. Exclusive distribution: where the producer restricts the sale of his products to a small number of carefully chosen intermediaries. These agencies may be granted exclusive distribution rights within particular areas, sometimes in return for an undertaking not to stock competing brands. By adopting such a strategy, a producer can exercise tight control over intermediaries, ensuring that they provide high levels of customer service and often adding to their product's prestige.

The intensity with which products are marketed at the bottom, usually retail, level of the channel affects the number of intermediaries used at higher levels in the channel. Where a producer wants his goods widely dispersed throughout the available retail outlets, it is expensive to deal directly with all the firms operating these stores, especially the smaller independent traders. Through direct contact, the producer can increase the probability of a retailer stocking his product, but in the case of outlets with a small turnover, such contact would not be cost-effective. By distributing the goods indirectly through wholesale intermediaries, a producer can achieve extensive retail exposure much more efficiently. The scale of the resulting improvement in transactional efficiency depends on the ratio of the numbers of wholesalers to retailers and varies both between market sectors and geographically. A producer opting for a more selective form of distribution would be able to rely more heavily on direct links with chosen retailers.

The directness of a marketing channel is partly a function of its intensity. Channels can be regarded as having a hierarchical structure whose height is related to the breadth of its base. In theory, the larger the number of agencies at the customer interface, the greater will be the demand for additional levels of intermediary between these agencies and the original sources of their supplies. In practice, however, most channels through which finished consumer products are distributed are short. A large proportion pass directly from producer to retailer and most of the remainder are channelled through only one wholesale intermediary. A small minority of products, such as garden produce and fish, can go through two wholesale stages before reaching the retailer. The additional level of wholesaling is usually found in trades where production is highly fragmented (Stacey and Wilson, 1958). The main task of the *primary wholesaler* is to assemble supplies from numerous sources. Having sorted the goods, he despatches them in consolidated bulk loads to *secondary wholesalers* who in turn supply retailers with small consignments of the desired product mix. The primary wholesaler may also take responsibility for functions such as grading and packaging which individual producers are too small to undertake economically themselves. As *dual wholesaling* is today comparatively rare in the UK, differentiating marketing channels on the basis of length really boils down to distinguishing direct producer-retailer links from indirect distribution via a single wholesaler.

Nature of channel participants.

Distinguishing channels simply in terms of the number of nodes and links they contain conceals important differences in the way functions are allocated between channel members. In channels of similar intensity and directness, for instance, wholesalers can differ markedly in the range of services they provide. Intermediaries can be differentiated, first, by whether they physically take possession of the goods in which they deal and, second, by the range of operations they perform on these goods. Intermediaries that do engage in physical distribution are often classified as providing either a *full service* or a *limited service*. Full-service wholesalers, for example, assemble, store, sort, promote and deliver goods, extend credit to retailers and, sometimes, provide them with advice on store management. Limited-service wholesalers transfer responsibility for some functions to their customers, thereby reducing their costs and offering lower prices. The typical cash and carry wholesaler, for example, withholds credit and requires trade customers to assemble and transport their purchases themselves. At a lower level in the marketing channel, 'non-store' retailers, such as mail-order firms, can be distinguished from conventional shop-based retailers. The latter can be further categorised into those with distribution facilities capable of receiving bulk supplies directly from producers and those dependent on the logistical support of wholesalers.

By taking account of the directness of channels as well as the nature of their component agencies, Guirdham (1972) identified eighteen separate channels for consumer goods in the UK. Many of these channels, particularly those with three intermediaries, today handle very little business.

Vertical integration has led to a shortening of marketing channels by concentrating functions in fewer agencies. For example, by absorbing many of the traditional functions of wholesalers, multiple retailers have been able to bypass wholesalers and trade directly with producers. By so doing, the multiples have converted the link between the shop and the warehouse that supplies it from a 'market' relationship to an 'organisational' one under their full control (McClelland, 1966). This has seldom been achieved by the merging of wholesale and retail businesses. Most multiples have expanded their role in physical distribution independently of the wholesale sector.

Channels have also been short-circuited by producers extending their control of physical distribution forward as far as the retail outlet. Some producers own shops through which part, or even all, of their output is sold, creating what McCammon and Bates (1965) have called a *corporate system* of distribution.

Channel relationships

The commercial relationships between agencies in a marketing channel can take various forms and provide a further basis for channel differentiation. To understand the nature of these relationships, one must examine the distribution of bargaining power among channel members. Where this power is quite evenly spread, as, for example, in trades composed of many small producers and intermediaries, *consensus channels* often develop, in which the various agencies work together harmoniously to their mutual benefit. Fisk (1967, p.237) defines a consensus channel as one in which 'there is no single agency that establishes policies or exercises administrative authority over the entire system'. In such channels, agencies remain independent and free of contractual obligations to other channel members. They co-operate merely because it is in their individual interests to do so.

In some trades, more formal contractual links have been formed between agencies at different levels in the channel, ensuring closer co-ordination of their distribution activities. *Contractual channels* are well exemplified by the wholesaler-sponsored voluntary groups that have arisen in many countries in response to mounting competition from multiple retailers (Fulop, 1962). Wholesalers and retailers belonging to these groups retain financial independence, but agree to various conditions in the wider interests of the group. Affiliated retailers, for example, undertake to purchase a large proportion of their supplies from a group wholesaler in return for such benefits as lower prices, advertising support and financial advice.

In contrast to consensus and contractual channels, some channels are dominated by large firms whose great buying power enables them to exercise a high degree of control over other channel members. Prior to the Second World War, these *commanded channels* were to be found mainly in industries where production was concentrated in a few large firms. Since then, the enormous growth of multiple retailing in many market sectors has given retail organisations the power either to countervail the influence of large producers on the channel, or, in trades where production is more fragmented, to dictate the nature of the distribution operation and even the style and quality of the merchandise. As multiple retailers make very little use of wholesalers, their purchasing power bears most heavily on their direct links with producers.

Channel selection

Channel selection is a key element in a firm's marketing strategy. As producers seldom distribute their entire output through a single channel, this generally involves selecting several channels and determining the optimum allocation of flow among them. By using several channels, producers can gain wider market exposure for their products, while reducing their dependence on particular types of intermediary. Overdependence on individual channels is usually resisted on the grounds that it increases the risk of distribution being disrupted and allows certain intermediaries to exercise excessive bargaining power. A multiple-channel strategy also enables a producer to undertake *differentiated marketing*, tailoring product, promotion, price and service level to the needs of particular market segments (Baker, 1985).

It is very difficult to generalise about firms' relative use of different types of marketing channel. Producers vary greatly in the number and types of channels they use and in the proportions of output they send along them. The pattern of channel usage can vary geographically, reflecting regional differences in the structure of the distributive system and in the demand for a firm's products. Taking this multidimensional view of channel selection, it appears that each producer is faced with an enormous number of channel options. In generalising about producers' choices of marketing channels, marketing analysts have often found it necessary to confine their attention to a single channel attribute, usually length. In most cases, short channels are equated with direct distribution to retailer (or consumers) and long channels with indirect distribution via wholesale intermediaries.

Channel preference has been associated with the nature of the product, the producer, the market and the channels themselves.

Product characteristics

Several attempts have been made to classify products in terms of their marketing requirements, offering producers guidance on their choice of marketing channels. The classificatory schemes that have been devised differ in the range of criteria they employ and in their degree of precision. The earliest, simplest and most widely quoted is that devised by Copeland (1924) at a time when manufacturers were beginning to see the need for a more systematic approach to marketing. Copeland proposed a three-fold classification based upon consumer purchasing behaviour:

1. Convenience goods: products, such as groceries, which people buy frequently, with a minimum of effort. If a particular brand is

unavailable at the first outlet visited, there is a high probability that the consumer will accept a substitute rather than look elsewhere or postpone their purchase. Empirical studies of purchasing behaviour have shown that customers' reactions to stock-outs differ between products (*Nielsen Researcher*, 1975). In the case of 'immediate use' food products, which people consume within a few days of purchase, the most common response is for customers to settle for an alternative brand. Producers of such products must, therefore, market them intensively at the retail level, minimising the distance consumers have to travel to obtain them and the number of occasions when the shops run out of stock.

2. Shopping (or comparison) goods: products which people purchase less frequently and are only likely to buy after comparing available alternatives. Customers are more keen to shop around for particular brands or styles and less willing to make do with substitutes. Non-food products such as clothing and crockery fall into this category. Producers of these products can market them through a smaller number of outlets in the knowledge that the consumer will probably visit several before making their purchase.

3. Speciality goods: products which are generally purchased infrequently and so closely tailored to consumers' particular tastes as to justify extensive shopping around. Their producers can limit distribution to a relatively small number of specialist outlets.

The definitions of these three categories of product were subsequently refined by Holton (1958) and Bucklin (1962). Holton clarified the distinction between convenience and shopping goods by introducing the concept of a trade-off between the increased satisfaction a consumer gained from comparing products prior to purchase and the time, effort and money expended in doing so. While extensive comparison was deemed to be cost-effective in the case of shopping goods, it was not for convenience goods. Bucklin employed the concept of the 'preference map' to differentiate shopping goods more clearly from speciality goods. He considered shopping goods to be those for which people had no explicit preference at the time they embarked on the shopping trip, making it necessary for them to look around at what was available. Consumers had much more clearly defined preferences for speciality goods at the outset and could, therefore, conduct a more focused search for the particular items they wanted. As Dommermuth and Cundiff (1967) note, however, the actual amount of searching customers undertake depends on their advance knowledge of what products particular outlets stock and this can be greatly expanded by experience and advertising. They suggest that 'advertising allows the buyer to pre-shop and perhaps reach a virtual buying decision before he or she ever leaves home' (p.32). Shop-related advertising can, therefore, reduce the intensity with which speciality products need to be marketed at the retail level.

As an aid to marketing management, Copeland's product classification is lacking in several respects. First, it gives no indication of how products should be distributed to retail outlets. For example, Copeland recommends that convenience goods be stocked by large numbers of retail outlets, but does not say whether this wide retail coverage should be supported by a system of direct distribution or distribution via wholesalers. Second, his classification is based on a narrow view of purchasing behaviour and fails to take account of other factors influencing the method of distribution. Third, the assignment of products to particular categories is based on subjective judgement and, therefore, lacking in rigour. Finally, the division of consumer goods into three discrete classes is unrealistic as differences between products can be as great within these classes as between them.

Each of these shortcomings was partly overcome by the *characteristics of goods* theory devised by Aspinwall (1958). This formed a basis for differentiating products along a continuous scale in relation to the following five criteria:

1. Replacement rate: frequency with which a product is purchased.
2. Level of service (or 'adjustment'): required during the distribution process to meet customer expectations.
3. Time taken to consume the product: although closely related to replacement rate, the two criteria are not perfectly correlated; a can of paint, for example, can be rapidly used, but may not be replaced until it becomes necessary to redecorate.
4. Searching time: the average time a consumer is prepared to spend shopping for a product.
5. Gross margin: the total cost of distributing a product from point of production to point of sale, including the profits earned by intermediaries.

Aspinwall argued that each of these characteristics could be quantified and empirically weighted, though he did not attempt to give his theory a 'mathematical setting' (p.436). Instead, he exploited the close association between the five variables in devising a system of colour coding for products. At one extreme are red products, which have a high replacement rate but low ratings for the other four criteria. Such products, which resemble Copeland's convenience goods, are likely to be channelled through wholesalers. At the other extreme, yellow products would have the opposite pattern of rating and be distributed directly from producer to retailer. There would be a gradation of products between these extremes, just as in the visible spectrum light rays grade continuously from red to yellow. Aspinwall gives no indication, however, of how the precise position of a product on this continuum might be determined or how this position would correspond to a particular channel requirement.

Another deficiency of Aspinwall's scheme is its neglect of several other product characteristics that have an important influence on channel choice (Dawson, 1979):

1. Perishability. It is preferable for highly perishable goods to be distributed through short, direct channels as this minimises the amount of intermediate handling and ensures rapid movement to the customer.
2. Bulk. As bulky goods are expensive to handle and store, there are cost advantages in delivering them directly from producer to retailer (or even final customer).
3. Degree of standardisation. Some products are tailored to the specifications of particular retailers or customers and therefore require direct distribution. Others need special adjustment, installation or servicing for which the producer prefers to take responsibility. The need for direct contact between producer and retailer (or customer) is much less strong in the case of standardised products.
4. Stage in the 'product life cycle'. The life cycle of the average product can be divided into separate stages, each characterised by a different sales trend and requiring a different distribution strategy (Kaminski and Rink, 1984). The generalised model of the product life cycle has four stages: introduction to the market, growth, maturity and decline. Immediately following its launch, the sales of a new product may not be large enough to justify direct distribution to retailers. While direct promotional links may be established with retailers in a few trial areas, wholesalers would form the main points of entry to the market. If the product proves successful and sales expand, direct distribution can become more cost-effective. The emergence of competitive brands by this time also strengthens the need for more active promotion at final point of sale. Dependence on wholesalers would consequently weaken during this growth stage. The relative use of direct and indirect channels would stabilise at the maturity stage. Market saturation coupled with intense competition from similar products causes sales to level off. The desire to contain selling costs discourages the firm from establishing additional direct links with retailers, but, at the same time, the need to maintain promotional pressure makes it unwise

to sever existing links. The final phase of declining sales is characterised by a desire to withdraw from contracting markets and to economise on distribution and promotion. This may entail a return to greater dependence on wholesalers but, nevertheless, a continuation of direct dealing with large retailers.

There are many circumstances under which the pattern of channel use would evolve differently. For example, a large producer with a well established product range might be able to market a new product intensively at the retail level from the start and make little use of wholesalers at all stages in its life cycle. In a trade dominated by large multiple retailers with centralised distribution systems, even a small producer can quickly develop a heavy dependence on a few direct retail links. It should also be noted that the product life cycle has a geographical dimension. As Dawson (1973, p.143) explains, 'a product will be at different stages in its life cycle at different points in space'. This contributes to regional variations in the relative use of different marketing channels.

Nature of the market

The choice of marketing channel can be strongly influenced by the number, size and location of retail outlets, in other words, the spatial pattern of retailing. This pattern is determined primarily by four factors:

1. spatial distribution of population;
2. level of personal mobility;
3. consumer purchasing behaviour;
4. cost structure of the retailing operation.

The last two factors are largely product related and have been discussed earlier. Within a particular country or region, the density of outlets selling a given product is largely a function of the spatial distribution of population. In rural areas, where population is sparse, outlets tend to be few in number, small and widely dispersed, making it expensive for producers to promote and distribute goods directly. Retail chains are less well developed in rural areas, denying producers the same opportunities there as in urban areas to offload responsibility for shop delivery onto multiple retailers. Producers tend, therefore, to make greater use of wholesalers in distributing their goods to rural customers.

The cost of dealing directly with retailers must be weighed against the additional revenue this is likely to generate. Direct contact with retailers can help to expand sales in two ways. First, it can increase the number of outlets stocking the firm's products. In the case of Mars confectionery, for example, regression analysis was used to establish a mathematical relationship between the proportion of the available outlets stocking the firm's products and the volume of sales (Nuttall, 1965). It was predicted that increasing this proportion from 40 to 50% would generate 17% more sales. Second, direct contact can raise the level of sales per outlet, as a producer's own sales staff usually promote his products more vigorously than intermediaries and as his shop delivery system can often ensure a higher level of product availability (Mallen, 1970). It is very difficult, however, to generalise about the sensitivity of sales volumes to variations in channel usage since this depends on the quality of distribution and sales support provided by particular channels. Furthermore, channel usage is only one of many factors influencing the level of sales.

Nature of the firm

A firm's relative dependence on different marketing channels is usually related to size, product range and corporate structure. In a study of 170 firms of widely varying size (measured by turnover) Weigand (1963) found that size correlated closely with channel usage. Larger firms are generally less reliant on wholesalers and more directly involved in direct distribution to customers. These firms generate enough sales to operate a direct system of distribution efficiently. They also have the resources needed to set up such a system. The relationship between firm size and channel dependence can, nevertheless, be distorted in various ways. For example, a manufacturer producing a diverse range of products destined for many different markets may lack the necessary sales volume in particular market sectors to justify direct distribution. Manufacturers' investment policies can also differ markedly. While some firms are prepared to invest heavily in distribution facilities, others prefer to concentrate resources on their main production activity, leaving much of the responsibility for distribution to outside agencies.

In the foregoing discussion, it has been assumed that producers are concerned with the complete marketing channel reaching as far as the retail outlet. This may be a valid assumption in the case of large firms, but does not apply to the many small and medium-sized producers who are only interested in their immediate trading links. McVey (1960, p.62) argues that a producer 'may little know nor care what becomes of his products after they leave the hands of some merchant middleman who has paid him for them'. He challenges the conventional view of channel selection which implies 'that it is the producer who selects all the links in the channel and establishes the working arrangements within them down to and including the outlet which sells his goods to the final user' (p.61). All but the larger producers, he claims, lack the power to exert influence on distributors with whom they do not deal directly.

The traditional approach to channel analysis can also be criticised for being excessively producer oriented, treating the producer as the active agency of channel formation and distributors as passive agents awaiting selection (Nilsson, 1977). In practice, many channels are today dominated by large distributors or held in balance by concentrations of selling and buying power at either end. This has enabled distributors to become more discriminating in their choice of suppliers and given them much more control over the way in which products are marketed. In recognition of this new situation, the focus of channel selection research has begun to shift down the marketing channel to investigate the factors affecting the buying decisions of large retail chains (McGoldrick and Douglas, 1983; Shipley, 1985).

Historical development of marketing channels

Prior to 1850, the production and distribution of most consumer products was highly localised. Food accounted for a large proportion of average household expenditure and most of this came in a raw and unpackaged state directly from local farms. Clothing, footwear and many household items were made to order by local craftsmen who combined the functions of producer and retailer. A large proportion of consumer expenditure went, therefore, on products marketed by their producers. Where marketing channels existed at all in these largely subsistent local economies, they were generally very short both organisationally and geographically.

During the second half of the nineteenth century, several changes occurred which had a major impact on the structure of marketing channels. Following the development of the railway network, agricultural production became more regionally specialised and diets became more varied as they ceased to be confined to what could be produced locally (Oddy and Miller, 1976). Dependence on local food supplies was further weakened by the large-scale migration of population from rural areas to the rapidly expanding towns and cities. From the 1860s onwards, there was a large influx of cheap food imports, their movement greatly facilitated by the advent of the steamship and improvements to the internal transport systems of the exporting countries. The food processing industry expanded rapidly after 1860 and became increasingly concentrated in factories. The production of other consumer products, such as knitwear and footwear, also became factory based, forcing the producer-retailer into decline and increasing the proportion of goods mass produced to standard design in advance of demand.

Each of these developments had the effect of lengthening the supply line from point of production to customer and increasing the time that elapsed between production and consumption. This created conditions conducive to the emergence of marketing intermediaries. As Bucklin (1972, p.8) observes:

> With higher levels of economic development and a shift from an agrarian economy to one of partial industrialisation, the distance between the producer and user widens. At some point, firms designed solely for the purpose of organising the rate and timing of product flow between the two appear to fill this gap. These firms become the middlemen of the economic system.

Wholesaling had existed in Britain for many centuries, but on a much smaller scale and providing a narrower range of services. In the early years of the twentieth century, wholesalers dominated the distribution of many consumer goods. By this time, however, the position of the wholesaler was already being undermined by the development of multiple retailing. Multiple retailing developed in the grocery trade from the 1870s onwards. This trade was particularly suited to the growth of multiples because, as food was a convenience product for which people preferred not to travel very far, it made more sense for the expanding food retailer to open new branches, thereby competing on the basis of proximity to the customer, rather than enlarge his existing premises. By 1910, multiple retailing was also quite well established in the footwear, clothing and household goods trades (Jefferys, 1954).

Another type of organisation which began to play a major role in distribution in the latter half of the nineteenth century was the co-operative society. Following the success of the first retail society founded in 1844 in Rochdale, many others sprang up around the country, catering mainly for the basic needs of the working classes. With the formation of the Co-operative Wholesale Society in 1864 in England (1867 in Scotland), the retail societies obtained, collectively, their own wholesaling and production agency. Thereafter, the retail and wholesale sides of the organisation were closely co-ordinated, though the institutional structure of the co-operative movement prevented retail and wholesale functions from being integrated to the same degree as in the multiples.

It was common practice for multiples at an early stage in their development to take over responsibility for logistical functions previously handled by wholesalers. Once they had sufficient turnover to deal directly with producers, retailers could receive supplies in bulk at a central depot or store. Having stored, sorted and sometimes packaged these goods centrally, the retailer then arranged their delivery to branch stores. This absorption of wholesale functions by the multiple retailer not only allowed them to internalise the wholesaler's profit margin, but also led 'to the reduction or elimination of some wholesaling costs, notably a reduction in risk taking and selling costs' (Fulop, 1964).

The integration of wholesaling and retailing took two forms. Many retailers engaged in the bulk distribution only of supplies destined for their own outlets. It was common, though, in trades such as those dealing in tobacco, confectionery, newspapers, groceries and cars, for some retailers to undertake wholesaling functions for others. Wholesaler-retailers could deal directly with producers, spread the cost of their 'in-house' wholesaling operation across a larger volume of business and supplement their retail profits with an extra margin earned from wholesaling. Such hybrid firms were by no means curiosities. Jefferys (1950) estimates that in 1938 there were almost as many wholesaler-retailers as 'pure' wholesalers. The dividing line between wholesaling and retailing was often poorly defined and in the early stages of their development, some firms switched sides in the pursuit of higher profits. Halfords, for example, began as a wholesaler of ironmongery and cycle parts before setting up a chain of retail outlets (Jones, 1982).

With the growth of multiple and co-operative retailing, competition for retail sales intensified. Owing to their more favourable cost structures, the larger organisations were able to offer lower prices and hence attract business away from the smaller independent outlets. In many trades, however, competition was constrained by resale price maintenance (RPM). Jefferys (1954) estimates that in 1938, between 27 and 35% of all consumer sales were subject to RPM, though the proportion was much higher in the grocery, confectionery, drug, book and stationery trades. By shielding independent shopkeepers against the full force of competition from the multiples, RPM indirectly helped to maintain the volume of flow through their wholesale suppliers (Yamey, 1966).

Though suspicious of multiples' increased buying power, most manufacturers found that they offered an effective and efficient means of giving their products wide retail exposure. In contrast, they became increasingly dissatisfied with the standard of service provided by wholesalers. As manufacturers expanded the scale of their operations and their market areas progressively overlapped, they began to pay much more attention to the marketing of their products. Jefferys (1954, p.12) explains that:

> The growing complexity of the production of consumer goods,
> the increased amounts of capital laid out on machinery and

buildings and the greater volume of output meant that the large scale producers could not afford, while planning their production, to leave the distribution of their goods unplanned and dependent on the whims and fancies of wholesalers, retailers and consumers.

To assist their marketing efforts, manufacturers standardised, packaged and branded their products to make them more identifiable and permit more intensive advertising. This led to a de-skilling of wholesaling and retailing in some trades, where it was no longer necessary for distributors to grade, prepare and package goods to customers' tastes. Manufacturers often felt, however, that wholesalers paid too little regard to brand names and failed to maintain stocks at an adequate level. Many then decided to bypass what they perceived to be the weakest link in the distributive chain and to trade directly with retailers. This gave them much greater control over the numbers and types of outlet selling their products and enabled them to focus promotional activity on the final point of sale, where it had its greatest impact. In the clothing and footwear trades, the application of mass-production methods to fashion merchandise shortly after the Second World War favoured direct links between producers and retailers. The speed with which fashions changed, the common desire of retailers to obtain exclusive lines and the large speculative risk involved in dealing in such merchandise, made it unsuitable for distribution via wholesalers (Fulop, 1962).

As Stern and El-Ansary (1982) observe, 'It is possible to eliminate the wholesaler...but it is impossible to eliminate his functions' (p.120). To be able to trade directly with retailers, manufacturers had to recruit teams of sales representatives to visit retailers and establish their own systems of physical distribution. This generally entailed setting up local depots and acquiring fleets of delivery vehicles. These developments are outlined more fully in Chapter 3. Some manufacturers, notably of stationery, sent out commercial travellers to retail outlets to promote their merchandise and collect orders, but left the physical supply of these orders in the hands of wholesalers (Braithwaite and Dobbs, 1932). It was possible, therefore, for producers to wrest control of the selling function without having to incur the high capital cost of setting up an elaborate system of physical distribution. Other manufacturers minimised distribution expenditure by confining direct trading links to the larger retailers, many of whom operated their own depots. Over the inter-war period, however, the larger manufacturers of consumer products built up the capability of supplying large numbers of retail outlets directly, including many operated by small independent shopkeepers (McKinnon, 1981b). In the grocery and confectionery trades, where there was an abundance of outlets, manufacturers' delivery networks became particularly dense. In 1922, for example, Peek Frean distributed biscuits to 40,000 outlets (Corley, 1972), while by 1938 Cadbury Bros was delivering its confectionery to around 100,000 outlets (Cadbury Bros, 1945). The practice of delivering directly became so prevalent that some multiples were able to scale down their physical distribution activities. For instance, so many of Marks and Spencer's suppliers (mainly of household goods and clothing) provided branch store delivery by 1927 that the firm was able to dispense with its warehouses (Rees, 1969).

Wholesalers' business thus contracted as a consequence of the absorption of their logistical functions by producers as well as multiple retailers. While distribution upstream of the shop was being restructured to the detriment of wholesalers, their main clients, the independent stores, were losing sales to the multiples and, to a smaller extent, the co-operative societies.

In the 1930s, many wholesalers reacted to the mounting external pressures on them in an essentially negative manner (Stacey and Wilson, 1958). In an effort to ease their financial burden, many reduced their stock levels by ordering smaller quantities more frequently from manufacturers. Such 'hand to mouth' purchasing, however, reduced the level of bulk discount they obtained and impaired the quality of service to customers. Some wholesalers, particularly in the clothing and textile trades, avoided holding stock completely by selling goods to retailers on the basis of samples and only buying supplies from producers once they had received firm orders from their retail customers. This shirking by wholesalers of their traditional stockholding and risk-bearing duties was severely criticised in a series of official reports in the 1940s. For many, it proved counter-productive as wholesalers' financial performance tended to correlate closely with their level of participation in the marketing channel (Beckman, 1949).

Jefferys (1950) warns, however, against exaggerating the plight of wholesalers in the 1930s. He points out that the decline of wholesaling was not uniform across all trades. Wholesalers in some commodities managed to maintain or even expand their volume of sales. The position of the wholesaler was most secure in channels containing large numbers of small producers and retailers, and handling low-value unbranded products (Jefferys, 1954).

The first large-scale survey of distribution in Great Britain was undertaken in 1938 and, unlike the later Censuses of Distribution in 1951, 1961 and 1971, it provided detailed information about the structure of marketing channels (Figure 2.2). It revealed that by 1938 only about 47% of the flow of consumer products (by value) was

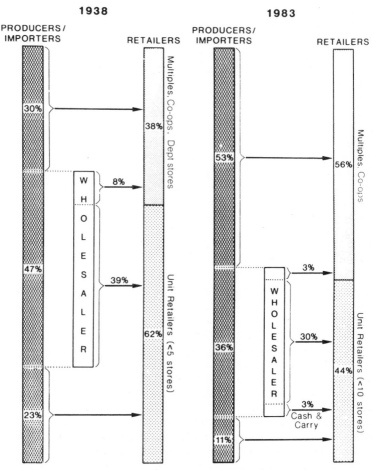

Figure 2.2 Allocation of retail sales among marketing channels: 1938 and 1983
Sources: Jefferys, 1950; NEDO, 1985; Office of Fair Trading, 1985.

passing through wholesalers. Multiple retailers and department stores were making very little use of wholesalers and even independent shops (or 'unit retailers') were receiving about a third of their supplies directly from producers. Direct producer-retailer links accounted for 57% of total sales to the public. Longer channels containing more than one wholesaler handled only a very small proportion of the total flow. In 1938, only about 7% of products (by value) experienced two or more stages of wholesaling. The subdivision of wholesaling was found

48

mainly in the distribution of fruit and vegetables, fish, eggs, wines and spirits and imported canned goods.

Inter-war trends in distribution were interrupted during the Second World War by the imposition of controls on consumption (rationing), manufacturing (concentration of production programme) and distribution ('sector' and 'zoning' schemes) (Hammond, 1951), but began to reassert themselves from the mid-1950s onwards. The multiples and co-operatives continued to increase their share of the retail market at the expense of smaller independent stores. They strengthened their competitive position by enlarging their outlets and, in some trades, introducing self-service. Legislation in 1964 eliminated RPM for all but a small number of products (such as books and pharmaceuticals) and heralded a new era of price competition when the small independent retailer was increasingly undercut by the larger operator. Nevertheless, the competitiveness of the independents was by this time enhanced both by the formation of retail buying groups and by two major wholesaling innovations.

Fulop (1962, p.15) defines a *retail buying group* as consisting of 'a handful of independent grocers bound simply by a gentleman's agreement to buy some of their supplies jointly'. By thus pooling their purchasing, members could deal directly with manufacturers and often qualify for bulk discounts. Associated buying by retailers developed mainly in the grocery trade where products were standardised and competition from multiples particularly intense.

New forms of wholesaling that appeared in Great Britain for the first time in the mid-1950s afforded the independent sector much greater and more lasting support. The negative tendencies exhibited by many wholesalers in the 1930s and 1940s gave way in the 1950s to more positive efforts to adjust to the changing market conditions. By setting up *voluntary groups*, wholesalers began to co-ordinate their activities more closely with those of their retail customers, effectively establishing consensus channels. Wholesaler-sponsored voluntary groups had existed in the US since the First World War and were already well established in several European countries. They had several important advantages. The agreement of affiliated retailers to purchase a substantial proportion of their supplies from a local group wholesaler allowed the latter to plan its operation more efficiently. By combining their orders, group wholesalers around the country could obtain their supplies collectively from producers at more favourable rates and thus charge retailers lower prices.

Early reluctance on the part of some manufacturers to deal with voluntary groups was quickly overcome. Once identified with a group's symbol (such as Spar, Mace or VG), retail members could also benefit from regional and national advertising campaigns comparable to those of the multiples. The main development of voluntary groups has occurred in the grocery trade, though they also exist in trades dealing in hardware, textiles, drugs, DIY and motor accessories.

The development of 'cash and carries' also represented a radical departure from conventional wholesaling. *Cash and carry wholesaling* was pioneered in North America in the 1930s, but did not appear in Great Britain until 1956. It effectively extended the practice of self-service into wholesaling (Kirby, 1974), offering retail customers lower prices by cutting back on the traditional wholesale functions of order picking, goods delivery and the provision of credit. As with voluntary group trading, the cash and carry principle has found its widest application in the grocery trade.

Despite these initiatives, small-scale retailing continued to decline, not only because of competition from the multiples, but also partly as a consequence of other developments, such as urban renewal and changes in the tax system (Dawson and Kirby, 1979). Many small shops also suffered from the growing tendency in the 1960s and 1970s for manufacturers, particularly in the food industry, to curtail the delivery of small quantities to shops. The contraction of manufacturers' distribution networks was partly a cost-cutting exercise and partly the result of a change in marketing policy. Many manufacturers recognised that, for several reasons, it was no longer necessary to trade directly with small retailers. Although these retailers' aggregate share of many consumer markets remained substantial, manufacturers were quite confident that severing direct links with them would not seriously jeopardise their sales. This confidence rested partly on the knowledge that alternative channels existed, in voluntary group and cash and carry wholesaling, through which the small shopkeeper could still obtain their products. Many manufacturers also believed that brand loyalty was now sufficiently strong to maintain sales through these outlets, even in the absence of a direct promotional link. Furthermore, television advertising now enabled manufacturers to stimulate consumer demand more directly. The withdrawal of manufacturers' deliveries to small independents created, in the early 1970s, a resurgence of demand for the services of wholesalers. This increase in business was short lived, however, as the independent sector continued to contract and as wholesalers, like manufacturers, found it necessary to cut back on the uneconomic delivery of small orders (Kirby, 1975). As the size threshold for entry into voluntary groups rose, increasing numbers of small independents were left almost entirely dependent on cash and carries for their supplies.

The main cause of the decline in wholesaling in recent decades has been the enormous growth of multiple retailing. Between 1966 and

Table 2.3 Proportion of total sales of selected products handled by wholesalers, 1983

Product class	Wholesaler's share (%)	Trend
Food and drink	38	down
Clothing	25	down
Tobacco	40	up
Housewares and DIY	45	down
Confectionery	45	stable
Periodicals	95	stable
Furniture	5	up
Toiletries	40	down
Floor coverings	25	down
Books	20	up
Footwear	20	down
Drugs	70	up

Source: NEDO, 1985.

1982, the multiples increased their share of total retail sales by roughly a third (Office of Fair Trading, 1985), winning sales from both independents and the co-operative societies. Within the multiple retailing sector, buying power has become increasingly concentrated, partly as a result of takeovers and mergers, and this has enabled the multiples to exert much greater influence over the way goods are distributed and the price paid for them. As a result of their wide geographical extent and heavy involvement in physical distribution, multiples can help small producers expand their market areas and greatly increase their volume of sales. By relieving these small producers of the high costs of establishing extensive retail delivery systems, the multiples are today fulfilling a similar role to that of wholesalers a century ago.

Having examined the structure of marketing channels in the north-east of England, NEDO (1971, p.12) concluded that 'business economists' requiems for the wholesaler, which are often heard, are in some cases premature'. In 1983, wholesalers still handled around 36% of total retail sales in the UK (Figure 2.2) and a much higher proportion of sales of particular products, such as periodicals, drugs and electrical goods (Table 2.3) (NEDO, 1985). In some trades, such as those of tobacco and books, they were increasing their share of business. Almost two-thirds of retail supplies, however, are now sold by their producer or importer directly to the retailer and this proportion is predicted to rise. The wholesaler's role in physical distribution will continue to diminish as control of this function passes increasingly into the hands of multiple retailers.

Chapter three

Physical distribution channels

A physical distribution (or logistical) channel is composed of terminal nodes, such as factories and shops, intermediate nodes, such as warehouses, and the links between them, represented by freight movements. It is a much less abstract concept than a marketing channel and much more observable on the ground. Figure 3.1 shows the main physical distribution channels through which finished goods pass *en route* from factory to shop. Like marketing channels, physical distribution channels have two dimensions:

1. Vertical dimension: the series of nodes and links that comprise the supply line from factory to shop.
2. Horizontal dimension: the number of similar nodes at a given stage in the supply line.

This chapter is concerned with the vertical structure of physical distribution channels. The horizontal dimension, particularly as it relates to stockholding, is considered in Chapter 4.

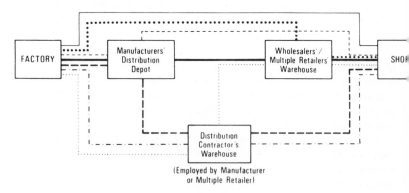

Figure 3.1 Physical distribution channels

Table 3.1   Proportion of output distributed directly from the factory: sample of food manufacturers

	\<20%	21-40%	41-60%	>60%	Total
	Proportion of output distributed directly from the factory				
No. of Firms	8	8	4	3	23
(%)	(35)	(35)	(17)	(13)	(100)

Goods passing through the same marketing channel can be routed through different physical distribution channels. This is because some members of marketing channels, mainly manufacturers and multiple retailers, have a choice of two physical distribution channels (Bowersox, 1978):

1. Direct channel: in the case of manufacturers, use of this channel entails transporting goods to customers straight from the factory, while for multiple retailers it involves receiving supplies at branch store level.
2. Echelon (or indirect) channel: in which stocks are held at one or more intermediate locations in the supply line. A manufacturer using an echelon channel directs its output through distribution depots. The corresponding action for a multiple retailer is to direct incoming supplies through a warehouse under its control.

In some firms' distribution systems, all flow is confined to one or other of these channels. It is much more common, however, for firms to make some use of both channels. Systems that combine direct deliveries with distribution via intermediate stockholding points are known as *dual or flexible systems*. Such hybrid systems can vary enormously in the relative proportions of flow allocated to the two types of channel. Table 3.1 shows how, even within a single industrial sector, firms can rely on direct, and by implication echelon, channels to widely differing degrees. In this chapter we shall consider what influences a firm's relative dependence on direct and echelon channels, and examine the nature of the linkage between those sections of physical distribution channels under the control of manufacturers and multiple retailers.

Little reference will be made to wholesalers at this stage because they seldom have a choice of physical distribution channel. They generally operate premises at only one level in the vertical physical distribution channel, through which they direct all the goods they handle.

Physical distribution systems

Manufacturer-controlled channels

Historical background

The evolution of manufacturers' distribution systems over the past century can be divided into three broad phases: the first characterised by heavy or complete dependence on direct channels, the second by the development of echelon channels and the third by a renewed emphasis on direct distribution. The following description of these three phases is based on the experience of British food processing firms, but also indicative of what has happened to manufacturers of other consumer products.

Expansion of the market area: dependence on direct channels

As manufacturers extended their market areas in the latter half of the nineteenth century, supply lines to customers radiated directly from their factories. Firms were heavily dependent on the railways for long-distance transport and on wholesalers for localised stockholding, merchandising and delivery. It was common for firms to use their own transport to distribute products directly to customers in the vicinity of the factory. The size of area served in this way was tightly constrained by the poor state of the road network and the limited range of horse-drawn carts. This similarly restricted the hinterland of the railway depots through which the remainder of manufacturers' output passed. The railway cartage services, for example, provided road delivery only within a radius of two or three miles (Reader, 1969).

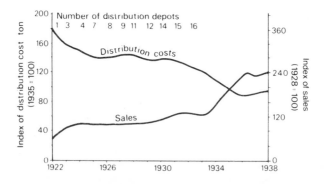

Figure 3.2 Cost and sales trends during the development of a distribution system: Cadbury Bros 1922–38
Source: Cadbury Bros, 1945.

Distribution at this time was characterised by small consignment size, slow carriage and limited stockholding at or near the point of sale. Because local delivery by road was difficult and costly, goods were generally trunked to the rail depot nearest to the customer before being transferred onto a road vehicle. The flow of goods through the railway network was, therefore, highly dispersed, distributing small, individually wrapped consignments through a large number of rail depots. Frequent marshalling and sorting of this traffic *en route* rendered transit times long and highly variable. In the late nineteenth century, more distant customers might have to wait several weeks for supplies ordered directly from the producer. By holding stocks locally, wholesalers could satisfy retailers' needs at much shorter notice, but, as noted in Chapter 2, they were often accused of carrying too little stock and not being sufficiently brand conscious. To be able to market their products more aggressively, manufacturers had to become more involved in the distribution process.

Market consolidation: development of echelon channels

In an effort to extend their control over the marketing and supply of their products many of the larger manufacturers developed echelon channels, principally during the inter-war period. This entailed setting up (or contracting) depots around the country where stock could be held much closer to retail customers and from which local delivery to shops could be more efficiently organised (McKinnon, 1981b). Sales operations were also decentralised at this time to help firms forge direct links with retailers.

The development of echelon systems was not motivated solely by manufacturers' desire to market their products more intensively at the retail level. It also enabled them to reduce their transport costs by making better use of the railway trunk haul. Instead of despatching goods in small consignments through numerous railway terminals, manufacturers could now send bulk loads to a much smaller number of their own stockholding depots. By consolidating trunk flows into large loads, manufacturers were able to obtain more favourable rates from the railway companies. The introduction of the motor vehicle permitted the expansion of depot delivery areas, as the lorry had a range roughly three times greater than that of the horse and cart (Jefferys, 1954). The new system of distribution also economised on packaging.

Cadbury Bros (1945) was the only large food manufacturer to publish a detailed record of its distribution operations in the inter-war period. Although it is not known how representative Cadbury's experience was at this time, the information the company has provided offers a good indication of the scale of benefits that manufacturers could obtain by developing a depot system. Between 1922 and 1938, Cadburys were able to reduce their distribution costs per unit by almost 50% while increasing total sales by around 650% (Figure 3.2). Between 1925 and 1931, savings in transport and packaging costs were largely offset by the heavy capital cost of setting up the new depots. From 1932 onwards, however, the rapid growth in sales volume, fostered by the new system of distribution, spread these overhead costs across a much larger depot throughput, bringing down the unit cost of distribution quite sharply.

Market rationalisation: reversion to direct distribution

Since the mid-1960s, many manufacturers have quite radically altered their distribution systems, putting into practice many of the principles of physical distribution management outlined in Chapter 1. When firms subjected their distribution activities to close scrutiny, often for the first time, many discovered that it was unprofitable to distribute small orders directly to retail outlets. For example, in the late 1960s, 34,000 of Associated Biscuit Manufacturer's 76,000 customers bought less than 100 cases 'and, therefore, hardly recompensed the

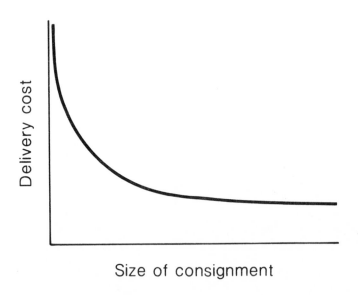

Figure 3.3 Relationship between consignment size and delivery cost

company for the cost of representatives' visits and deliveries' (Corley, 1972, p.283). It has been shown that there is a negative exponential relationship between delivery costs and order size (Williams, 1975; McConkey, 1979) (Figure 3.3). Once the high cost of distributing small orders was taken into account, it was found that maximising sales did not maximise profit (Figure 3.4). Many companies reacted to these findings by cutting back on the delivery of small quantities. They did this either by raising *minimum drop size* (the minimum amount they were prepared to deliver) or by imposing prohibitive surcharges on small orders (Walters, 1976; Lambert, Bennion and Taylor, 1983).

Table 3.2 shows how, over the period 1960-78, a group of large British food manufacturers reduced the number of outlets they supplied. This contraction of their delivery networks effectively reversed the inter-war policy of trading directly with as many retailers as possible. The severance of many of these direct trading links was

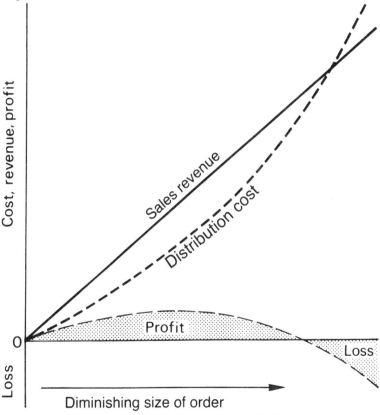

Figure 3.4 Relationship between order size and profitability

Table 3.2 Reduction in the number of outlets served: sample of food manufacturers

Dominant Product	1960	1964	1968	1970	1972	1974	1978
Sugar	90,000						30,500
Margarine	31,000			23,000			10,300
Biscuits		19,000					11,000
Confectionery			32,000				22,000
Biscuits			170,000				60,000
Breakfast Cereal				12,000			7,000
Canned Vegetables					11,000		5,600
Tea						85,500	17,000

now considered acceptable for reasons that were outlined in Chapter 2. The number of delivery points was also diminishing as a result of other developments outside the manufacturers' direct control, most notably:

1. the widespread closure of small shops;
2. the development of superstores and hypermarkets;
3. concentration in the wholesale sector;
4. multiple retailers' growing preference for central warehouse delivery.

The spatial concentration of demand for manufacturers' products at the wholesale and retail levels has enabled them to distribute an increasing proportion of their output in bulk loads directly from the factory. There has been a corresponding decline in the use of echelon channels, with many manufacturers reducing the capacity of decentralised storage and delivery systems. The trend back towards direct delivery has been reinforced by the desire to reduce inventory by concentrating it in fewer locations.

Factors affecting channel allocation

To a manufacturer, the use of a direct physical distribution channel is associated with the concentration of stock at the factory site; the use of an echelon channel with its dispersal to regional depots. The choice of physical distribution channel is, therefore, conditioned by the decision on whether to centralise or decentralise the inventory of finished goods. In making this decision, firms must weigh up the advantages and disadvantages of each strategy.

By centralising stock, firms can reduce the total amount of stock they need to hold to maintain a given level of customer service. As there are economies of scale in warehousing, the unit cost of storing goods is lower in one large warehouse than in several smaller ones. Both these relationships are discussed more fully in Chapter 4. Holding stocks centrally at the factory site also enables manufacturers to avoid the *speculative risk* involved in allocating too much stock to regional depots (Alderson, 1950). This allocation is generally based on forecasts of the future level of sales in the areas served by the depots. If sales in a particular area fall below the anticipated level, the firm has three options:

1. Sell off the surplus stock at discounted prices.
2. Redistribute it to areas of higher demand.
3. Store it at the regional depot until required.

Each of these options erodes profitability: the first by reducing sales revenue, the second and third by inflating distribution costs. This gives firms an incentive to postpone committing stocks to particular market sectors as long as possible (Bowersox, 1983). Such postponement also carries a risk, however — that of being unable to satisfy sudden increases in demand in particular areas and as a result losing potential sales (Bucklin, 1965). The magnitude of this *risk of postponement*, which is inherent in the centralisation of inventory, depends on the size of the market area, the quality of the transport system and the demand characteristics of the firms' products. In deciding whether to concentrate or disperse stocks manufacturers must strike a balance between the risks of speculation and postponement.

The nature of the demand for products, which in Chapter 2 was shown to influence the selection of marketing channels, also affects manufacturers' choice of physical distribution channels. Convenience goods, particularly those characterised by low brand loyalty and high substitutability, are best stored within echelon systems, where stocks are held within easy reach of final demand. In contrast, supplies of higher-order shopping goods, for which customers are prepared to wait or shop elsewhere, can usually be replenished quickly enough from centrally held stock.

Products with a fast turnover rate typically require decentralised storage, permitting rapid delivery to customers from local stockholding points. Although daily storage costs are higher in small local depots, fast-moving products spend little time there, keeping total storage costs within acceptable bounds. The urgency with which these goods are required limits the scope for holding back orders at a factory or central depot until a sufficiently large load has accumulated to fill a trunk vehicle. On the other hand, slower-moving items, which on average spend a longer time in storage, are more economically stored in a large central facility and offer greater opportunity for consolidation into bulk loads.

Table 3.3 ABC system of product classification

Product category	% of product items	% of total sales	Cumulative % of items	Cumulative % of sales
A	20	80	20	80
B	30	15	50	95
C	50	5	100	100

Turnover rates usually vary widely across an individual firm's product range. This means that some products account for a much larger share of total sales than others. In fact, it is commonly found that 80% of total sales are generated by only 20% of the product range. This *Pareto relationship* occurs widely throughout industry and commerce and is extensively used in the classification of products for inventory management purposes. Products are normally ranked in descending order according to their sales volume and given an A, B or C designation as shown in Table 3.3. Ballou (1973) gives this ABC classification a spatial dimension by ranking products not simply on the basis of their contribution to total sales volume, but also in terms of their relative transport, storage and service opportunity costs at different levels in the physical distribution channel. In his scheme, A products are those which can be distributed at minimum cost through decentralised systems, comprising numerous local depots, whereas C products are distributed most cost-effectively from a single large warehouse. B products fall between these extremes and, according to Ballou, are best located in a few regional warehouses. Ballou, therefore, envisages a three-tier distribution system to correspond to the traditional three-fold classification of products by turnover rate. In practice, however, most manufacturers, particularly in smaller countries such as the UK, dispense with either the local or regional level of stockholding. Ballou's stock location model also fails to allow for the possibility that stock of a particular product may be held at more than one level in the physical distribution channel.

The vertical structure of physical distribution channels is also influenced by the number, size and spatial distribution of customer delivery points. Manufacturers channelling their products through wholesalers or the central warehouses of retail chains can transport their output efficiently in bulk loads directly from the factory. The delivery of small consignments to retail outlets directly from the factory is only economical over short distances. To serve shops located beyond the immediate hinterland of the factory efficiently, it is necessary to split the freight movement into *trunk (or line-) haul* and *local delivery* sections. Goods are then transported in bulk loads from the factory to break-bulk points where these loads are disaggregated

Table 3.4 Number of outlets served: sample of food manufacturers

| | Number of outlets | | | | | |
	<5,000	5-10,000	11-20,000	21-30,000	>30,000	Total
No. of Firms	6	5	6	5	3	25
%	(24)	(20)	(24)	(20)	(12)	(100)

into individual orders for final delivery. It is not necessary to hold stock at these break-bulk points, as demonstrated by the distribution operations of firms such as Lyons-Tetley and General Foods; however, where decentralised stockholding is justified on other grounds, manufacturers usually combine storage and break-bulk functions at local depots.

Direct channels are used mainly for the bulk delivery of goods to the warehouses of wholesalers and multiple retailers, whereas echelon channels generally handle shop deliveries. One might, therefore, expect the allocation of product flow between direct and echelon channels to correlate with the relative numbers of warehouses and shops supplied. An attempt was made to test this hypothesis using data collected from a sample of 25 food manufacturers. Almost all the firms consulted were able to estimate the total number of outlets served (Table 3.4), but very few could disaggregate this figure by outlet type. There was found to be a weak, but significant, relationship ($r = -0.484$; significance level = 99%) between the total number of outlets these firms supplied and their relative dependence on direct, ex-factory delivery.

The food manufacturers surveyed differed widely in the number of outlets to which they delivered their products. The number of outlets served by a manufacturer's distribution system depends on four factors:

1. The spatial extent of the market area.
2. The density of wholesale and retail outlets in this area.
3. The degree of market penetration at the wholesale and retail levels.
4. The relative proportions of output distributed to warehouses and shops.

As all the manufacturers in the sample marketed their products nationally, the first and second factors were of little concern. The wide variations in the numbers of outlets served were, therefore, a function of the third and fourth factors. In respect of the third factor, it could reasonably be assumed that the manufacturers in question achieved a

Table 3.5 Proportion of grocery stores stocking the three best-selling brands of grocery and related products

	% of grocery stores
No. 1 Brands	76
No. 2 Brands	53
No. 3 Brands	48

Note: Based on the following products: baked beans, instant cereals, ready to eat cereals, coffee, canned evaporated milk, soup, chocolate biscuits, cat food, dog food, toothpaste, household cleaner, detergents, men's hairdressing, shampoos, soap.

Source: Nielsen Researcher, 1975.

high level of market penetration. Most of them produced at least one leading brand and, as shown in Table 3.5, the top brands of grocery and related products are typically sold through roughly three-quarters of the total number of retail outlets (*Nielsen Researcher*, 1975). It appears likely, therefore, that observed differences in the numbers of outlets served are attributable more to variations in the ratio of warehouse to shop deliveries than to variations in the degree of market penetration.

Table 3.6 presents estimates of the numbers of grocery stores and warehouses in operation at the time of the survey and estimates of the proportions of grocery trade they handled. It can be seen that a

Table 3.6 Numbers of grocery warehouses and shops with the proportions of trade handled, 1979[a]

Organisation	Approx. no. of warehouses	% of grocery turnover through warehouses	Approx. no. of shops	% of turnover direct from supplier
Multiples	100 ———— 26 ———→		7,000 ◄——— 27	
Co-op Wholesale/ Retail Societies	150 ———— 7 ———→		6,000 ◄——— 8	
Wholesalers (Delivered Trade)	240 ◄——— 11 ———→ 3		21,000[b] ◄——— 3	
Cash and Carry Wholesalers	590 ◄——— 11 ———→ 1		52,000[b] ◄——— 3	
	1,080 ———— 55 ———→		86,000 ◄——— 41	

Notes: a. Sales of groceries through mixed retail businesses and department stores are excluded. These represented approx. 4-5% of the total.
     b. Independent stores affiliated to voluntary groups.
     c. Unaffiliated independent stores.

Sources: Institute of Grocery Distribution; Co-operative Union; Co-operative Wholesale Society; Economist Intelligence Unit, 1980; Mintel, 1979.

Table 3.7 Approximate ratios of shops to warehouses in the grocery trade, 1979

Type of organisation	Ratio
Multiples	70 : 1
Co-operative Wholesale Society	165 : 1
Voluntary Group Wholesalers	87 : 1
Cash and Carry Wholesalers[a]	100 : 1

Note: a. Assumes that 80% of independent stores used cash and carries (Mintel, 1979).

Sources: Same as Table 3.6.

manufacturer relying totally on direct distribution from the factory could despatch goods to a maximum of roughly 2,000 warehouses plus around 150 superstores and hypermarkets. A manufacturer seeking to maximise market coverage through a system of shop delivery would have to distribute its products to around 50,000 outlets. Such a system would, of course, increase the chances of each outlet actually stocking the firm's products. The ratios of stores to warehouses in Table 3.7 give a measure of the extent to which a manufacturer could reduce the density of its distribution network by delivering to warehouses rather than shops and help to explain wide disparities in the number of outlets served.

Companies which distributed their products to numbers of outlets between the extremes of 2,000 and 50,000 made use of both direct and indirect channels, though to varying degrees. Few producers delivered to the 52,000 unaffiliated independents which were generally very small and had a low turnover. Only suppliers of perishable products requiring fast and frequent delivery dealt directly with these independent stores, often by means of a van sales operation. By this time, many voluntary group stores were also deemed to be too small to receive direct deliveries. Through a combination of pricing policies and the imposition of minimum drop restrictions, many of the large food manufacturers had reduced the total number of shops eligible for direct delivery to around 20,000. These 20,000 stores, however, accounted for over three-quarters of total grocery sales. It is necessary, therefore, not only to consider the total numbers of outlets in each category, but also their proportion of total grocery sales. There was a marked concentration of grocery turnover in a comparatively small number of both warehouses and shops. Madigan (1980) estimated that roughly 70% of grocery sales were channelled through around 4,000 retail outlets. The multiples, for example, in 1980 operated only 9% of grocery stores but held 55% of the grocery market (Institute of Grocery Distribution, 1982). At a higher level in the distributive channel, they controlled only 8% of all grocery warehouses, but these premises handled around 44% of total grocery turnover. On the other hand, the 60% of grocery stores that fell into the 'unaffiliated independent' category generated only 15-16% of grocery sales and the 590 cash and carry warehouses, from which they drew most of their supplies, accounted for less than a quarter of total grocery warehouse throughput (Economist Intelligence Unit, 1980).

It was estimated, in 1979, that grocery suppliers sold 81% of their total output through 285 buying points, mainly retailers' and wholesalers' head offices (*Nielsen Researcher*, 1979). The concentration of individual manufacturers' sales was even more pronounced. In 1978, for instance, 84% of Tate and Lyle's sales to the public were channelled through only 16 retailers, while 80% of Cadbury-Typhoo's sales were handled by 20 (Price Commission, 1978a, b). It can be seen, therefore, that the total number of outlets to which a manufacturer delivers its products, and hence its relative use of direct and echelon channels, can largely depend on the manner in which major retail customers are supplied. The nature of the supply links between manufacturers and their large retail customers is examined in detail later in this chapter.

The division of output between direct and echelon channels is also related to firm size. Small firms are more dependent on direct distribution because they lack the financial resources to develop their own systems of regional depots and, moreover, the volumes they distribute would be insufficient to make economic use of an echelon system (Mintel, 1977). By employing contractors, small manufacturers can effectively establish echelon channels without having to invest heavily in regional depots, though to obtain competitive rates from contractors they must generate a certain minimum volume of traffic.

Some manufacturers are constrained in the extent to which they can distribute output directly to customers by the geography of their production. Where different products are made in different plants, it may not be possible to assemble at any single plant orders large enough to justify direct delivery. Some firms mix product ranges manufactured at different locations in special warehouses, or by means of interplant transfers. Orders thus consolidated may be large enough to bypass distribution depots and be delivered 'directly' to the customer. Several multiplant firms, however, find it difficult to operate a system of bulk mixing efficiently and as a result only distribute mixed orders through local distribution depots. Their dependence on the echelon channel is likely to be greater, therefore, than it would have been had the entire range been produced at a single factory. The logistics of bulk distribution in multiplant firms is discussed at greater length in Chapter 7.

Retailer-controlled channels

Few multiple retailers passively await the arrival of all their supplies at their branch stores. Most intervene at an earlier stage in their distribution to centralise stocks in separate warehouses, consolidate orders for branch store delivery and even collect supplies from producers' premises. As outlined in Chapter 2, the internalisation of the traditional logistical functions of wholesalers has given multiples a major economic advantage over independent retailers and helped them expand their share of total retail sales. Over the past 20 years, multiple retailers have substantially increased their involvement in intermediate storage and transport as a result of two related trends. The first has been the increase, in most trades, in the multiples' share of retail sales. While expanding their market share and partly to help

Table 3.8 Variations in the proportion of turnover channelled through retailer-controlled warehouses

(a) Multisectoral Survey of 200 Large Retailers: ·

% through warehouse	% of retailers
>80	54
50 – 80	25
1 – 50	15
0	6

(b) Variations by trade sector, 1983:

Sector	% through warehouse
Electrical goods	48
Alcoholic drinks	49
Clothing	57
Footwear	59
Food	62
Furniture	73
Tobacco	73

(c) Variations among grocery retailers, 1984:

Supermarket chain	% through warehouse
Safeway	93
Sainsbury	85
Kwiksave	80
Waitrose	80
Tesco	50
Fine Fare	45
Dee	40

Sources: (a) Simpkin *et al.* 1987.
(b) NEDO, 1985.
(c) Institute of Grocery Distribution, 1985.

them do so, many multiples have increased the proportion of supplies channelled through the warehouses they control (usually called *central warehouses* or *regional distribution centres* (RDCs)). The extent of multiple retailers' influence over intermediate distribution is generally measured by the proportion of turnover passing through these warehouses; in other words, flowing through what from the retail standpoint can be regarded as echelon channels. In 1983, about 35% of total retail sales in the UK were channelled through these warehouses, making them, in terms of aggregate throughput, more important nodes than depots operated by either wholesalers or manufacturers (NEDO, 1985). As multiples accounted for 56% of all retail sales in that year, it can be deduced that they directed about two-thirds of their supplies (by value) through central warehouses. A more recent survey of 200 large British retailers by Simpkin, Maier and Lee (1987) found that the majority handled more than 80% of their supplies centrally (Table 3.8a) with only 6% relying totally on direct deliveries from manufacturers.

Some multiples, most notably mixed-retail businesses such as British Home Stores (BhS) and Woolworth, also organise the collection of supplies from producers' premises. By extending their control further back along the supply chain they can improve the reliability of incoming flows while obtaining goods more cheaply on an *ex-works* basis (McKinnon, 1986d). These benefits can outweigh the extra transport costs the retailer incurs, especially where, as in the case of BhS (Hawes, 1979), the collection of supplies provides back-loads for delivery vehicles returning from branch stores.

Advantages of centralised delivery

It is not surprising that multiple retailers have become so involved in physical distribution 'upstream' of the shop as it confers a host of economic and operational benefits. These benefits can be grouped under three headings (McKinnon, 1986a):

Strengthening of retailers' negotiating position with suppliers

By receiving goods in bulk loads into their warehouses, multiple retailers can qualify for bulk discounts. The nature and scale of these discounts are discussed later in this chapter. It should be noted at this stage, however, that these discounts are never large enough to finance multiples' warehouse and transport operations. Thorpe and Shepherd (1977), for example, estimated that, in the case of supermarket chains, the cost of these operations averages around 3-4% of turnover, whereas suppliers' discounts for bulk deliveries of groceries seldom exceed 1-2% of selling price. To justify their additional net expenditure on physical distribution, multiple retailers must, therefore, derive other benefits from centralised distribution.

It can give them additional leverage in trade negotiations in other ways. Retailers whose shops have poor reception facilities, 'backdoor' congestion problems and high delivery refusal rates can improve the efficiency of manufacturers' delivery operations by diverting the inflow of supplies to a central warehouse. Suppliers can be expected to pass on at least some of the resulting cost saving in lower prices.

The centralisation of the distribution operation generally entails the centralisation of the buying function, allowing the retailer to negotiate much more professionally and aggressively with suppliers at head-office level and curb the tendency for individual store managers to overorder.

Improving the efficiency of the retailing operation

By centralising deliveries, multiple retailers can raise labour productivity in branch stores, both at goods handling and management levels. Labour costs account for roughly 50% of the total operating costs of a supermarket (Dawson, 1982), and around 40% of these costs are associated with the physical handling of goods. These costs can be significantly reduced by replacing numerous deliveries from suppliers with a few large consolidated drops from a central warehouse. Studies of the pattern of delivery to supermarkets have shown how consolidation can greatly rationalise the inflow of supplies. In the case of one London supermarket, 50% of supplies arrived in large consolidated loads from a central warehouse and took a total of 45 minutes to offload. The remainder came in 132 separate deliveries from suppliers and took around 25 hours to unload. A similar survey by the GLC (1975) found that deliveries to a supermarket from a central warehouse comprised on average 740 cases, whereas orders received directly from suppliers averaged only 26 cases. The impact of consolidation on labour productivity is indicated by Kirby (1975), who states that one order of 500 packs is 31% quicker to assemble and 47% quicker to unload than five orders of 100 packs. Productivity is further enhanced by the more careful scheduling of deliveries under the retailer's direct control and by the use of handling systems tailored to the size, layout and trading characteristics of branch stores. By controlling the flow of supplies into shops, retailers can reduce stock loss through theft and damage. Management and clerical staff can also be more effectively employed. The amount of time shop managers spend meeting sales representatives and compiling orders is reduced, allowing them to direct more attention to the internal running of their stores. Centralised processing of orders also enables the multiple to concentrate clerical work at head office where it can be performed more efficiently.

The concentration of a retailer's inventory in a central warehouse yields similar benefits to those of a manufacturer centralising stock at the factory. It reduces the total amount of 'safety' stock required to maintain a given level of product availability, and enables the retailer to postpone committing stock to particular outlets until justified by customer demand. This is particularly advantageous in trades where changes in fashion and seasonal variations in demand make it difficult to manage stocks efficiently at the retail level. Across all sectors of the retail trade, the centralisation of inventory makes for much tighter stock control, minimising retailers' investment in working capital and associated interest payments. As the profitability of retailing is critically dependent on the rate of stockturn (usually defined as the ratio of annual sales to the value of stock held at the end of the financial year), it is important for retailers not only to maximise sales but also to minimise stock levels. Partly as a result of rapid distribution, some retailers are today able to 'turn' stock so rapidly that it is sold before the supplier has been paid. This means that the retailer benefits not only from having its stockholding financed by the supplier, but also from a positive cash flow. Morever, retailers with centralised systems of distribution and ordering are well placed to exploit the advantages of laser scanning at *electronic points of sale* (EPOS) and thereby further reduce stock levels relative to turnover.

In addition to cutting stock levels, the centralisation of retailers' inventory geographically redistributes it away from shops in expensive sites to warehouses in more peripheral locations where storage space can be provided much more cheaply. This enables firms to improve the shop *conversion ratio* (i.e. the ratio of sales area to floorspace used for storage and other purposes), releasing valuable space for display purposes.

Improving customer appeal

Centralised distribution helps retailers compete more effectively on the basis of customer service. Where they can supply branch store orders more rapidly from their warehouse than a producer can deliver them, they reduce the risk of their shops running out of particular items. The quality of supplies can also be more effectively monitored when they pass through a central warehouse. Multiples with central warehouses can extend their product ranges by purchasing supplies from producers that are too small to provide extensive branch store delivery. Such suppliers can be a valuable source of more specialist lines. Multiples wishing to develop a range of own-label products must also be prepared to assume responsibility for their intermediate distribution.

Variations in the relative use of central warehouses

Despite the numerous benefits of centralised delivery, multiple retailers differ widely in the proportion of turnover they send through their central warehouses (Table 3.8a). Intertrade variations in average dependence on central warehouses (Table 3.8b) can be partly ascribed to differences in the marketing and handling characteristics of products and the structure of the industries that supply them.

Even within a single trade, closely competing retailers can operate very different distribution strategies. Table 3.8c shows how across a sample of supermarket chains there were wide disparities in the proportion of turnover channelled through a central warehouse (Robson, 1985). The existence of such wide disparities can be interpreted in two ways. It can suggest either that there is no single optimum level of centralised delivery or that distribution policy has little bearing on competitiveness and profitability, allowing retailers with markedly different policies to co-exist. The latter interpretation can be contested on the grounds that the centralisation of deliveries has helped many retailers to increase their net margins.

Thorpe, Kirby and Thompson (1973) list eight characteristics of retail chains which they believe affect dependence on central warehouses: degree of vertical integration, the number, size and dispersal of branch stores, sales density, site costs, growth history and product mix. These create different conditions for the optimisation of distribution strategies, confirming that there is no single optimum level of centralisation. Thorpe *et al.* depict the relationship between these factors and the level of centralised delivery in a series of highly generalised graphs. They do not, however, fully explain these relationships, nor attempt to test them empirically.

As the degree of vertical integration is really just another way of describing the relative use of central warehouses, it cannot be used as an explanatory variable. The question still remains as to why some retailers choose to become more involved in the intermediate storage and movement of their supplies than others. Some retailers clearly attach more importance to physical distribution than others and are prepared to allocate a greater proportion of capital investment and managerial effort to this ancillary function. This is sometimes attributed to imponderable differences in 'business philosophy', but further investigation reveals that other more tangible factors shape retailers' distribution strategies.

The number and sizes of branch stores together determine a chain's total turnover and this has to exceed a certain minimum level to justify the establishment of a central warehouse. Firms generating their turnover through large numbers of small outlets have greater cause to use central warehouses than those that concentrate sales in larger stores capable of receiving bulk deliveries directly from suppliers.

Thorpe *et al.* postulated that the greater the dispersal of branch stores, the lower would be the level of centralised delivery. This is presumably based on the reasoning that, other things being equal, it is more costly to distribute supplies from central warehouses to widely scattered branch stores, particularly where many of them are located beyond the maximum daily range of a delivery vehicle. Research on grocery retailing casts doubt on this hypothesis (McKinnon, 1985). Most grocery chains with centralised delivery systems were found to have all their branches within the daily delivery range. 94% of the branches operated by a sample of eight multiples were within 100 miles of the central warehouse that supplied them. Across this sample there was no significant relationship between dependence on a central warehouse and the dispersal of branch stores.

At a smaller spatial scale, Thorpe *et al.* claim that shop occupancy costs will affect the relative use of central warehouses. Chains composed of stores located in town centres where site costs are high might be likely to make heavier use of central warehouses, reducing the amount of premium space in shops devoted to storage. By comparison, chains of suburban or out-of-town stores would not be under the same pressure from retail site costs to centralise stocks in a peripheral depot. Though plausible, this hypothesis is difficult to test for three reasons. First, many chains operate stores in different parts of the urban area. Second, site costs can vary as much between urban areas as within them, and, third, the siting of a store is usually related to its size, making it difficult to separate the effects of size from those of siting.

The way in which retail chains have grown has clearly been an important factor in the evolution of their supporting systems of physical distribution. Retail chains can expand either by setting up new stores (*organic or unitary growth*) or by the acquisition of existing outlets. Organic growth allows a multiple to co-ordinate the development of its distribution system more closely with the enlargement of its retailing operation. In the case of a small-scale acquisition, a few shops can easily be integrated into an existing distribution system. Larger-scale takeovers are usually followed by a process of rationalisation. This often entails the closure of many of the smaller stores in the acquired chain. Where the areas served by the acquiring and acquired chains overlap, it is necessary to eliminate competitive stores. The geography of the two chains can, therefore, be radically altered by such a takeover, making it essential to reorganise the system of centralised distribution. This reorganisation can be complicated by the associated acquisition of central warehouse capacity. Roughly a third of the central warehouses operated by a sample of 23 grocery multiples were obtained through the acquisition of other chains. The integration of two chains' distribution systems is even more complicated where they previously differed in their relative use of central warehousing by a significant margin. All this makes it difficult for multiples growing principally by acquisition to phase the long-term development of a centralised system of delivery. These multiples tend, therefore, to channel a smaller proportion of supplies through a central warehouse than chains characterised by a long period of organic growth. There are, nevertheless, notable exceptions to this simple dichotomy. The Argyll supermarket chain, for example, which is the product of a long sequence of mergers and takeovers, has completely restructured its distribution system to enable it to increase sharply the proportion of turnover channelled through central warehouses (Christensen, 1986). Allowance should also be made for retailers undertaking 'external growth' (Davies and Sparks, 1986), where they acquire firms in other retail sectors, dealing in completely different products. Retail conglomerates formed in this way, such as Ward White, often do not attempt to integrate the distribution systems of the firms they acquire and allow them to fix the level of centralised delivery autonomously.

The overall proportion of supplies passing through a central warehouse is the net result of the retailer's reception policy for many different classes of product. As some product classes are more suited to centralised handling than others, the relative importance of central warehouse deliveries partly depends upon the range of goods stocked and their relative contribution to total turnover.

Some products are typically distributed via a central warehouse. Imported goods are often transported in bulk loads from the ports to the retailer's central warehouse. As multiple retailers take responsibility for distributing and merchandising own-label products, they generally have little choice but to receive them into their warehouses. A multiple's policy on the development of own-label products can, therefore, carry important implications for physical distribution (Institute of Grocery Distribution (IGD), 1986a). Decisions on which of the remaining products to channel through the central warehouse are based on a range of criteria including value density, turnover rate, perishability, handling characteristics, product compatibility and the level of discount offered for bulk delivery.

In the late 1970s, there was considerable uncertainty about future trends in delivery operations. A survey of food manufacturers by Mintel (1977) found that similar numbers anticipated increases as reductions in the proportion of output delivered in bulk to retailers' warehouses. Among a combined sample of food manufacturers and retailers surveyed by the present author in 1978/9, the majority opinion was that there would be a further net diversion of grocery flow away from manufacturers' distribution depots towards multiples' central warehouses, but that this process was nearing its conclusion. One distribution executive at the time suggested that the allocation of flow between manufacturers' and retailers' warehouses had entered a phase of 'dynamic equilibrium'. During the 1980s, however, the centralisation of retail deliveries has gathered momentum, particularly in the grocery trade. Several of the large chains, such as Tesco (Kirkwood, 1984), whose relative use of central warehouses was previously below average, have greatly increased the proportion of centralised delivery (Sparks, 1986). Contrary to earlier expectation, the development of superstores, many of which are capable of receiving bulk deliveries directly from the factory, has neither reversed nor arrested this trend. Increasing pressure on superstore operators to maximise the conversion ratio in these outlets, stemming partly from the increasing cost of superstore sites and partly from the expansion of sales through these outlets, is promoting greater use of central warehousing facilities. The trend towards greater centralisation is also evident in other trades, though this has received less attention. For example, chains such as Littlewoods (Taylor, 1982), House of Fraser (McKibbin, 1983), Mothercare (Roadway, 1986) and Comet (Malloy, 1987) have also established new centralised systems of distribution.

Interconnection of physical distribution channels

So far we have examined the sections of the logistical channel controlled by manufacturers and multiple retailers separately. We can now look at the way in which these two channel sections connect. There are four possible channel arrangements:

1. Directly from factory to shop.
2. Via distribution depot under the manufacturer's control.
3. Via central warehouse under the retailer's control.
4. Via both manufacturer-controlled depot and retailer-controlled warehouse.

There are no published data available on the allocation of flow among these physical distribution channels. As only a small minority of retail outlets are large enough to receive supplies in bulk loads directly from factories, channel 1 is lightly used. Channel 4 also handles a small, and declining, proportion of retail supplies as retailers' central warehouses are generally large enough (in storage capacity and turnover) to receive bulk shipments from the factory. Indeed, a major reason for multiple retailers operating central warehouses is to obtain the favourable buying terms associated with direct ex-factory delivery. The vast majority of retail supplies pass along channels 2 and 3.

It is possible to examine the pattern of delivery in the grocery trade using data collected from samples of 18 food manufacturers and 22 supermarket chains. Each of the multiples purchased supplies from each of the manufacturers, generating a total of 396 trading links (or *dyads*). Information about delivery arrangements was obtained for 374 of these dyads and is presented in Figure 3.5. The organisation of the delivery data in this matrix is based upon two statistically significant relationships:

1. between the extent to which a manufacturer distributes goods to the central warehouses of the 22 supermarket chains and the percentage of its output delivered directly from the factory ($r = 0.722$, significance level = 0.99);
2. between the percentage of a chain's supplies passing through its central warehouse and the proportion of the manufacturers sampled delivering into its central warehouse(s) ($r = 0.479$, significance level = 0.95).

One might hypothesise that the nature of the delivery will largely reflect the strength of these two relationships. Figure 3.5 has been constructed in such a way as to shed light on, though not rigorously test, this hypothesis. Manufacturers are aligned along the vertical axis in terms of the proportion of output they delivered directly from the factory (Y). Multiple retailers are arranged along the horizontal axis so that the percentage of supplies channelled through their central warehouses (X) declines from left to right. Quite fortuitously, both sets of sample values grade reasonably gently over a wide range.

One would expect to find a preponderance of store deliveries above the leading diagonal (running from top left to bottom right) and a preponderance of warehouse deliveries below it. While there are concentrations of store and warehouse deliveries in the top right and bottom left corners respectively, the central section of the matrix does not display any clear pattern. Only in extreme cases would it be possible to predict with any accuracy the nature of the delivery arrangement for a particular dyad on the basis of the X and Y variables.

To explain why no clear pattern emerged, one must examine the factors that influence the choice between warehouse and shop delivery.

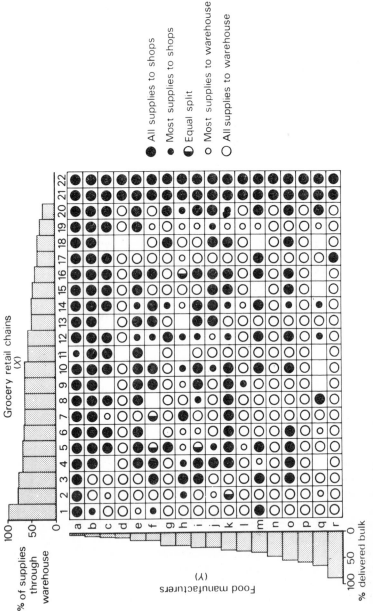

Figure 3.5 Delivery arrangements between samples of manufacturers and multiple retailers

Factors affecting channel linkage

The final choice of delivery rests with the retailer, though the supplier can influence this decision by adjusting the following variables:

1. prices and discounts;
2. minimum drop size;
3. standard of delivery service.

1. Pricing

Lösch (1954, p.165) considered the pricing system to be 'the most important regulator of a rational spatial arrangement'. Similarly, one might suppose that if price differences reflected distribution costs, this would generate a 'rational' pattern of distribution. It must be asked, therefore, to what extent the price mechanism fulfils this task.

Before a firm can relate prices to distribution costs, it must first ascertain how these costs vary between different types of delivery. Available evidence suggests that many companies have scant knowledge of their distribution costs. This can be partly attributed to the fact that responsibility for distribution has traditionally been divided between different branches of management and so, for the purposes of cost accountancy, distribution costs have not been calculated in consolidated form (Murphy, 1978). Even where firms do estimate their total distribution costs, they often differ in the range of activities they include in the cost calculation. Differences in accounting schemes result partly from disagreement over what actually constitutes distribution (Ray and Gattorna, 1980). It appears that the main areas of disagreement are over the inclusion of stockholding, order processing and packaging in the distribution cost calculation. The addition of these items can effectively double the distribution cost estimate (McKibbin, 1982).

Cost differences between distribution channels stem mainly from the transport and stockholding functions. Transport costs vary with respect to the distance travelled and the consignment size. Most consumer goods industries employ an *equalised (or uniform) delivered pricing* scheme. This means that the price charged for a certain quantity of goods remains constant regardless of the distance between factory and customer. This system has the advantages of greatly simplifying the producer's price structure and allowing products to be advertised nationally at a single price. Customers located near the factory effectively cross-subsidise more costly deliveries to customers further afield. Coates, Johnson and Knox (1977) contend that the amount of cross-subsidy is small, partly

Table 3.9 Costs of delivering bulk orders to retailers' warehouses: canned food products

Warehouse location	Distance (km)	Cost/tonne (£)	Cost/tonne/km (pence)
Farnborough	27	2.70	10.0
Waltham Cross	43	3.40	7.9
Aylesford	70	4.00	5.7
Winsford	240	10.20	4.3

because, in the case of the higher-value finished goods most affected by this pricing scheme, transport costs generally represent a small proportion of final selling price, and partly because unit transport costs 'taper' as journey length increases.

Although transport costs vary less than proportionally with distance, the cost of delivery can still vary significantly between customers. Table 3.9, for example, shows how the cost of delivering canned products in bulk loads from a manufacturer's warehouse to four retailers' central warehouses varied substantially over a comparatively short-distance range, despite a pronounced tapering of the transport rate per tonne-kilometre. Shop delivery costs are subject to an even greater degree of spatial variation. If pricing schemes reflected these cost differences, they could affect a retailer's decision on whether or not to channel supplies through its central warehouse. For example, a multiple operating a widely dispersed chain in a region distant from a supplier's factory might be quoted a high rate for direct branch store delivery and thereby encouraged to take bulk deliveries into its central warehouse. The spatial uniformity of delivery costs ensures, however, that retailers are not subject to such geographically discriminating pressures.

Manufacturers' pricing schemes take much more account of variations in the cost of delivering different sizes of order. These cost variations can be very wide: one large food manufacturer estimated that the cost of distributing a palletised load of 7,000 units to a central warehouse represented 2.3% of the average selling price of its products, while the cost of delivering 5 units to a shop represented 15.2% (Monopolies and Mergers Commission, 1981). As explained earlier, delivery costs vary inversely and exponentially with drop size. There is a limit, however, in the extent to which manufacturers can translate distribution costs into prices. It is generally considered impractical, for example, to vary prices in accordance with the size of individual shop deliveries. Allocating distribution costs to particular consignments is notoriously difficult and inevitably involves a large measure of subjective judgement (Buxton, 1975). Systems for allocating cost on the basis of drop size have, nevertheless, been

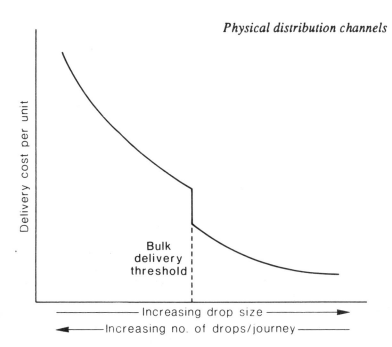

Figure 3.6 Relationship between drop size and unit delivery cost over wide size range

developed and successfully implemented (Barrett and Wilkinson, 1977). Some manufacturers take the average size of drops to a multiple's branch stores into account in deciding what level of discount to grant. It is much more common for manufacturers' pricing schemes to distinguish between local deliveries of relatively small quantities from depots, to which Figure 3.3 relates, and large bulk deliveries direct from the factory. Figure 3.6 extends the cost curve depicted on Figure 3.3 to show how drop size eventually becomes large enough to qualify for direct delivery from the factory. The switch from ex-depot to ex-factory delivery is represented as a discontinuity on the cost curve because these larger direct deliveries avoid the costs of storage and handling at distribution depots. Direct delivery from the factory is, therefore, much cheaper per unit than distribution in smaller consignments via depots. Two large food manufacturers have estimated that the costs of direct delivery are 68% and 65% cheaper than the cost of 'indirect' distribution via depots. Such large cost savings give manufacturers a strong incentive to promote direct bulk deliveries by means of their pricing policy.

Thorpe *et al.* devised a generalised cost model to establish the critical volume required for direct, ex-factory delivery. It was based on the ratio of manufacturers' branch store delivery costs to the costs retailers incur in channelling supplies through a central warehouse. This model has limited practical relevance, however, for several reasons. In the first place, suppliers and retailers do not have access to each others' cost data nor, as will be seen later, does the price mechanism permit an effective trade-off between these cost elements. Second, it can be extremely difficult for a supplier to isolate the costs of delivering its products to the branch stores of a single retailer. Third, the model makes no allowance for the various marketing considerations that often dominate the choice of delivery method.

A view commonly expressed by distribution managers is that it is almost impossible to say what proportion of a retailer's total discount is attributable to its acceptance of warehouse delivery. Some food manufacturers offer a fixed discount of around 1% to customers taking a full lorry load, regardless of whether it is delivered to a store or a warehouse. Fifteen out of twenty food manufacturers consulted by the author claimed that the prices charged made little or no allowance for differences in distribution costs. The five companies which said prices were sensitive to distribution costs delivered less than 10% of their output to retail outlets. Hollander (1980, p.65) complains that manufacturers 'do not always bring to the bargaining tables the knowledge of the real economies (of large drop size) both for suppliers and retailers, with a view to getting these reflected in trade terms'. In fact, fewer than half the manufacturers surveyed by the Monopolies and Mergers Commission (1981) had even attempted to assess differences in the cost of distributing their products to particular customers.

Most firms have a price list which quotes prices on the basis of product type and quantity purchased. The quantity rates set out in the published price list are 'non-cumulative' in the sense that they relate to each order separately. It is these bulk rates which correspond most closely to distribution costs. Those firms that claim to gear prices to distribution costs are those that adhere rigidly to the published price list. The majority of manufacturers, however, supplement this price list with a series of 'cumulative' or 'patronage' discounts (often known as 'over-riders'), which relate to the total purchases a customer makes over a period of time. These are designed to encourage the customer to maximise his total purchases and are not affected by the frequency or size of individual orders. The Monopolies and Mergers Commission (1981, p.25) observed that 'over-riders tended to be regarded by manufacturers as a tool of marketing and not to be cost-related in any tangible way'. In most cases, over-riders exceed discounts for bulk delivery by a considerable margin. In the grocery trade, for example, the cheapest form of delivery, that of direct bulk delivery to central warehouses, attracts a discount of only 1-2% out of total discounts of over 10% for the larger supermarket chains (Office of Fair Trading, 1985). There is, therefore, no clear and direct relationship between the prices a food manufacturer quotes and the type of delivery he provides.

Manufacturers offering little or no discount for bulk deliveries to central warehouses often justify this policy on the grounds that they wish to retain an extensive system of direct delivery to branch stores so that their sales representatives can continue to market their products intensively at store level. These firms fear that the switch to centralised buying which generally accompanies the change to central warehouse delivery would result in a loss of sales, particularly where a competitor continued to deal with and deliver directly to branch stores. Some manufacturers also argue that, as their depot delivery systems are encumbered with a large element of fixed cost, the redirection of a multiple retailer's orders from branch stores to a central warehouse yields only a small net saving in distribution costs in the short term. It is frequently stated that around 80% of distribution costs are fixed (Crawford, 1972; Barber, 1976; Monopolies and Mergers Commission, 1981). Small discounts for central warehouse delivery can, therefore, reflect limited scope for cost reduction (Millar, 1983). In the longer term, a manufacturer might wish to reduce the capacity of its depot system, thereby releasing capital previously tied up in distribution. It might then promote direct deliveries from the factory by offering more generous bulk discounts. A manufacturer's pricing scheme can, therefore, reflect longer-term distribution objectives.

In its reports on Tate and Lyle, Cadbury-Schweppes Foods Ltd and CPC (UK) Ltd, the Price Commission (1978a, b, c) expressed concern about the discounting practices these firms employed. It was suggested at this time that legislation similar to the Robinson-Patman Act in the US might have to be enacted in the UK 'to prevent large buyers from securing excessive advantages over their smaller competitors by virtue of their size and purchasing power' (Hill, 1978). The Robinson-Patman Act of 1936 stipulated that any discounts offered to customers must be cost related, thus outlawing discrimination between customers simply on the basis of total quantity purchased. Suppliers have since had to demonstrate that price differentials are justified with respect to differences in manufacturing, marketing and distribution costs. As Matz, Curry and Frank (1967, p.751) explain, however, the opportunities for discriminating between customers 'fall chiefly in the field of distribution cost'. The Robinson-Patman Act has inspired a great deal of interest in distribution cost analysis and is generally believed to have succeeded in bringing prices more into line with distribution costs, though at the expense of much litigation.

Table 3.10 Minimum drop sizes: sample of food manufacturers

| | Number of cases | | | | | |
	<10	10-20	21-30	31-40	>40	Total
No. of firms	3	10	5	3	2	23
(%)	(13)	(42)	(21)	(13)	(8)	

In 1981, however, the Monopolies and Mergers Commission denied that there was a need for Robinson-Patman-type legislation in the UK. It broadly approved of current trading practices in the grocery trade, arguing that, on the whole, they were beneficial to consumers. The Commission conceded that it is difficult for manufacturers to quantify differences in the cost of distributing their products to particular customers and accepted the case for cumulative discounts that bore little relation to delivery costs. The Commission's findings have since been endorsed by the Office of Fair Trading (1985).

2. Minimum drop sizes

Manufacturers can constrain a retailer's choice between branch store and central warehouse delivery by imposing minimum drop (or order) sizes on the two types of delivery. Minimum drop sizes for bulk ex-factory deliveries are usually expressed in relation to the capacity of a trunk vehicle. Many manufacturers require a customer to take a full lorry load to qualify for this type of delivery. Minimum drop sizes for shop delivery via a distribution depot are much more variable (Table 3.10). It is difficult to assess the extent to which these variations are product related because many firms manufacture diverse product ranges, yet stipulate the same minimum size for orders regardless of their composition.

Although minimum drop size is partly influenced by the breadth of a manufacturer's product range and by the value, handling characteristics and turnover rates of the products, it is often decided primarily on the basis of marketing considerations. Minimum drop size is a critical parameter in the trade-off between maximising revenue and minimising distribution costs (Lambert, Bennion and Taylor, 1983) and is thus a frequent source of contention between marketing, sales and distribution departments. A firm wishing to market its products intensively at the retail level must be prepared to deliver comparatively small amounts to numerous outlets. In contrast, a manufacturer who does not value direct trading links with shops so highly would tend to discourage small, relatively uneconomic branch store deliveries by fixing minimum order size at a higher level.

Increasing awareness of the high cost of delivering small orders has led to a general raising of minimum drop sizes. This trend has been reinforced by the concentration of retail sales in larger outlets. On the other hand, the increased use of third-party consolidation services has made shop deliveries more economical and probably eased the upward pressure on minimum drop size.

3. Standard of delivery service

Several studies have established that retailers and wholesalers attach great importance to delivery reliability and order lead time in choosing suppliers (Christopher, Schary and Skjøtt-Larsen, 1979; McGoldrick and Douglas, 1983; Shipley, 1985). In their research on factors influencing grocery distributors' choice of crisp suppliers, McGoldrick and Douglas found that 47% of the distributors consulted regarded 'the ability to comply precisely with delivery arrangements' to be of 'primary importance' (p.21). They cite the case of one retailer rejecting some manufacturers because they could not provide weekly delivery to branch stores. Some multiples would not consider poor delivery service to be sufficient grounds for dismissing an otherwise good supplier, but would take this into account in deciding whether or not to channel its products through a central warehouse. Manufacturers can, therefore, gain some leverage on retailers' choice of delivery arrangement by adjusting the quality of distribution to shops and warehouses.

The mechanism by which service level influences retailers' behaviour is imperfect, though, as most retailers do not properly evaluate suppliers' delivery performance or compare it with that of their own centralised operation. Retailers, nevertheless, often assert that they can provide their shops with faster and more frequent delivery than suppliers, thereby reducing in-store stock levels and the risk of stock-outs. Conversely, manufacturers committed to branch store delivery often argue that this enables them to maintain a higher level of product availability in shops. Research by Thorpe *et al.* (1973) casts doubt on both retailers' and manufacturers' claims. Across a range of 81 grocery products, they could find no significant relationship between the proportion of supplies delivered directly to a branch store and the frequency of stock-outs. This led Thorpe *et al.* (p.137) to conclude that:

> Although sales, through the influence of lack of stock, can be affected by distribution arrangements, the relation is by no means clear cut. Indeed it varies substantially from one retailer to another and is likely to vary from one product to another.

It is, therefore, difficult to generalise about the effect of service level on the choice of delivery type.

The need for co-ordination

There appears to be no effective mechanism to ensure that the allocation of product flow between physical distribution channels maximises the efficiency of the system as a whole. It is possible that 'efforts by one company to improve productivity in physical distribution activities may simply result in diseconomies in supplier or customer firms' (Bloom, 1983, p.5). Where a multiple instructs a supplier to switch from branch store to central warehouse delivery, the resulting increase in the multiple's distribution costs may exceed the savings that the supplier is able to make. The net increase in overall distribution costs must then be borne by the consumer. Conversely, some retailers impair the efficiency of the distribution channel by ordering supplies in small quantities at short intervals in an effort to push responsibility for stockholding onto the manufacturer (Lambert *et al.*, 1983). These situations could be averted if suppliers and retailers co-operated more closely in the management of the complete channel from factory to shop. Hollander (1980, p.65) argues that

> the selection and design of the best means of supporting the store
> system, through the best distribution channel for the
> purpose...must be based on the true costs through the chain of
> events and be a decision for both parties to develop together.

This would require suppliers and distributors to 'develop mutual understanding of the economics of the various distribution channels'. This endorses the view of the NEDO (1976, p.6) that 'the probing of total distribution costs from the factory needs to be an essential part of the customer/supplier relationship' and that the 'probing should be a joint effort in the interests of both'.

There have so far been few instances of suppliers and retailers exchanging distribution cost data, but they have co-operated in other ways. Food manufacturers and grocery retailers in the US, for example, have jointly investigated the possibility of sharing regional distribution centres (Heskett, Glaskowsky and Ivie, 1973). The development of *electronic data interchange* (EDI) is also establishing closer ties between producers, wholesalers and retailers and creating new opportunities for the co-ordination of logistical operations. Agencies will only co-ordinate their distribution activities, though, if they consider it to be to their mutual advantage and if the benefits are equitably distributed. Even so, in many trades, traditional inter-organisational rivalries will prove difficult to overcome.

Chapter four

Pattern of stockholding

At any given time the systems of production and distribution contain large amounts of stock, most of it required to balance variations in the rates at which goods are produced and consumed. In managing their stocks, firms at each level in the marketing channel aim to provide the desired level of product availability with the minimum amount of stock. Of the numerous inventory management decisions they make, those concerning the spatial distribution of stocks are particularly important as they have a strong bearing both on the cost of stockholding and on the speed with which stocks can be marshalled to meet customer demands.

The spatial distribution of inventory can be conceptualised within the two-dimensional structure of a physical distribution channel outlined in the previous chapter. Stocks must be allocated between the various nodes in the vertical channel, ranging from the factory through intervening depots to retail outlets. At each level in the physical distribution channel, there is a horizontal dispersal of stock to similar nodes in different locations. In this chapter, we shall examine this two-dimensional pattern of stockholding, concentrating on the mechanisms that regulate the amount of stock at each level in the vertical channel and the factors influencing the decentralisation of stock at intermediate levels.

For the purposes of statistical accounting, stocks are divided into three categories on the basis of their physical form:

1. Raw materials and fuels, awaiting input into the production process.
2. Work in progress ('in-process inventory'), undergoing processing or in a semi-finished state awaiting further processing.
3. Finished goods, ready for distribution to final customers.

Although this book is focusing on the distribution of finished goods, many of the inventory management principles that will be advanced in this chapter are equally applicable to the storage of raw materials and semi-finished products at earlier stages in the logistical channel. The overall ownership of finished stock is divided fairly evenly between producers, wholesalers and retailers, though the pattern of ownership varies between product sectors. No comparable data are available to show the allocation of stock between nodes in the physical distribution channel. One cannot, for example, ascertain, at a general level, what proportion of manufacturers' finished stock is held at factories as opposed to distribution depots.

In the next section we shall examine the procedures that firms employ to allocate stock to different points in the vertical channel.

Vertical dimension: stock replenishment

Stock replenishment policy must provide answers to two fundamental questions:

1. When should stocks be replenished?
2. How much should be reordered?

Traditionally, factory, depot and shop managers have exercised considerable autonomy in deciding these matters. In some cases, orders are transmitted to a higher-level supply point within the same organisation, triggering an internal movement of stock as, for example, between factory and depot or between a retailer's warehouse and branch store. Other orders are placed with outside suppliers and effect a change of ownership. Similar stock replenishment procedures can be employed in each case. These procedures will be illustrated with reference to a manufacturer's distribution depot drawing supplies of a single product from a factory warehouse.

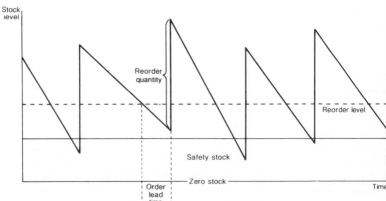

Figure 4.1 Stock level fluctuations (Continuous Review System)

It is important to distinguish quantities of stock held for different purposes. The main distinction is between *cycle (or working) stock* and *safety (or buffer) stock*. Cycle stock is that which is required to satisfy the average level of demand during the period between the placing of an order and the arrival of the goods at the depot (i.e. *order lead time*). The depot essentially regulates the flow of goods through the distributive channel. Goods arrive infrequently in bulk loads, but flow out more gradually in small consignments. This causes the level of stock in a depot to fluctuate. When expressed graphically, these fluctuations exhibit a 'saw tooth' profile similar to that in Figure 4.1. The depot manager must ensure that stocks are replenished soon enough to prevent them running out (i.e. to avert a stock-out). In so doing, he must take account of the rate at which products are selling as well as the order lead time. If it could be assumed that both of these parameters were constant, the depot would only need to hold cycle stock, because the reordering of supplies could then be precisely planned so that additional supplies arrived just as existing stocks were exhausted. If one relaxes the assumption that demand remains constant, reliance on cycle stock alone no longer guarantees that there will always be adequate stock on hand to meet demand. During periods of above-average demand stock can run out before fresh supplies arrive. It is necessary, therefore, to supplement cycle stock with safety stock to cater for these higher levels of demand. The addition of safety stock effectively displaces the 'saw tooth' profile upwards, reducing the number of occasions when it dips below the horizontal, 'zero-stock' axis (Figure 4.1). In determining how large the margin of safety stock should be, the depot manager must know how great a risk of stock-out the firm is prepared to tolerate. This risk is one of the key determinants of the level of customer service. Many firms define customer service very narrowly and would simply interpret a 5% stock-out risk to be a 95% service level.

So far, cycle stock has been defined only in relation to demand, considering it to be 'pulled' down the physical distribution channel by final demand. The volume of cycle stock can also be affected, however, by the rate at which goods are produced. They are usually manufactured in large batches, mainly to obtain economies of scale, but sometimes in response to seasonal variations in the availability of raw materials. The total volume of goods manufactured during a production cycle can exceed the available storage capacity at the factory site, making it necessary to 'push' surplus stock out to regional depots. The depots then receive more stock than is strictly required to meet demand during the period between orders. The amount of stock in a depot can also exceed the normal provision of cycle and safety stock where additional stock is held speculatively in anticipation of some future contingency, such as a reduction in the rate of value-added tax or the withdrawal of a competitor from the market. As the amount of additional stock 'overflowing' from a factory warehouse depends on the particular circumstances of individual firms, and as speculative stockholding is a response to exceptional demand or supply conditions, it is difficult to generalise about these forms of stockholding. Attention will, therefore, be confined to the management of cycle and safety stocks to meet the 'normal' pattern of demand.

Two general systems of stock replenishment are widely applied in industry:

1. Continuous review system: stock levels are continuously monitored and when they fall below a specified reorder level, an order is placed for a fixed quantity of replenishment stock. The period between orders is, therefore, variable, whereas the amount ordered each time remains fixed. This is also known as the *fixed order quantity* or *fixed reorder point system.*
2. Periodic review system: orders are placed at a fixed interval, regardless of the amount of stock on hand, and must be of sufficient size to bring stocks up to some predetermined level. In this case, the time interval between orders is fixed, whereas the order quantity can vary. This is sometimes called the *fixed interval system.*

The continuous review system is generally deemed to be the more efficient and is the more commonly used. Simpkin, Maier and Lee (1987) found that it was employed by 56% of a sample of 200 large British retailers.

To operationalise these systems, it is necessary in each case to find values for two parameters. For the continuous review system, one must specify the reorder level and order quantity, while for the periodic review system one must establish the time interval between stock reviews (or 'stock-takes') and the level to which stocks must be 'topped-up'.

Continuous review system

Reorder level

The reorder level must be set high enough to ensure that at the time of reordering the depot has sufficient stock to meet average demand during the order lead time (cycle stock) and most of the demand variation in excess of this average (safety stock). (We shall assume, for the moment, that deliveries are perfectly reliable and order lead times constant.) The cycle stock component (C) is calculated by multiplying the average sales per day (S) by the number of days it takes for the order to arrive (L):

$$C = SL. \tag{4.1}$$

To determine the safety stock requirement, firms typically assume that demand fluctuates randomly about a constant mean and in accordance with the normal distribution. The assumption of normality makes it possible to establish a direct relationship between the extent to which demand deviates from the mean (measured in terms of the standard deviation) and the probability of a stock-out occurring. This is illustrated by Figure 4.2, which focuses on the sloping section of one 'saw tooth' in the inventory profile. Stock is gradually sold off until at time T the amount of stock remaining falls to the reorder level. More goods are then ordered from the factory, but these take Y days to arrive,

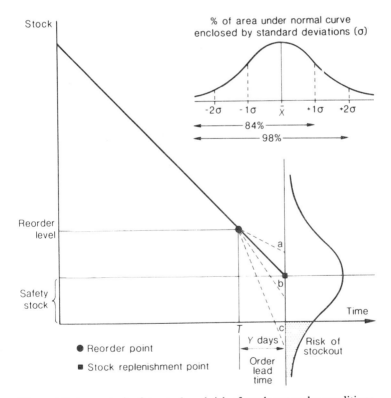

Figure 4.2 Amount of safety stock and risk of stock-out under conditions of normally distributed demand
Adapted from Buxton, 1975.

during which time sales continue to deplete the depot's stocks. The thick solid line represents a situation in which goods are sold off and stocks depleted at an average rate. The broken lines, labelled a, b and c, depict situations in which, during the order lead time, goods sell more slowly (a) or more quickly than the average rate (b and c). The classic bell shape of the normal distribution (Figure 4.2 inset) means that, over most order cycles, demand deviates only marginally on either side of the mean (X). The larger the deviation, the less frequently it occurs. By referring to normal probability tables, it is possible to predict the frequency with which particular sizes of deviation will occur. On 68% of occasions, for example, demand variations will lie within one standard deviation on either side of the mean. In deciding the margin of safety stock, the depot manager will only be interested in deviations above the mean, as below average sales will be more than covered by cycle stocks. Since the normal distribution is symmetrical about the mean, it can be deduced that on 16% of occasions demand will exceed the mean by more than one standard deviation. If, therefore, the volume of safety stock were equivalent to the standard deviation (σ) of the level of demand, it would fail to meet demand on 16% of occasions. The probability of this happening corresponds to the area enclosed by the tail section of the normal curve falling below the horizontal axis. If enough safety stock were held to accommodate demand deviations of up to 1σ, this tail section would constitute 16% of the total area under the curve. Increasing the margin of safety stock to 2σ, would effectively raise the normal curve until only about 2% of the area enclosed under the curve fell below the axis. This would correspond to a product availability level of 98%. As the tail section of the normal curve tapers, the reduction in the stock-out risk diminishes with each successive increment in safety stock (Ray and Millman, 1979). When one weighs the marginal cost of increasing safety stock against the economic benefits of marginally reducing the stock-out risk, reducing this risk below 2% seldom proves cost-effective.

A stock-out risk of 2% may appear very small, but would only relate to a single product. If a customer order comprised, say, twelve different products, each of which was subject to a 2% stock-out risk, then, *ceteris paribus*, the probability of the customer obtaining a full order from stock would be 0.785 (i.e. $(1 - 0.02)^{12}$). This would correspond to an order fill rate of only 78.5%. An apparently high level of availability for individual products can still result, therefore, in a substantial proportion of heterogeneous orders lacking one or more items (Christopher *et al.*, 1979).

The amount of safety stock required therefore depends on the extent to which demand varies about the mean (measured by the standard deviation) and the desired level of customer service. Both these factors are incorporated in the standard formula for safety stock (*B*):

$$B = k\sigma \sqrt{L} \qquad (4.2)$$

where σ is the standard deviation of the level of demand and k is the number of standard deviations above mean demand corresponding to the desired service level.

Combining the formulae for cycle and safety stock, one obtains the following expression for the minimum amount of stock that should be on hand at the time of reordering, that is, the reorder level (R_L):

$$R_L = SL + k\sigma \sqrt{L} \qquad (4.3)$$

Order quantity

The optimum size of order, or *economic order quantity* (EOQ), is determined by the trade-off between the cost of holding stock and the cost of procuring supplies (McClelland, 1960).

1. Stockholding costs: In holding stock, firms incur four types of cost:
   (i) Financial costs: While goods are in storage they represent an investment of working capital. If the firm finances its stockholding with capital borrowed from financial institutions, it must pay the commercial rate of interest (usually several percentage points above bank base rate). If, on the other hand, it ties up some of its own assets in stock, then it foregoes interest that could have been earned on this capital had it been invested elsewhere at prevailing market interest rates. The financial cost of stockholding is often measured, therefore, in relation to the general level of interest rates in the economy. In many cases, however, this underestimates the true opportunity cost of investing capital in stocks, because it fails to allow for the fact that a firm might be able to earn an even higher return on this capital by investing it in some other sphere of its operations (La Londe and Lambert, 1977).
   (ii) Physical storage costs: These are the costs of providing, equipping and operating storage facilities to accommodate stock.
   (iii) Depreciation: While in storage, stock can lose value in several ways. It can physically deteriorate through time, or be damaged or stolen. Insuring against these contingencies can add significantly to stockholding costs, particularly in the case of higher-value goods. Changes in styles and tastes during the storage period can reduce demand for the stock or even render it

obsolete, further depressing its value. It should be noted, however, that stock can also appreciate in value, where, for example, its quality improves with time, as in the case of whisky, or over periods of high price inflation.

(iv) Taxes: In some countries, goods are taxed while in storage. Many states in America, for example, impose a tax levy on all or part of the stock held in warehouses (Ballou, 1978). This has the desirable effect of depressing stock levels. In contrast, the British tax system positively favoured stockholding between 1974 and 1982. Today, in the UK, stocks are neither taxed nor granted tax allowances.

Surveys in several countries, including the UK (Kearney, 1980) and the US (Lambert, 1975), have revealed that management often underestimates the full cost of stockholding, excluding some cost elements from the calculation and undervaluing others. The sharp increase in interest rates in the early 1980s prompted many firms to subject their inventory carrying costs to much more careful scrutiny.

Total stockholding costs increase in direct proportion to order size. Where stocks are replenished infrequently and in large quantities, they must be maintained at a high average level. If a depot manager's sole objective were to minimise stockholding costs, they would seek to minimise order size and maximise the frequency with which orders were placed. Such a policy would, however, result in very high procurement costs.

2. Procurement (or ordering costs): These comprise mainly administrative and clerical costs, and are generally more difficult to estimate than stockholding costs (Howard, 1984). Information processing costs vary with the number of orders placed but are largely unaffected by the size of each order. To minimise these costs, one must therefore minimise the frequency with which supplies are ordered and maximise order size. This also yields economies of scale in the physical handling and movement of orders, and can secure larger discounts from suppliers. Ordering costs thus follow the opposite trend to stockholding costs.

The EOQ is defined as that which minimises the sum of stockholding and procurement costs, as indicated in Figure 4.3. It can be calculated by means of the following formula (Thomas, 1980):

$$EOQ = \sqrt{2DP/IV} \qquad (4.4)$$

where D is the number of units demanded annually, P the procurement cost per order, I the ratio of the annual stockholding cost to the value of the product and V the unit value of the product.

It was stated above that in the continuous review system, the order quantity was fixed. Clearly, however, there are cost elements in the EOQ calculation which can vary substantially through time. The financial cost of stockholding, for example, has in recent years been particularly volatile. EOQ is best regarded, therefore, as only being fixed in the short term.

Periodic review system

Review period

This can be established by calculating the EOQ in the manner outlined above and dividing this figure into the annual demand. If, for instance, 1,000 *stock-keeping units* (SKUs) were sold annually and the EOQ

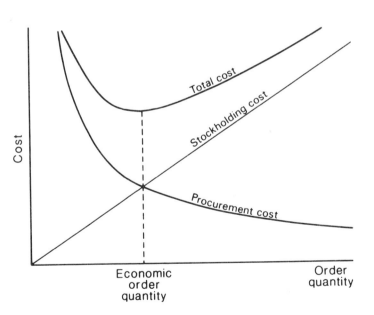

Figure 4.3 Relationship between stockholding and order procurement costs
Source: McClelland, 1960.

estimated to be 50 units, the optimum reorder period would be about 18 days (i.e. 365 + 1000/50). The reorder period is often rounded to a certain number of days or weeks for administrative convenience.

Replenishment level

This can be determined in a similar fashion to the reorder level by working out cycle and safety stock requirements. In this case, however, these stocks must be large enough to meet demand not only during the order lead time (L) but also the period between orders (T). The top-up level of stock (R_t) can thus be calculated as follows:

$$R_t = S(L + T) + k\sigma \sqrt{(L + T)}. \tag{4.5}$$

Since, under this system, stocks must accommodate variations in demand over a longer period, the volume of safety stock must be higher than under the continuous review system. This is confirmed by a comparison of formulae (4.3) and (4.5). The periodic review system is, therefore, less responsive to demand and, as it relieves staff of the need to monitor stock levels closely, often leads to careless inventory management. Its main advantages are that it is easier to manage and permits tighter scheduling of vehicle movements between factory and depot.

So far, in outlining the main methods of stock replenishment, three major assumptions have been made. First, it has been assumed that order lead times remain constant. This is not necessarily so. Outside suppliers often cannot be relied upon to deliver orders at a specified time, and even internal stock movements within a single firm need not adhere to a rigid timetable. Where order lead times vary significantly, an additional margin of safety stock may be required to cover possible delays. Magson (1979) has developed a method of calculating stock requirements that allows for variations in lead time.

Second, demand variations have been assumed to conform to the normal distribution. Where this does not occur in practice, the stock replenishment calculations outlined earlier can substantially under or overestimate stock requirements. Mentzer and Krishman (1985) advise firms to analyse the actual pattern of demand for their products and be prepared to base their inventory calculations on other statistical distributions. As Howard (1984, p.17) points out, though, 'An identifiable pattern of variation is fundamental to the discussion of safety stocks and service levels'.

The third assumption has been that demand fluctuates about a stable average. In practice, average demand, calculated on a weekly or monthly basis, may be subject to seasonal variations and, underlying these variations, may be a longer-term trend towards higher or lower sales. An attempt must be made to forecast these trends and adjust stock levels accordingly. There are several approaches to the forecasting of sales, differing in their complexity, assumptions and dependence on subjective judgement. Short-term fluctuations in the level of sales can be mathematically 'smoothed' to reveal longer-term trends. This can be done by calculating moving averages or fitting trend lines to past sales data by means of multiple regression analysis or exponential smoothing (Schary, 1984). Once identified, trends can then be extrapolated into the future on the assumption that the underlying conditions will remain unaltered. For the purposes of short-term inventory control, such extrapolatory forecasts usually suffice. The forecasting of longer-term trends is more soundly based if rooted in an understanding of what causes demand to vary and a foreknowledge of future events likely to affect sales. This requires detailed market research and an appreciation of wider economic and social trends. The relevant information can either be interpreted subjectively or more formally incorporated into mathematical models. As it is difficult and costly to quantify the relationship between the level of sales and a host of causal factors, most firms adopt a subjective approach to longer-term forecasting.

Stock-out costs

The optimal level of safety stock is determined by the trade-off between the cost of holding this stock and sales losses resulting from stock-outs. The stockholding cost element in the trade-off has already been considered. We shall now turn our attention to the more formidable problem of establishing the cost of a stock-out.

Table 4.1 Possible consumer reaction to stock-outs: consequences for retailers and manufacturers

Consumer reaction	Consequence for:	
	Retailer	Manufacturer
1. Buy a different size of the same brand	o	—
2. Buy another brand	o	—
3. Buy a substitute product	o	—
4. Postpone the purchase	?	?
5. Search elsewhere for the desired item	—	o
6. No purchase	—	—

o little or no effect
— short-run profit loss, potential loss of brand/store loyalty
? depends on action ultimately taken

Source: Miklas, 1979, p.215.

Table 4.2 Actual consumer reaction to a desired product being out of stock

| | Food | | Non-food |
	Extended use	Immediate use	
Bought a substitute	32%	48%	26%
Returned to buy in same store later	23%	21%	33%
Bought elsewhere	45%	31%	41%

Source: Nielsen Researcher, 1975.

Most of the research on customer response to stock-outs has focused on the behaviour of final consumers when they are unable to obtain a particular product in a given shop. Under these circumstances, the consumer can react in one of six ways (Table 4.1), three of which result in a loss to the manufacturer, two in a loss to the retailer and one whose effects are indeterminate (Miklas, 1979). Ray and Millman (1979) show, by means of a theoretical example, how one can calculate the probability of customers reacting in different ways to a stock-out and assess the cost implications of each outcome. Several studies have collected data that could be used in such probability calculations (e.g. *Nielsen Researcher*, 1975; Schary and Christopher, 1979). Most of these studies have been concerned with consumers' immediate responses to stock-outs (Table 4.2) rather than the longer-term erosion of their loyalty to particular brands and outlets. The disruption of the supply of certain brands of beer to Seattle, as the result of a strike, gave Schary and Becker (1978) the opportunity of examining consumer reactions to the non-availability of products over a longer period. Analysis of changes in the market shares of different brands of beer over three four-month periods (before, after and during the strike) suggested that, 'Removal of a product from a competitive market because of supply failures can significantly alter market shares. Even though the temporal effects are strongest in the short-run, they persist with measurable effect over a long period of time' (p.40).

The cost of stock-outs further back along the distribution channel depends on the nature of the buyer's response and the vendor's back-order policy. Where an organisational buyer, such as a wholesaler or retailer, is prepared to wait for the requested products and the back-order is delivered with the next regular order, the supplier may incur little additional cost. Some vendors have a policy of delivering back-orders as soon as they become available, thereby trying to win customer goodwill at the expense of higher transport costs. In some cases, the customer will obtain the unavailable items from an alternative supplier, resulting in a loss of revenue to the original supplier. Persistent stock-outs usually erode customer loyalty, undermining demand for the firm's products in the longer term. In a survey of the buying decisions of 216 firms, Perreault and Russ (1976) found that on 32% of the occasions when an order could not be supplied in full, a purchase was made from an alternative supplier. Underlying this average, however, was a wide variation in firms' propensity to transfer their patronage to different vendors. The research revealed that roughly three-quarters of the respondents cancelled back-orders less than 25% of the time, but the remainder took this action much more frequently, and in fact accounted for around 72% of all back-order cancellations. This suggests that suppliers might be able to reduce the impact of stock-outs on total sales by identifying the minority of customers that are highly sensitive to the non-availability of products and giving them priority treatment.

Variable customer response to stock-outs, over different time-scales, makes it difficult to express stock-out costs in a form that readily permits their incorporation into inventory planning calculations. Morgan and Wagner (1978) used a simulation modelling exercise to explore the relationship between back-order percentage and variable distribution cost. Most firms, however, baulk at the practical difficulties of formally estimating stock-out costs and instead decide what is an acceptable level of stock-out risk, and hence possible sales loss, merely on the basis of intuition.

Requirements planning

Attention has so far been confined to the stock replenishment policy of a single node in the physical distribution channel. We shall now take a broader view of the allocation of stock to different levels in the vertical channel. This channel might contain a distribution depot under the manufacturer's control, a local wholesaler's warehouse and an independent retail outlet. At each of these three stockholding points, stock is reordered using one of the two procedures described above. Each node acts independently, responding only to demands generated by the node immediately below it in the channel or, in the case of the shop, by final customers. This means that changes in consumer demand take a while to register at higher levels in the channel. As information about a change in demand is only relayed at the time of reordering, it may take several weeks for the effects of this change to be felt at the factory. Adherence to fixed reordering rules at each level of the channel makes the time-lag cumulative. This, coupled with the fact that higher-order nodes reorder supplies in larger quantities, results in demand variations being amplified as they work their way up the channel. Forrester (1961) developed a theoretical model to illustrate this effect and showed how a 10% increase in retail sales could give rise to a 16% increase in the volume ordered from a wholesaler, a 28% increase in the amount the wholesaler ordered from the producer and a 40% increase in production. The amplification of demand fluctuations is most pronounced in channels where communication is difficult and the processing of orders slow. It creates a need for excessive volumes of safety stock at the upper levels of the channel, and by inducing wide fluctuations in the rate of production, impairs the efficiency of the manufacturing operation as well.

This effect can be suppressed by transmitting information about changes in final demand directly from the final point of sale to each of the higher-level nodes in the channel. According to the *base stock plan*, each channel level is kept regularly informed about variations in final demand (Schary, 1984). Each node, therefore, receives advance warning about demand variations rippling back along the channel and can adjust stock levels accordingly. This makes for much tighter stock control, particularly in the upper echelons of the channel. Inventories can be even more carefully controlled where the manager of a stockholding point knows how much stock is being held at each of the lower nodes in the channel. This gives an indication of the likely impact of the demand change on stock levels further down the channel, from which future demands on the depot can be more accurately projected. In a base stock system, however, each node in the channel continues to replenish supplies and manage stocks autonomously. As a consequence, demand projections made at the upper levels of the channel can still be rendered inaccurate by inconsistencies in reordering decisions taken at lower levels.

Ideally, the rapid dissemination of sales data should be complemented by a close co-ordination of stock control at all levels in the vertical channel. This is what *distribution requirements planning* (DRP) tries to achieve. Modelled on a system of ordering and inventory control first applied to the inflow of raw materials and components into factories, known as *materials requirements planning* (MRP) (Orlicky, 1975), DRP can minimise inventory across the physical distribution channel as a whole by carefully phasing the replenishment of stock at each level.

DRP is generally undertaken centrally, with all relevant inventory data collected and processed by a central computer. The aim is to find the optimum allocation of stock among the various nodes in the channel. An important distinction is made between nodes which satisfy demands determined by external market forces (i.e. *independent demand*) and those which meet the needs of other nodes within the DRP system (i.e. *dependent demand*). Where ordering and inventory control are co-ordinated across a complete distribution channel from factory to shop, only the shop, at the interface with the

Table 4.3   Application of distribution requirements planning

	Week 1	Week 2	Week 3	Week 4	Week 5
Demand forecast	100	160	80	260	120
Customer orders already received	60	20		200	
Stock at start of week	110	300	140	310	300
Stock at end of week	50	140	60	50	180
Incoming supplies from factory		250		250	250
Orders to be placed		250	250		

Minimum Order Quantity = 250 Safety Stock = 50 Order Lead Time = 2 weeks

final consumer, experiences independent demand. Sales forecasts are used to determine inventory requirements at this end point in the channel. Demands upon stockholding points further back along the supply chain are then established relative to the predicted needs of the retail outlet, and product flows phased accordingly. Table 4.3 shows how inventory would be managed at one of these points (e.g. a manufacturer's distribution depot) using DRP. In this example, stock replenishment is planned over a five-week period on the basis of a series of weekly demand forecasts. These forecasts would be based on the predicted level of sales at the retail outlet. Three parameters must be established in advance: minimum order quantity, the order lead time for supplies entering the depot and the amount of safety stock required to accommodate demand forecasting errors. In Week 1, actual customer orders (60 units) fall short of forecast demand (100 units) and can be comfortably supplied from stock carried over from the previous week (110 units). At the time when the DRP exercise is being undertaken, orders for only 20 units have been received for Week 2. The inventory requirement must still be planned, however, on the basis of the demand forecast of 160 units. At the start of Week 2 there are 300 units of stock on hand (50 surplus to requirement in Week 1 plus a delivery of 250 units ordered two weeks previously). Assuming that the forecast demand for 160 units materialises, the depot will be left with a stock of 140 units at the end of Week 2, more than enough to meet the safety stock requirement. These 140 units would also meet forecast demand in Week 3, with 60 units of safety stock to spare. In the absence of any new supplies, a shortfall would occur in Week 4. Given that the order lead time is two weeks, it is necessary to reorder in Week 2. A minimum order of 250 units would raise the stock level at the start of Week 4 to 310 units, satisfying the forecast demand of 260 units and the safety stock requirement. A further order for 250

97

units would have to be placed in Week 3 to meet forecast demand in Week 5. Similar calculations could be carried out for other stockholding points in the physical distribution channel.

DRP is essentially forward looking, planning inventory levels in relation to projections of future demand, in contrast to the fixed order quantity or interval procedures which merely respond to past variations in sales. It can, as a result, yield large reductions in cycle and safety stock, particularly in the case of slower-moving lines (Martin, 1983). By delaying the transfer of stock down the channel to more dispersed locations, it has the beneficial effect of centralising stocks in higher-order nodes, permitting a net reduction both in stock levels and unit stockholding costs. The advantages of inventory centralisation are discussed later in this chapter.

To most firms, however, DRP presents a major challenge. Like MRP, it imposes heavy demands on a firm's computer system. It also requires accurate sales forecasting and a commitment by staff to adhere closely to ordering schedules. Above all, it demands a rapid flow of information between stockholding points at different levels in the distribution channel.

Advances in telecommunications and computing have greatly facilitated the implementation of DRP. Electronic points of sale (EPOS) continuously monitor the outflow of goods from shops. Electronically recorded sales data can be relayed either to warehouses under the retailer's control or directly to suppliers by means of electronic data interchange (EDI). Special computer networks have been developed to handle the transmission of orders between different levels in the distribution channel. In Britain, the Tradanet system, launched by ICL and the Article Number Association (ANA) in 1985, links, through a common network, the computer systems of manufacturers such as Proctor and Gamble, United Biscuits and Brooke-Bond-Oxo with those of retail chains such as Tesco, J. Sainsbury and Waitrose. Anderson (1986, p.I-1) describes as logistics data interchange (LDI) 'the use of any computerised network system to electronically transmit logistics information within a company or with external suppliers, transportation carriers or customers'. He defines 'logistics information' very broadly to include 'inbound materials flows, production status, product inventories, customer shipments and incoming orders'. He describes the extensive LDI network developed by the large US drug distributor, McKesson, which links its 52 distribution centres with most of its 15,000 trade customers and all of its 2,000 suppliers. EDI/LDI greatly accelerates the transfer of information and enables firms to reduce both cycle and safety stocks. It effectively substitutes information for inventory (Christopher, 1986).

Now that the necessary computing and communications technology is available, the main obstacle to a channel-wide introduction of DRP is the lack of co-operation between the various agencies in the distribution channel. Retailers and wholesalers are often unwilling to relay sales data back to producers and very reluctant to divulge information about their current stock position. Indeed in many trades, the relationship between producers and distributors is essentially adversarial, with each group trying to push as much of the responsibility for stockholding as possible onto the other. Each firm's efforts to minimise its own stockholding therefore conflict with the greater goal of minimising inventory across the channel as a whole. Where interagency rivalry makes channel-wide co-ordination impossible, a more limited form of DRP can be practised by a single firm, such as a manufacturer or multiple retailer, and applied to the particular section of the channel under its immediate control. Where manufacturers are denied up-to-date information about retail sales, however, they are unable to exploit the full benefits of DRP. There are, nevertheless, several instances in the UK of manufacturers and multiple retailers working together to streamline inventory management. Marks and Spencer, for example, has established close links with many of its suppliers, such as Corah, rapidly passing on sales data and in return demanding fast and reliable replenishment of stock. Close co-operation between supplier and retailer also underpins the innovative 'Quickship' operation developed by the Australian department store chain, Grace Bros, to expedite the distribution of furniture, electrical appliances and other merchandise (Campbell, 1987).

The next stage in the rationalisation of inventory management is to integrate DRP with MRP to co-ordinate the movement of stock throughout the logistical channel from raw material source to final point of sale. Christopher (1986, p.121) sees this as the 'final consummation of the requirements planning logic' and suggests that it be termed '*logistics requirements planning*'. While there are already some examples of LRP in existence, its widespread application is still some way off.

Horizontal dimension: stock dispersal

The previous section examined the vertical allocation of stock between nodes at different levels in the physical distribution channel. We shall now consider how many stockholding points there should be at particular levels in the channel.

Producers employing echelon channels disperse a substantial proportion of their finished stock to distribution depots. In Chapter 3,

Table 4.4 Number of stock locations in food manufacturers' distribution systems

| | Number of Stock Locations | | | | | | |
	1	*2-5*	*6-10*	*11-15*	*16-20*	*>20*	*Total*
No. of firms	3	3	9	9	2	3	29
(%)	(10)	(10)	(31)	(31)	(7)	(10)	

this decentralisation of the stockholding function was contrasted with its centralisation at the factory site. Firms differ, however, in the degree to which they decentralise their stockholding, as revealed by variations in the numbers of depots they employ. The number of depots a manufacturer uses depends partly on the size of its market, both in terms of its geographical extent and sales volume. Firms with similarly sized markets, though, can still differ markedly in their depot numbers, even within the same industrial sector. Thorpe *et al.* (1973), for example, found wide disparities in the numbers of depots used by a sample of 44 food manufacturers distributing their products nationally. A later survey by the author of 29 firms in the same industry also discovered great variability in depot numbers, though within a narrower range (Table 4.4). To explain these variations, one must examine the factors that influence the decentralisation of inventory.

Cost minimisation is usually the dominant objective behind efforts to optimise the number of stockholding points in a distribution system. The two main distribution cost elements of stockholding/storage and transport are both sensitive to variations in depot numbers.

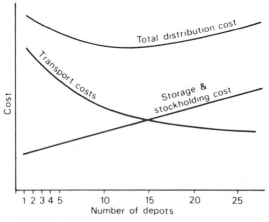

Figure 4.4 Relationship between depot numbers and total distribution costs

Concentrating inventory in fewer locations carries the double benefit of reducing the total amount of stock that needs to be held (to provide a given level of service) and the unit costs of physically accommodating this stock. In most cases, however, these benefits are won at the expense of higher transport costs. Given this inverse relationship, optimising the number of stock locations largely involves finding the trade-off between stockholding/storage and transport costs that minimises the total cost of distribution (Figure 4.4).

Benefits of centralising inventory

Starr and Miller (1962) demonstrate that by centralising safety stock (or 'reserve stock' as they call it), one can reduce the total amount required to maintain a given level of 'protection' against demand variations. It was shown earlier in this chapter how the level of safety stock is typically calculated in relation to the standard deviation of variations in demand. Let us suppose that a firm initially serves its market from ten depots, each with its own exclusive hinterland. The amount of safety stock in each depot would be conditioned by the standard deviation of demand in the area it served. This demand is assumed to vary randomly. By centralising stock and serving the whole market area from a single location, all the randomly varying demands in the separate hinterlands are aggregated. When this happens the standard deviation does not increase in direct proportion to the combined demand. It increases by a smaller margin, equivalent to the square root of the number of depots in the decentralised system. As the required volume of safety stock is determined by the standard deviation, it increases at a similar rate. The ratio of stock held in decentralised and centralised systems can thus be expressed as follows:

$$S_d / S_c = \sqrt{n} \qquad (4.6)$$

where S_d is the amount of safety stock in the decentralised system, S_c the amount of safety stock in the centralised system and n the number of depots in the decentralised system. Since n will always be greater than 1, a centralised system will invariably need less safety stock than a decentralised system. The reduction in safety stock resulting from centralisation (W) can be calculated by the following formula:

$$W = S_d (1 - 1/\sqrt{n}). \qquad (4.7)$$

Moving from a decentralised system containing ten depots to a completely centralised system would, in theory, reduce the safety stock requirement by 68%. Figure 4.5 uses this general relationship (which is widely known as the *square root law*) to show the extent to

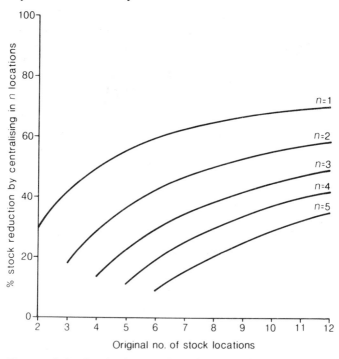

Figure 4.5 Stock reductions resulting from centralisation

which safety stock can be reduced by concentrating it in fewer locations. It has so far been assumed that demand is divided evenly among the depots in the decentralised system. The square root law can also be applied to the much more realistic situation in which the level of demand varies between depots (Table 4.5).

Maister (1976) provides a mathematical proof of the square root law and argues that it can be extended to cover cycle stock. His reasoning, however, is underpinned by several important assumptions, some of which are acceptable, but others much more questionable. The following assumptions present little difficulty:

1. All depots in the decentralised system fix the level of safety stock in relation to the same number of standard deviations above mean demand. In other words, they all maintain the same level of cover against variations in demand. This is a reasonable assumption, as a firm would tend to standardise service level across its distribution system.

2. Unit stockholding and procurement costs are the same in centralised and decentralised systems. As there are economies of

Table 4.5 Effect of inventory decentralisation on the level of safety stock

| % of Total Demand | | | Relative Amount of Safety Stock |
Depot 1	Depot 2	Depot 3	(centralised [c] = 100)
100	—	—	100
20	80	—	134
50	50	—	142
50	40	10	166
40	30	30	173
x	y	z	$(\sqrt{x} + \sqrt{y} + \sqrt{z})$ $c/10$

scale both in stockholding and ordering, this assumption initially appears unrealistic. As shown in Figure 4.3, however, stockholding and procurement costs vary inversely as order size increases. The economies of scale tend, therefore, to cancel each other out and do not significantly distort the 'square root' relationship (Maister, 1976).

The remaining assumptions cast more serious doubt on the validity of the relationship:

3. Demands at each depot in the decentralised system must be uncorrelated. Where this condition does not hold, safety stock reductions from centralisation will be less than the square root law predicts; the stronger the correlation, the smaller will be the reduction. It is quite common for demands in different parts of a market area to be correlated, in some cases, very strongly.
4. Demand at each depot must be subject to the same degree of variability. Where this is not so, reductions in safety stock resulting from centralisation will be less than indicated by the square root law. In practice, spatial variations in economic circumstances, customer loyalty and the effectiveness of promotional campaigns make demand more variable in some depot hinterlands than others.

Assumptions 3 and 4 have the effect of maximising the amount of safety stock in the decentralised system and, therefore, maximising the possible reductions from centralisation (Das, 1978). As defined by Maister, the decentralised system is a special case, very unlikely to occur in reality and, when compared with a centralised system, likely to exaggerate the safety stock differential. Sussams (1986), nevertheless, claims that, when tested in '24 different situations', the square root law quite accurately predicted safety stock reductions. He concludes that 'subject to reservations concerning the normality of the demand pattern, the square root law may be used with confidence to estimate differences in buffer stock requirements for different configurations of depots' (p.10).

5. The application of the square root law to cycle stocks rests on the assumption that these stocks should be uniformly distributed to all depots in the decentralised system. This condition maximises the amount of cycle stock in the decentralised system, again creating an unrealistic and unfair basis of comparison with the centralised system. In practice, the mean level of demand is likely to vary between depot hinterlands, causing firms to allocate cycle stock differentially between depots.

As inventory centralisation allows firms to economise mainly on safety stock, its impact on the total volume of inventory depends on the ratio of safety stock to cycle stock. The potential reduction in inventory is greatest where order lead times are short, keeping cycle stocks low, and demand is highly variable, creating the need for large safety stocks. Overall stock reductions can be substantial, as demonstrated by the case of an office equipment supplier that achieved a 40% reduction in inventory investment by closing twelve regional depots and centralising stock in a single location (Newson, 1978).

6. Total demand must be unaffected by the centralisation of inventory. This, too, can be disputed on the grounds that as it usually takes longer for orders to be supplied from a central facility, some sales may be lost. The magnitude of these sales losses depends partly on the scale of the resulting deterioration in the delivery service and partly on the sensitivity of demand to changes in the level of product availability. The former can, of course, be minimised by employing faster means of transport to distribute goods from the central depot, but this inflates delivery costs and offsets some of the savings in inventory costs. We shall consider the relationship between stock location and sales more fully in a later section.

Warehousing systems

Centralised inventory can also be stored more economically. As there are economies of scale in warehousing, storage costs per unit decline as warehouse throughput increases (Figure 4.6). In a survey of food wholesale warehouses, Williams (1975) found that storage cost per case fell as throughput increased up to a level of about 225,000 cases

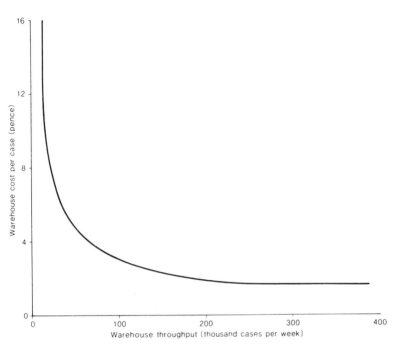

Figure 4.6 Relationship between warehouse throughput and unit storage costs
Source: Williams, 1975.

per week. For a given product range, the actual relationship between unit storage costs and throughput depends on the nature of the warehousing operation, particularly the following:

1. Warehouse layout

In designing the internal layout of a warehouse, firms must balance the conflicting objectives of maximising *cube utilisation* and minimising product handling and movement. If the efficient use of space were the sole objective, 'block stacking' of goods in a solid mass would be ideal. Retrieving stock from a densely packed block would, however, require an excessive amount of multiple handling. It is preferable, therefore, to insert aisles (or gangways) to provide easy access to all SKUs. The width of these aisles, and hence the trade-off between cube utilisation and handling efficiency, depends on the nature of the picking operation and the types of equipment used. Investment in more advanced forms of handling equipment, such as reach trucks, which require narrower aisles, can be more easily justified in centralised warehouses with higher throughputs.

2. Height

Construction costs per unit of storage space decline as warehouse height increases up to around 10-12 metres, when diseconomies set in (Williams, 1981). This height limit does not apply to 'roof-on-rack' structures which are supported by the internal racking and covered with a flimsy metal cladding. Williams estimates that the cost of storage space in these premises is around a third lower than in conventional warehouse buildings of comparable size. 'High bay' warehouses also use land much more intensively, especially as the trucks and cranes employed to lift goods onto high-level racking can operate in narrow aisles.

3. Storage system

In deciding where to place individual SKUs within a warehouse, firms generally adopt either a fixed location or a random location approach (or some combination of these two approaches). In a *fixed location system*, the storage space is divided into zones and each assigned a separate product or product group. The allocation and location of space for particular products is determined on the basis of past stock levels and turnover rates. Such a system is easily managed but usually prodigal in its use of storage space. Under the alternative *random location system*, any product can be placed in any location. As positions become vacant they are filled with incoming stock of any type. This system uses storage space more efficiently, but requires a much more elaborate and reliable information recording and processing system. The computerisation of warehouse documentation has promoted the more widespread use of the random location approach and thereby helped firms to substitute information for storage space as well as inventory (Christopher, 1986).

Transport implications

The transport cost curve in Figure 4.4, like that of stockholding, is a composite curve. It combines two separate relationships: between the number of depots and (i) local delivery costs and (ii) trunking costs.

Local delivery costs are partly a function of distance. Delivery distances are conventionally regarded as comprising a stem component (distance from the depot to the zone in which drops are made) and a zonal component (distance travelled between delivery points within this drop zone). The zonal distance is a function of the number of delivery points per unit area (i.e. the *drop density*) and is generally calculated as the square root of the area required to generate a full load for a delivery vehicle (Waller, 1983). Thus defined, a drop zone is small relative to the total area served by a depot. For this reason, the zonal distance is usually considered to be unaffected by variations in depot numbers and hence hinterland size. In contrast, the stem distance is very sensitive to differences in depot numbers. The larger the number of depots, the smaller are their hinterlands and shorter the stem distances. Marginal reductions in stem distances, and hence delivery costs, diminish as the number of depots increases, causing the cost curve to taper. The actual configuration of a local delivery cost curve is influenced by other factors, principally the drop density, drop sizes, the physical characteristics of the product and the nature of customers' reception facilities.

Variations in depot numbers have a much greater effect on local delivery costs than on the cost of trunking goods from the factory. Generally speaking, all the transport cost savings that accrue from an increase in depot numbers are the result of improved efficiency at local delivery level. Decentralising the stockholding function causes the pattern of bulk flow to become more dispersed and this can increase trunking costs. The addition of depots can also increase the average length of trunk hauls, though, as transport costs taper over longer distances, the resulting increments in bulk freight costs are usually small. Overall, increases in trunking costs tend to be very small and far exceeded by savings in delivery costs. In fact, so limited is the sensitivity of trunking costs to the number of depots that they are often excluded from the cost trade-off calculations.

Total distribution costs

It is found in practice that the total distribution cost curve produced by the summation of transport and stockholding costs is fairly flat across its central section, indicating that there is no single, optimum number of depots, but rather an optimal range. One food manufacturer which undertook a detailed cost trade-off analysis found little variation in total distribution costs across the range 9-16 depots, though the optimal range is often narrower than this. Cadbury-Schweppes, for example, found that the difference in cost between operating 7 depots and 10 depots was only about 0.2% of total distribution costs (Beattie, 1973). The shallowness of the total distribution cost function around the optimum offers firms flexibility in the design of their distribution systems and allows other factors, excluded from the cost analysis, to influence the actual number of depots finally chosen. This flexibility can be enhanced by the use of separate break-bulk facilities.

Break-bulk operations

Most stockholding depots also act as break-bulk points. The key to minimising the cost of a freight movement lies in maximising its trunk-haul component, over which goods are transported in bulk loads, and minimising the local delivery distance, over which they move more expensively in small consignments.

This is achieved by breaking bulk as close as possible to the customer and hence maximising the number of break-bulk points. The minimisation of stockholding costs, on the other hand, requires the concentration of stock in as few locations as possible. The locational pressures of the two main depot functions of stockholding and the breaking of bulk are, therefore, in conflict.

As a result, it is often desirable to divorce these functions and perform them in separate locations. Stocks are then held in a small number of large warehouses from which goods are despatched in bulk loads to a much larger number of stockless, break-bulk points. This spatial separation of the stockholding and break-bulk functions is not a recent phenomenon. In 1929, for example, Huntley-Palmer, the biscuit manufacturer, supplemented its network of 26 stockholding depots with a further 21 non-stockholding 'transfer sheds' (Corley, 1972).

Break-bulk systems can take various forms. The main distinction is between systems that employ depots and those that do not.

1. Depot systems

Depots that hold neither cycle nor safety stock and act solely as break-bulk points are known by a variety of names such as transit, transhipment, satellite or stockless depots. Goods passing through these premises have already been ordered and are *en route* to specific customers. They are held there only long enough for loads to be disaggregated and sorted, and for local delivery to be arranged. Firms vary enormously in their relative use of separate break-bulk depots. There was found to be a significant inverse correlation between the numbers of break-bulk and stockholding depots employed by a sample of 20 food manufacturers ($r = -0.64$). Clearly, though, variations in the numbers of stockholding depots cannot be explained simply by the substitution of break-bulk depots for storage premises. Firms can be classified into four general categories in terms of their relative use of 'transit depots':

(i) Firms that distribute their entire output in bulk loads to customers directly from the factory and therefore have no need for break-bulk facilities, or indeed decentralised storage.

The following three categories contain manufacturers that distribute a significant part of their output to small outlets and, hence, do require to break-bulk:

(ii) Firms that centralise stocks at a single location and break-bulk at numerous points around the country. In deciding how many transit depots to use, these firms must ensure that levels of flow on each link in the trunk network permit efficient utilisation of vehicles and depots. Firms contracting out break-bulk operations often spread the risks of service disruption across many separate contractors in different locations.

(iii) Firms with highly decentralised stockholding systems that make little use of separate break-bulk facilities. Satellite depots are then only justified where the hinterlands of particular depots are exceptionally large or irregularly shaped.

(iv) Firms that fall between categories (ii) and (iii), which concentrate stock to a moderate degree, giving most stockholding depots such wide hinterlands that they require one or more satellite break-bulk points.

In the case of firms in the last two categories, break-bulk depots constitute additional nodes in the echelon channel. To be economically justified they must reduce transport costs by a large enough margin to offset the extra terminal and handling costs they impose.

2. Depotless systems

It is possible to dispense with depots and break-bulk 'out of doors' by employing road semi-trailers or demountables. In some countries, it is possible for a single tractor unit to trunk haul two or more trailers to a 'decoupling point', from which local deliveries can be made by each trailer separately. Such 'road train' formations are illegal in the UK, but it is permissible for a rigid vehicle to haul a single drawbar-trailer. Drawbar-trailer combinations can be equipped with *demountable vehicle bodies* (or 'swap bodies') which are easily removed from the chassis of the rigid lorry or trailer and left standing on retractable legs. Demountable bodies can be manually transferred between the chassis of rigid vehicles and trailers by a single driver. In the UK, most demountable operations have a similar trunk haul, comprising the outward movement of a drawbar-trailer combination to a transfer point, such as a lorry park or other 'hard standing'. From there, the two units distribute orders separately, usually in multiple-drop rounds. The nature of the local delivery operation can vary, depending on whether an outbased vehicle is available at the transfer point and, if so, how it is used.

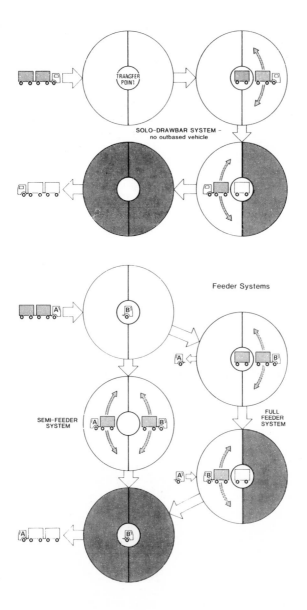

Figure 4.7 Road-based demountable systems

The three main delivery strategies are illustrated in Figure 4.7 (Cooper and Doganis, 1982). Each of the circles represents a local delivery area split into two zones and with a centrally located transfer point. In the *solo-drawbar system*, all trunk haulage and local delivery work is performed by a single rigid lorry. Feeder systems employ an outbased vehicle (B), either to handle all deliveries within the local area (*full feeder system*) or to share them with the 'trunk-haul' rigid (A) (*semi-feeder system*). Demountable systems allow firms to avoid the expense of setting up their own break-bulk depots or using contractors' premises. As they only break-bulk into fixed unit loads, however, they do not offer the same flexibility as a depot operation.

In recent years, there has been a sharp increase in the number of firms employing demountables and this trend is likely to continue. Where the use of demountables permits the closure of depots and centralisation of stock, the potential savings in inventory can be impressive. Diversey, for example, managed to reduce its total stockholding by 40% by replacing a network of 15 depots with a demountable system based on a single warehouse (*Motor Transport*, 7 July 1987).

Customer service level

The spatial distribution of inventory is not solely determined by the desire to minimise stockholding and transport costs. Consideration must also be given to the level of customer service, and in particular the speed with which orders can be delivered. In theory, the more centralised the inventory, the greater the average distance between supply point and customer, and hence the longer the order lead time. If the level of sales is inversely related to order lead time, it is likely to decline as a consequence of the centralisation of inventory. The typical relationship between depot numbers and sales revenue is shown by the uppermost curve in Figure 4.8. The gap between this curve and the total distribution cost curve is a crude measure of profitability. If optimisation is defined as profit maximisation, the optimum number of stockholding points occurs where this gap is at its widest and need not minimise distribution costs. In practice, however, the number of depots does not influence sales revenue in such a clear and direct manner as Figure 4.8 suggests. The conventional view that more dispersed stockholding leads to higher sales is based on two hypotheses:

1. reducing delivery times generates additional sales;
2. decentralising the stockholding function reduces delivery times.

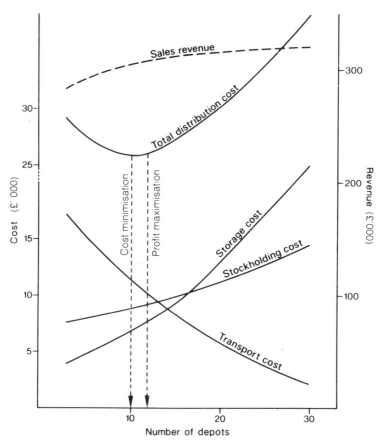

Figure 4.8 Determining the optimum number of depots on the basis of distribution costs and sales revenue
Adapted from Rand, 1976.

The first hypothesis is difficult to test empirically because one can seldom isolate the effect of a change in delivery times from the influence of other factors. In a survey of head-office buyers in a small sample of wholesale and retail organisations, Christopher *et al.* (1979) enquired about the factors affecting their evaluation of suppliers and hence likely to influence their level of purchases. Delivery time rated sixth equal in rank order, well behind such criteria as product availability, promotional activity and representation. In another part of their study, the reliability of deliveries was shown to be a critical variable in most buyers' estimation. This accords with the finding of Shipley (1985) that, for a range of convenience and shopping goods,

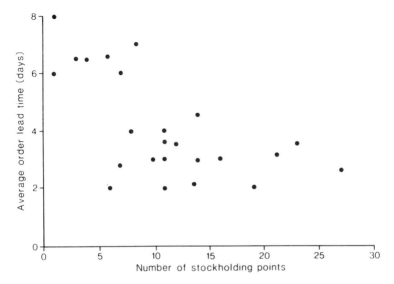

Figure 4.9 The number of stockholding points and average order lead times

the reliability of deliveries was deemed to be more important than quoted delivery times. McGoldrick and Douglas (1983) also established that delivery reliability was the main factor affecting multiple retailers' decisions on which brands of potato crisp to stock. On the basis of this evidence, one might hypothesise that, so long as a manufacturer adheres rigidly to a delivery timetable, customers may be prepared to accept slightly longer lead times.

None of the studies cited above attempt to relate the opinions buyers express to their actual purchasing behaviour. Ozment and Chard (1986), on the other hand, use historical data, provided by 'a division of a billion dollar corporation' selling mainly convenience goods to wholesalers, to analyse the relationship between sales and several customer service variables, including order cycle time. Although their definition of order cycle time excludes transit times, their research is still pertinent. Having allowed for varying degrees of time-lag and taking account of other major service variables such as price and promotion, Ozment and Chard discovered that there was a significant relationship between order cycle time and sales. Their work, however, gives little indication of the sensitivity of sales to variations in order cycle time.

Information collected from 24 food manufacturers on average order lead times and numbers of stockholding points casts doubt on the validity of the second hypothesis. Six of the firms achieving delivery times of under five days operated 'nominated day' schemes, whereby customers adhere to a timetable for the submission of orders. Even allowing for the slight bias that this introduced, it appeared that there was little relationship between service level and depot numbers (Figure 4.9). The seven firms with the longest lead times (over five days) did operate comparatively few depots. Across the range one to five days, however, within which the average delivery times of 70% of the firms fell, there was no significant relationship between lead time and depot numbers. This contradicts the frequent claim that a wide dispersal of stocks is necessary to provide customers with fast delivery. Stock dispersal is only one of a number of factors affecting order lead times. Christopher *et al.* found that most of the variation in order lead time stemmed from differences in the rate at which firms handled documentation. According to Sweet (1984), the centralisation of stockholding enabled Elida Gibbs, the personal products division of Unilever, to accelerate order processing and thereby reduce order lead times. The centralised facility also maintained a higher level of product availability, despite the fact that it held only half as much stock as was previously dispersed in regional depots. On the basis of wide consultancy experience in this area, Bevington (1979, p.67) observes that, 'The more dispersed stock is, the less likely it is to be subject to careful control. Stock levels are, therefore, higher than necessary without any corresponding increase in customer service'. It should also be remembered that firms can compensate for centralised stockholding by using faster transport modes or having sufficient transport capacity available to despatch orders to customers at short notice. One may conclude, therefore, that the centralisation of inventory need not carry sales penalties and, on the contrary, may actually help generate additional revenue.

Sales staff sometimes argue that, regardless of its effects on actual delivery times, merely having a depot in a particular area has a favourable psychological effect on customers, making them feel that stock is readily available nearby upon which they can draw in an emergency. This raises more general questions about how buyers perceive the standard of delivery a supplier provides and how closely their perceptions correspond to actual delivery performance. Christopher *et al.* (p.186) argue that 'subjective perception of a supplier's service offering may differ substantially from the objective reality'.

Powell (1976) concludes that, as it is very difficult for a firm to establish in advance how much additional sales revenue an extra depot will generate, depots should be justified only on cost minimisation grounds. Costs can only be minimised, though, in relation to a defined standard of delivery service. Christopher *et al.* (p.3) note that, 'Service has become a minimal performance constraint against which the total costs should then be minimised'.

Since the impact of depot changes on sales is uncertain, customer service level tends not to be formally incorporated in cost trade-off analysis.

Spatial concentration of inventory

Over the past 25 years, stock has become concentrated in fewer locations. This spatial concentration has been the result of three processes.

1. Internal rationalisation of individual firms' stockholding systems

There is much anecdotal evidence to show that firms have substantially reduced their depot numbers in recent years in the UK and other developed countries. Few general surveys have been done, however, to discover how pronounced and widespread this trend has become. Sample surveys of the distribution systems of large food manufacturers by Thorpe *et al.* in 1972/3 and the author in 1978/9 indicated that over the intervening period there had been a reduction in the average number of stockholding depots from 16.1 to 10.6. Twenty-four of the firms surveyed in 1978/9 provided historical data on the numbers of depots they employed at various times since 1945 (Figure 4.10). All these firms had reduced depot numbers while expanding their volume of sales. These desultory time series data indicate that several firms embarked on a programme of depot rationalisation in the 1960s, confirming the observation of the NEDO (1967) that the spatial concentration of stockholding was well underway in the UK by the mid-1960s. For the majority of firms, however, the main phase of depot closure was in the 1970s and these firms generally compressed depot rationalisation into a shorter time-span. A survey of 266 warehouses in the East Midlands region found that 42% of the premises opened in the previous ten years had replaced two or more warehouses and represented a spatial concentration of storage space (McKinnon and Pratt, 1985).

2. Changes in the organisational structure of industry and commerce

In most industrial and trade sectors, business has become more concentrated in a smaller number of firms and this has promoted the centralisation of stockholding, as well as production and sales, in the premises of the dominant firms.

3. Reallocation of trade between marketing channels

Since the early 1960s, there has been a diversion of product flows away from marketing channels characterised by dispersed

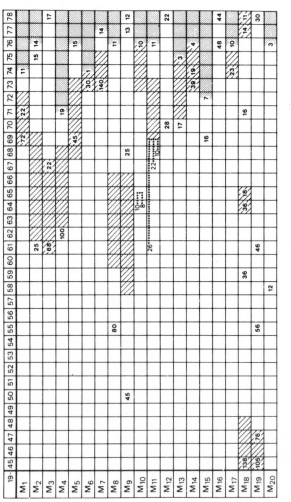

M Manufacturer

Main phase of reduction in depot numbers

Depot numbers constant

······ Company merger

Figure 4.10 Reduction in depot numbers, 1945–78: sample of food manufacturers

stockholding towards channels in which inventory tends to be more spatially concentrated. This has resulted mainly from the growth of multiple retailers and the increase in the proportion of supplies channelled through their central warehouses. In some trades, most notably the grocery trade, multiple retailers centralise their stock to a greater extent than wholesalers and manufacturers (McKinnon, 1986a). They tend to organise their physical distribution on a national or regional scale, whereas wholesaling and the distribution operations of many manufacturers have remained more localised, though they too have become more spatially concentrated. Statistics compiled for the Institute of Grocery Distribution (1984) show wholesale depots increasing in size while declining in numbers. Indeed many manufacturers and wholesalers have adjusted their distribution systems to the loss of traffic to multiple retailers by closing depots and concentrating storage capacity in fewer locations. Furthermore, as multiple retailers' warehouses are relatively large they can receive bulk loads directly from factories, allowing flows to bypass manufacturers' depots and promoting the centralisation of stock at points of production. This trend has been reinforced by the development of superstores, hypermarkets and retail warehouses, which can also accept bulk loads directly from factories.

The spatial concentration of inventory has been a response to several cost pressures. The cost of financing stockholding has risen in line with real interest rates and exerted a downward pressure on stock levels. Much destocking has been accomplished in the short term by reducing stocks in existing premises. High and fluctuating interest rates have also induced a longer-term reduction in stock levels and this has been partly achieved by inventory centralisation. Large increases in the cost of borrowing have also given firms greater incentive to release working capital from stockholding for investment in more productive activities. Major advances in warehouse construction, materials handling and information processing have augmented economies of scale in warehousing. Indeed, the installation of many sophisticated handling systems is only justified in warehouses with a large throughput. New technology has, therefore, reinforced the trend towards more centralised patterns of storage. The centralisation of inventory nevertheless carries a transport cost penalty as it tends to increase delivery distances. It is likely to have been a major cause of the large increase in the average length of freight hauls in recent years. Between 1967/8 and 1984, the average length of haul by road and rail in the UK rose by over 50% (McKinnon, 1986b). The average length of road movements went up by roughly 60% despite the fact that over this period the real cost of operating lorries increased sharply.

117

Table 4.6   Increases in maximum lorry weights and dimensions, 1955-87

| | Articulated | | | Rigid | | |
	Weight (tonnes)	Length (m)	Width (m)	Weight (tonnes)	Length (m)	Width (m)
1955	24.4	10.7	2.4	24.4	9.1	2.4
1987	38.0	15.5	2.5	30.5	12.0	2.5
% change	55.8	45.3	2.5	25.0	31.9	2.5

Increases in vehicle operating costs might have been expected to constrain the centralisation of inventory as they inflate the marginal cost of the resulting increase in average journey length. The effect of these cost increases has been mitigated, however, by the use of larger vehicles improvements to the road network and the structure of vehicle operating costs.

1. Use of larger vehicles

Larger-size classes of goods vehicle have similar operating costs per kilometre to smaller-size classes, mainly because their higher 'standing' costs are spread over the much greater distance they travel annually (Cundill and Shane, 1980). As larger lorries carry heavier loads, they have lower costs per tonne-kilometre. Legal limits on the weight and size of rigid and articulated lorries have risen substantially since the mid-1950s (Table 4.6). Between 1966 and 1984 the proportion of commercial vehicles with gross weights in excess of 24 tonnes increased from 3.4% to 29.1%. Between 1974 and 1984, these vehicles increased their share of the total tonnage carried on the road network from roughly 40% to 69% (Department of Transport, 1985). This dramatic increase in the use of heavier vehicles has helped to compensate for the general increase in operating costs and average length of haul. Increased use of these vehicles has been closely associated with the spatial concentration of stockholding and consolidation of deliveries, because these trends have aggregated consignments into bulkier loads. The design and location of centralised storage facilities are also well suited to the collection and delivery of goods in large vehicles.

2. Improvements to the road network

Since 1962, the length of motorway in Britain has increased from 240 km to over 2800 km and much of the remaining trunk-road network has been upgraded to dual-carriageway standard. This extensive road development has promoted the acceleration of freight movement by road, allowing lorries to travel longer distances within the 'driving day'. This has enabled operators to increase delivery distances significantly without incurring the high marginal costs that arise when a round trip cannot be completed within daily driving restrictions. Partly as a result of road improvements, firms have been able to maintain or extend delivery ranges despite Britain's adoption of tighter EC rules on drivers' hours in 1981. (These rules were relaxed in 1987 when the legal driving day increased from 8 to 9 hours.) Better road links have made it possible for firms to provide similar or even improved standards of delivery service from more centralised stockholding points.

3. Operating cost structure

For all but the largest sizes of lorry, 'standing costs' account for more than 50% of total operating costs, and this proportion has tended to increase. Total vehicle operating costs are therefore relatively insensitive to changes in journey length and, for many types of vehicle, this sensitivity has been diminishing.

In summary, it appears that firms have been altering the trade-off between stockholding and transport costs, reducing the former partly at the expense of the latter. Despite the upward trend in vehicle operating costs, firms have been able to hold the transport cost penalty associated with the centralisation of inventory at an acceptable level mainly by using larger vehicles and taking advantage of new road development. Some of the economic benefits of road improvements and increases in vehicle size and productivity have therefore been internalised in more efficient patterns of stockholding.

Chapter five

Depot location

Firms commonly decide how many stockholding points they require and then, quite independently, try to optimise their locations. This strategy facilitates the distribution planning exercise, but fails to take account of the fact that the numbers and locations of depots are interacting variables (Stasch, 1968). To calculate accurately the cost of differing degrees of stock dispersal, one needs information about the actual locations at which stock is to be held. For each level of stock decentralisation, different sets of depot locations should be evaluated in an effort to optimise depot numbers and locations jointly. In practice, however, this approach is often judged to be impractical as it requires excessive amounts of data and computation. Instead, firms typically resolve the question of depot numbers on the basis of the reasoning outlined in the previous chapter, and then establish depot locations either by subjective judgement or, increasingly, with the aid of quantitative techniques. In this chapter we shall review the main locational techniques available, consider the factors that cause depots to deviate from theoretically optimal locations and examine the actual patterns of location that have emerged.

Optimisation criteria

The dominant objective in depot location exercises is generally the minimisation of total distribution costs. These exercises differ in the range of cost elements included in the calculation and in the nature of the cost functions they employ. Eilon, Watson-Gandy and Christofides (1971) differentiate six levels of sophistication in the modelling of distribution costs. At the lowest level, only the cost of delivering goods outward from the depot is considered and expressed as a linear function of the direct distances to customers. Higher-level models refine the delivery cost function, incorporate trunk haulage costs and allow for spatial variations in warehousing costs. The minimisation of distribution costs in isolation, however accurately these costs are represented, cannot, of course, guarantee profit maximisation. Rand (1976) notes that such an outcome would only occur where sales revenue was completely unaffected by depot location. In fact, through its influence on order lead times, the location of a depot can affect a firm's ability to generate sales in a particular area. Mercer (1970) found, for example, that, in the case of a firm supplying a 'service product', market share diminished as distance from the depot increased. While this distance decay effect is likely to be less pronounced in the case of most consumer goods, it can still be of sufficient importance to merit consideration in depot location decisions, especially where the distribution system is highly centralised and depots serve wide hinterlands. Several attempts have been made to incorporate estimates of revenue generation into locational models, but this is seldom done in practice.

As Mole (1975, p.34) explains, 'The influence of warehouse configuration on revenue generation is obscure and this does tend to result in a reluctance to accept any criterion other than cost'. As noted in the previous chapter, it can prove extremely difficult to measure the effect on sales of changes in the distribution system. It has become common practice for service levels to be fixed in advance, in accordance with marketing and sales policies, and for depots to be located at points where the stipulated level of service can be provided at minimum cost.

The time-frame within which depot locations are optimised can vary. Most location models are static, in the sense that they only indicate where the optimal location(s) will be at a particular time. Attempts have, nevertheless, been made to develop dynamic locational models that show how stock should be relocated through time, mainly in response to spatial variations in the level of demand. The aim of these models is to find the pattern of depot location and relocation required to maximise profits or return on assets over a specified planning period. Ballou (1968) devised a method of determining the initial location of a single depot and the subsequent relocations required to maximise cumulative profits over a number of years. His method involves establishing static optimal locations for each year and then, by comparing the profits generated by each of these locations (discounted to the starting date), indicates when a move is justified and to which location. Meyer (1974) employs a mixed integer programming method to show how locations can be found for several facilities and their development phased over a specified time period so as to maximise return on investment.

The critical problem one encounters in trying to optimise depot location(s) over time is that of minimising the risk of changes in the pattern of demand, rendering locations chosen early in the planning period grossly inefficient. Rosenhead, Elton and Gupta (1972) propose a method of assessing the 'robustness' of selected locations, that is, the probability of them remaining efficient through time. They calculate the costs of many different sets of locations over the planning period and identify those locations which appear most frequently in sets yielding low costs. In their case study, Rosenhead *et al.* found that out of 297 sets of five locations, 31 had total costs within 5% of the cheapest. The location occurring most often in these 31 sets was deemed to be the most robust and would be the first to receive a facility. At later stages, facilities would be assigned to other locations in descending order of robustness. When used in distribution planning, this strategy need not maximise profits but can help to minimise the risk of a firm's depot locations becoming seriously suboptimal through time. Stoker (1980) has shown that the optimality of an existing set of depot locations is unlikely to be significantly reduced by the siting of additional depots. This suggests, therefore, that it is possible to decompose the multiple-location problem and optimise each location separately without fear of impairing the efficiency of the system as a whole. This is fortuitous, as firms are seldom able or willing to redesign their entire depot system from scratch. Most locational decisions relate to individual depots in particular areas.

Pattern of demand

Most of the research on depot location has been concerned primarily with the type of depots Bowersox (1969) classifies as being 'market-oriented'. Their locations are determined principally by the spatial distribution of the outlets they supply, in contrast to 'production-' and 'intermediate-oriented' depots whose locations are tied more closely to points of production. Depot location models either ignore the backward linkages from depots to the factories that supply them or accord them very little importance. As locations are optimised mainly with respect to the pattern of demand, it is necessary to consider the way in which demand is represented in locational models.

In the case of finished goods destined for consumers, demand can be expressed either in relation to population or in terms of actual sales data. This is an important distinction because spatial variations in population and sales need not be closely correlated. Per capita sales of a firm's products can vary significantly across its market area as a result of differences in affluence, tastes and the level of competition. Furthermore, sales data are generally collected where people shop, whereas population census figures relate to their places of residence. The relationship between the population of an area and its level of retail sales partly depends, therefore, on the distribution of retail outlets and the spatial pattern of consumer behaviour, together constituting what Sussams (1969, p.34) has called the 'shopping centre factor'.

It should be noted too that in depot location exercises the relevant measure of sales is not total sales but rather the volume of sales passing through distribution depots. The proportion of a manufacturer's sales distributed via depots can vary across its market area, reflecting geographical variations in its relative dependence on different physical distribution channels. For example, multiple retailers account for a much larger share of grocery sales in the south-east of England than in other parts of the country (Office of Fair Trading, 1985), and most of the larger chains supplying this region channel a relatively high proportion of their supplies through central warehouses. A large proportion of food manufacturers' sales in this region are, therefore, distributed directly in bulk loads to retailers' warehouses. Spatial variations in channel allocation can further weaken the relationship between an area's population and the demands it imposes on a local distribution depot.

Population is often used as a basis for demand calculations where a firm is setting up or rapidly expanding its business and hence more interested in potential demand than in past sales performance. It is also particularly relevant to firms producing convenience goods and marketing them intensively at the retail level. Population data are obtained from the national census, aggregated either by administrative districts or by grid squares. In their crudest form, population figures can be translated into measures of demand by multiplying them by an estimate of per capita consumption based on past sales data or market research findings. It is now possible to refine demand calculations based on population by taking account of spatial variations in its demographic and socio-economic characteristics. Consumer data bases, such as that developed in the UK by CACI, provide detailed information about the composition of the population in particular zones (Rowley, 1984). These can be used, in association with market research data, to build up a more accurate picture of the spatial pattern of demand. Although such data bases are being used increasingly in localised shop location studies and in the targeting of areas for direct marketing, they have as yet found little application in depot location exercises.

It is more common for firms to define the pattern of demand with reference to their own sales data. Where a firm's depots serve a large number of small outlets, sales data are usually aggregated either on a zonal basis or less systematically with respect to the clustering of outlets in particular areas. Sales are then assumed to arise at a central point (or centroid) in the zone or cluster. By cutting down on the number of demand points, this spatial aggregation reduces the scale of the problem. Where the number of outlets is relatively small there may be sufficient data and computing capacity available to treat them as separate locations, each with its own particular demand weighting.

In depot location models, demand is also simplified with respect to the time dimension. Some allowance is generally made for the growth in total demand over the planning period, but the spatial distribution of this demand is assumed to remain constant. Eilon *et al.* (1971) relax this assumption and let both the set of customers to be served and the size of their demands vary randomly. They show how one can estimate ton mileage, and hence transport costs, where the pattern of demand is subject to random variation. The practical advantages of this approach are, nevertheless, questionable because the assumption that the pattern of demand varies randomly can be as unrealistic as the assumption that it remains fixed.

Measurement of distance

The way in which distance is measured is of major importance in depot location exercises as most aim primarily to minimise distance-related costs. It is possible to approximate the measurement of distance in three ways.

First, where demand is spatially aggregated, distance need be measured only to a weighted centre point in a zone or customer grouping and not to each customer separately. Areal data are then effectively collapsed onto a point and intrazonal distances ignored.

Second, straight-line (crow-fly) distance can be used rather than network distances. This generally results in an underestimation of distances travelled since movement across transport networks entails some deviation from the straight-line path. In the UK, a correction factor of 1.2 is commonly used to convert crow-fly distances into network distances and some allowance made for geographical barriers, such as rivers, estuaries and mountains. An analysis of tachograph records has provided empirical support for a correction factor of this magnitude (Cooper, 1983a). Some depot location models take more explicit account of the structure of transport networks and use graph theoretic measures of distance. Maranzana (1964), for example, regards all the nodes on a transport network as possible depot locations and uses a shortest-path algorithm to measure the network distances between depots and customers. Today, an algorithm of this type can be used in association with a computerised road network data base to yield very accurate distance measurements

(Beasley, 1982). Several of these data bases have been employed in connection with depot location models, though their main application has been in the field of route planning (see Chapter 7).

Third, it is generally assumed that deliveries are made to each customer separately and directly, whereas in practice many of the deliveries originating at depots take the form of multiple-drop rounds. In 1984, roughly 27% of all lorry journeys in the UK were classified as 'multiple stop', as the vehicle stopped more than once to deliver or collect consignments. Approximately 37% of the journeys made by goods vehicles within the range most used for depot deliveries (3.5 - 16 tonnes gvw) had five or more stops. Clearly, therefore, for a substantial proportion of deliveries, direct radial distances misrepresent the actual logistics of the freight movement. Webb (1968) argues that, where deliveries are of the multiple-drop type, the length of the planned route, or 'planned distance', is a more accurate basis for calculating transport costs than direct distance. He compared the results of depot location exercises based on radial distances and route distances planned using a vehicle routeing algorithm and found that they differed, in some cases quite markedly. Eilon *et al.* (1971), however, question the validity of this comparison on the grounds that it relates to only four particular examples, that the vehicle routeing algorithm used often yields suboptimal routes and that Webb undermines the mathematical consistency of the calculation by allowing a critical parameter to vary. They go on to demonstrate that there is a close relationship between radial and route distances and show that, under certain circumstances, the same depot locations would approximately minimise cost functions based on either metric. This would happen either where, as a result of capacity and operating constraints, delivery vehicles are able to serve only a small number of customers per journey, or where the hinterland has a high customer density. When neither of these conditions apply, it would be advantageous to follow the example of Wren and Holliday (1972) and incorporate a vehicle routeing algorithm within the depot location model. Perl and Daskin (1984) have developed a mathematical programming model which can optimise depot location and vehicle routeing simultaneously. They demonstrate that this unified location-routeing model can 'handle real-life distribution system design problems' (p.92) and see it as 'a step towards the development of an integrated approach to the analysis of distribution systems' (p.109). Very few firms, however, attempt to optimise routes in the manner that Perl and Daskin suggest, for reasons outlined in Chapter 7. Widespread application of their methodology will, therefore, require a fundamental change in the way firms plan vehicle movements.

In the next section, attention will be confined to models which aim to optimise depot location independently of vehicle routeing.

Methods of optimisation

A major distinction must be drawn between continuous (or infinite-set) methods which permit an unrestricted choice of locations and discrete (or feasible-set) methods which confine the search to a preselected list of possible locations. Both approaches have advantages and disadvantages (Eilon *et al.*, 1971). The greatest shortcoming of the continuous approach is its failure to distinguish possible from impossible locations. In distribution circles, anecdotes abound about infinite-set models yielding ridiculous results. A large supermarket chain, for example, found that it should serve shops in the London area from a warehouse on Waterloo Bridge, while, in the case of a major food manufacturer, Lundy Island in the Severn Estuary was pinpointed as the best location from which to supply south-west England! Distribution managers frequently cite such ludicrous examples as grounds for dismissing this type of optimising model, or even models in general. This is unfair, however, as firms should not expect to be able to locate depots at the precise locations established by the model. Even where depot location is decided intuitively, firms must still search over a reasonably wide area for a suitable site. Searches are typically conducted over areas with a radius of 30-40 miles, but some have been much more extensive. W.H. Smith, for instance, considered numerous locations in a broad arc from Bristol to Peterborough before basing its national distribution centre at Swindon (Loasby, 1973). As the distribution cost function is generally very shallow in the vicinity of the optimum location 'some latitude in the choice of location is possible at little extra cost' (Willis, 1977, p.150). In the early stages of the depot location exercise firms need an indication of the general area in which to look for sites and this can be adequately provided by infinite-set models.

While feasible-set models exclude impossible locations from consideration, their success depends on the thoroughness with which possible locations are preselected. There is always the danger that the best possible location will be overlooked at the preselection stage. One can minimise the chance of this happening by defining a very large set of feasible locations, but this greatly increases the data requirements. On the whole, the discrete approach requires more data than the continuous approach. It demands large amounts of information specific to particular locations, whereas infinite-set methods can make greater use of spatially continuous cost functions. Such cost functions are often highly generalised, though, and lack the precision of point-specific data.

Discrete methods

All discrete methods of depot location can be divided into three stages:

1. preselection of possible locations;
2. evaluation of these locations;
3. search for optimal or near-optimal location(s).

The preselection can be carried out in various ways. As depots tend to gravitate to major population centres, all settlements with population in excess of a certain figure might be considered possible locations. Points of high accessibility on transport networks should also be included. Alternatively one can eschew these more objective criteria and rely more heavily on intuition and experience. In the UK, for example, distribution managers have long recognised that regional centres are particularly good bases for storage and distribution (Braithwaite and Dobbs, 1932). Where a firm wishes to modify an existing depot system, the list of feasible sites will, of course, include the locations at which it already has depots.

The manner in which a model evaluates locations depends on its optimisation criteria and cost functions. There tends to be an inverse relationship between the complexity of the cost functions used and the thoroughness of the search procedure (Rand, 1976). At one extreme are simulation techniques, such as that of Shycon and Maffie (1960), which can model a firm's distribution system with great accuracy, but offer no guidance on how to find an optimal or near-optimal pattern of depot location. The use of such techniques entails generating large numbers of potential locations, subjectively or by means of a random process, in the hope that the one which yields the lowest cost (or maximum profit) is near optimal. In the absence of a systematic search procedure, simulation methods are highly inefficient and offer no guarantee that a near-optimal set of locations will be found. At the other extreme are various forms of mathematical programming that can converge quite rapidly on optimal or near-optimal locations (e.g. Efroymson and Ray, 1966). Some branch and bound methods, for example, can be relied upon to yield exact solutions to the depot location problem, achieving optimisation on every occasion (Khumawala, 1972). As Khumawala and Whybark (1973, p.197) point out, however, 'they are exact only in a mathematical framework'. Their use of highly generalised cost functions and numerous simplifying assumptions casts doubt on the true optimality of the locations they identify. Between these extremes lie various heuristic methods which do not necessarily establish optimal locations but offer an efficient means of achieving a near-optimal solution. They can accommodate more operating constraints and more complex cost functions than integer programming methods, giving them greater versatility and realism.

The first major heuristic method of solving the depot location problem was developed by Kuehn and Hamburger (1963). This method makes use of three lists of locations. The first is a list of potential sites; the second, an intermediate 'buffer' containing a subset of possible sites to be subjected to detailed evaluation; and the third, a list of locations provisionally assigned a depot. The size of the intermediate list must be decided at the outset, though no limit is imposed on the number of locations finally receiving a depot.

It is assumed at the outset that there are no depots in existence and that all customers are supplied directly from the factory. By setting up depots at several locations in the market area, it should be possible both to reduce distribution costs and to generate additional sales. Kuehn and Hamburger subsume the objective of maximising revenue within a cost minimisation framework by expressing additional sales in terms of the opportunity costs of losing these sales as a result of slow delivery from more distant locations. Those potential locations that reduce the cost of supplying customers in their local hinterlands by the greatest margin are placed in the intermediate list. Each of these locations is then individually evaluated in terms of the extent to which a depot located there would reduce the cost of the distribution system as a whole. The location yielding the largest cost saving (which we shall call X) is transferred to the third list and is deemed, provisionally, to become a depot site. If a location does not produce a cost saving in excess of the fixed cost of establishing a depot there, it is excluded from further consideration. The remaining locations in the buffer list are then returned to the general list of potential sites for further consideration at a later stage. At the end of this first stage of the procedure, one depot has been provisionally located and, possibly, some of the potential sites discarded. The second stage begins, like the first, by selecting potential sites from the buffer list, though this time the existence of a depot at location X will result in a different set of locations being chosen. The evaluation of these locations proceeds as before and, again, the one yielding the largest cost saving is assigned a depot. This operation continues until the list of potential sites is exhausted. Most will be eliminated at some stage in the procedure because they fail to yield cost savings in excess of fixed costs; the remainder will have been provisionally assigned depots. Kuehn and

Hamburger then apply what they call a 'bump-shift' routine to this pattern of depot location to achieve a lower cost solution. It is possible that some of the locations assigned depots by the earlier procedure are superfluous, as a result of their close proximity to other, superior locations. These are eliminated by the 'bump' part of the routine. In other cases, it might be possible to make a further cost saving by relocating a depot at another potential site in the vicinity. The 'shift' part of the routine makes marginal readjustments of this type.

The Kuehn and Hamburger method has several desirable features:

1. It simultaneously establishes the numbers and locations of depots.
2. It makes allowance for the effect of depot location on the level of sales, though very crudely.
3. By only evaluating a subset of the potential locations at any given time, it economises on computation.
4. The quality of its results compares favourably with other feasible-set methods, some of which require much more calculation.

Various refinements have been made to the Kuehn and Hamburger method. Feldman, Lehrer and Ray (1966), for example, found it advantageous to reverse the procedure, starting from a position in which all the potential locations were deemed to have depots and approaching the optimal pattern by removing these depots one at a time. They also used a more realistic depot cost function that allowed for economies of scale in depot operations.

Continuous approach

This approach to facility location has a much longer history than the feasible-set approach. Attempts to optimise location on this basis date back over three centuries (Cooper, 1963). In the early stages, the objective was to find a point that minimised total radial distance to a small number of given locations. Weber (1909) examined the problem in the context of industrial location, considering the simple situation of a plant drawing raw materials from two sources and supplying finished goods to a single market, each represented by a point. These points were weighted in terms of the volume of goods they supplied or received. Initially, Weber defined the optimum location for the plant as that which minimised total transport costs, assuming that these costs varied in direct proportion to the weight of goods transported multiplied by the distance moved (traditionally expressed as *ton mileage*). The depot location problem can be formulated in a similar manner. Factories can be substituted for raw material sources.

Alternatively, where the aim is solely to minimise the outward delivery costs, only customer locations need be considered. The number of customer locations can also be greatly increased, relaxing Weber's assumption that all demand is concentrated at a single point.

In some of the physical distribution literature it is claimed that, under these circumstances, transport costs would be minimised if the depot were located at the *weighted mean centre* (or *centre of gravity*), whose x and y co-ordinates are calculated as follows:

$$x = \sum_j x_j w_j / \sum_j w_j \qquad y = \sum_j y_j w_j / \sum_j w_j \qquad (5.1)$$

where x and y define the location of customer j and w is the weight of goods demanded by customer j.

As Vergin and Rogers (1967) and Watson-Gandy (1972) prove, however, the weighted mean centre is not necessarily the point of minimum ton mileage. There are three situations in which this is unlikely to be the case (Van Auken, 1974):

1. where there is a dominant customer, receiving a large proportion of total supplies;
2. where numerous heavily weighted customers are clustered in the same area;
3. where customers are distributed asymmetrically across the market area.

To ensure that ton mileage is minimised, it is necessary to establish the *weighted mean distance centre* (or *ton-mile centre*) by applying differential calculus to the basic ton-mile equation. This method of calculating the ton-mile centre was first devised by Miehle (1958), though similar procedures were proposed by Kuhn and Kuenne (1962) and Cooper (1963). As with the centre of gravity calculation, there are separate formulae for the x and y co-ordinates of the depot location:

$$x = \sum_j (x_j w_j / d_{ij}) / \sum_j (w_j / d_{ij}) \qquad y = \sum_j (y_j w_j / d_{ij}) / \sum_j (w_j / d_{ij}) \quad (5.2)$$

where d_{ij} is the distance between depot location i and customer j.

Unlike the centre of gravity calculation, this algorithm converges on the solution by working through a series of iterations. One begins by suggesting a starting location for the depot i. This can be done subjectively or randomly because, regardless of the starting position, the formulae will, in the end, always yield the same optimal pair of co-ordinates. A good initial location will require fewer iterations and thereby economise on the amount of calculation. The straight-line distances between the starting location and each of the customers is

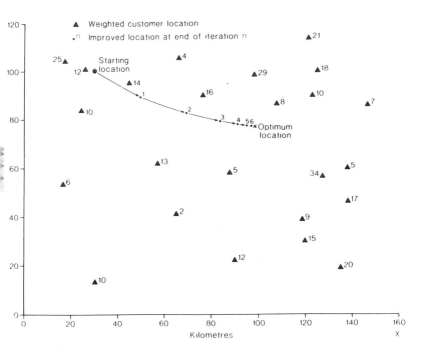

Figure 5.1 Convergence on optimum location (weighted mean distance centre)

measured, usually by means of Pythagoras' Theorem, and these *d* values inserted in the formulae. At the end of the first iteration, the formulae yield a new set of *x* and *y* co-ordinates that define an improved location for the depot. Distribution from this new location would generate less ton mileage than from the starting location. In the second iteration, distances are measured from the new location (again denoted by *i*) to each of the customers and the formulae recalculated accordingly to produce an even more efficient set of *x* and *y* co-ordinates. Figure 5.1 shows how, with each successive iteration, there is a gradual convergence on the optimum location. The distance the depot 'shifts' diminishes each time as does the reduction in total ton mileage (Figure 5.2). When the saving in ton mileage from one iteration to the next becomes negligible, the calculation ceases and the last calculated location adopted as the optimum.

A revenue-generation element can be built into this model to counterbalance the cost minimisation objective and permit an assessment of the profitability of a depot location. Mossman and Morton (1965) abandon the conventional assumption that customer

131

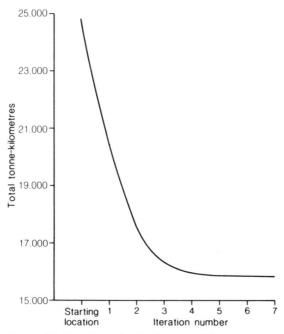

Figure 5.2 Iterative reduction in tonne-kilometres

demands are fixed and allow them instead to vary in relation to delivery times. Customer demand then becomes a dependent variable determined within the model by a service elasticity function. The *service elasticity of demand* (E) is defined as follows:

$$E = \propto \frac{t}{t_c} \log q \qquad (5.3)$$

where t is the firm's delivery time, t_c an average of competitors' delivery times, q the quantity demanded when the delivery time is t and $\propto$ a 'proportionality factor' specific to particular areas.

The speed with which lorries travel from depot to customers must be specified to allow the conversion of distances into travel times. Once vehicle speed and competitors' delivery times have been established, revenue generation, like the cost of transport, becomes a function of distance. While this model has obvious theoretical attractions, its success in practice depends on the accuracy with which the service elasticity of demand can be empirically derived. Furthermore, as transit time usually represents only a small proportion of total order lead time (Christopher *et al.*, 1979), especially in a comparatively small country like the UK, its relationship to the level of sales can be fairly tenuous. A similar criticism can be levelled at Stoker's (1978) multiple-location model. This model incorporates a revenue-generation function and searches for locations that maximise either profit or return on investment. It allows sales to decline outwards from the depot at a variable rate, determined by the number of competitors and their relative attractiveness. In practice, spatial variations in sales revenue seldom conform to such a simple relationship, making it very difficult to operationalise this model.

In multiple-location modelling, the objective is to optimise simultaneously the locations of several depots. With more than one depot serving the market area, consideration must be given to the allocation of customers to depots. The multiple-location problem is often referred to, therefore, as the location-allocation problem. The complexity of the allocation part of the exercise largely depends upon whether constraints are imposed on depot capacity. In the absence of such capacity constraints, any number of customers can be assigned to each depot, making it possible to allocate them simply on the basis of proximity. Where, on the other hand, capacity constraints are in force, optimising customer allocation generally requires the use of linear programming. We shall consider first the much simpler uncapacitated problem.

Unlike the feasible-set procedure devised by Kuehn and Hamburger (1963), none of the infinite-set methods indicate how many depots there should be in a distribution system. Depot numbers must, therefore, be determined at the start, taking account of the cost trade-offs and service level requirements described in the previous chapter. Starting locations must be specified for the desired number of depots, and customers allocated to these depot locations on the basis of proximity. The ton-mile centre formula (5.2) is then applied to each depot separately to improve its location relative to its customers. If one follows the *alternative location-allocation method* proposed by Cooper (1963), each depot location is separately optimised with respect to the initial allocation of customers. Customers are then reallocated among these new depot locations, again on the basis of proximity. A further round of ton-mile centre calculations ensues, moving each depot into a new location optimised relative to the reallocated set of customers. This procedure, of alternating between optimising locations and reallocating customers, continues until it ceases to yield a significant reduction in total ton mileage. Eilon *et al.* (1971) present a modified version of this algorithm, which they call the *adaptive location-allocation method*. This differs from Cooper's algorithm in reallocating customers at the end of each iteration in the ton-mile centre calculation rather than allowing the optimisation procedure to run full cycle before reallocating them. The main advantage of this method is that it reduces the number of iterations required to reach a solution.

Neither of these algorithms, however, ensures that the final solution minimises transport costs overall. Individual depots often gravitate to local optimal locations which, taken together, do not yield a global optimum. None of the methods currently in existence guarantee a globally optimal solution to the multiple-location problem. As one cannot rely on these algorithms to achieve full optimality first time, it is necessary to rework them several times using different sets of starting locations. The results of these trials are then compared and the set of locations yielding the lowest cost adopted as the global solution. Baxter (1981) has developed a set of heuristics to facilitate the search for a global optimum. This involves 'dislodging a system from a non-globally optimal solution' (p.819) by inserting 'hazards' in the vicinity of locations identified by this solution. Baxter defines these hazards as circular zones of given dimensions, each carrying a transport cost penalty. The presence of these hazards perturbs the original solution and can cause some depots to move from locally optimal positions into locations that yield lower costs for the system as a whole. Having 'shaken' these depots out of globally suboptimal locations, the hazards are removed and the optimisation procedure allowed to run its course as before. By applying these heuristics to the adaptive location-allocation method, Baxter was able both to reduce deviations from the global optimum and increase the probability of a global solution being achieved on any particular trial.

Multiple-location algorithms based on the ton-mile centre calculation generally ignore revenue generation and employ simplified cost functions. Stoker's (1978) model is exceptional in taking into account the affect of depot configurations on sales and hence profitability. The heuristic method developed by Lawrence and Pengilly (1969), on the other hand, is solely concerned with cost minimisation, but permits the use of more realistic cost functions.

So far it has been assumed that no restriction is imposed on the capacity of individual depots. Once depot locations are established, customers are assigned to the nearest depot and their demands aggregated to indicate how large the depot should be. Depot capacities are, therefore, automatically determined by depot locations. Often, however, capacity constraints are present, where, for example, a firm wishes to continue to use some of its existing depots or from experience has found that diseconomies of scale arise when a depot exceeds a certain size. Limited capacity may then prevent a depot from meeting in full the demands of the customers nearest to it. Some of these customers must, therefore, receive all or part of their supplies from other more distant depots. Under these circumstances, one encounters not only the multiple-location problem but also the classic transportation problem of allocating flows between supply and demand points in a manner that minimises total transport costs. Cooper (1976) has called this combined problem the transportation-location problem and shown how it can be solved reasonably efficiently using a heuristic algorithm. He tested this algorithm on 120 problems and found it yielded optimal solutions in every case.

Considerable effort has gone into developing and refining depot location methods. For firms wishing to base their locational decisions on rigorous analysis, there is a range of sophisticated techniques available. There is evidence that a growing number of firms are making use of computerised depot location models (National Computing Centre, 1968; Robson, 1982). It was estimated in 1968 that these models could yield potential savings of 5-15% over 'good manual methods' of depot location (Atkins and Shriver, 1968). Improvements to model design and computing facilities since then have probably widened this gap. Nevertheless, many distribution executives continue to view these models with scepticism. Like Murphy (1978, p.229), many argue that 'while the techniques developed were and are of undoubted value in their theoretical solution, they very often fall short in their practical application'. As Sussams (1971, p.32) explains, 'In practice, the optimum solution is usually of academic interest only because there is so much variability in the system that the conditions which make a particular solution optimal seldom ever apply'. Even the most complex of the models currently available are unable to accommodate all the factors influencing the location decision and must rely on a host of simplifying assumptions. There has been a tendency to 'bend the problem to fit known techniques' and to 'assume away a major part of the problem, albeit unintentionally' (Khumawala and Whybark, 1971, p.5). In the light of these inadequacies, Chentnik (1974, p.23) suggests that the theoretical optimum that these methods establish should be regarded as a 'starting point from which to bring in some of the non-quantifiable or difficult to express quantitative variables before making a final decision'. In the next section, we shall consider some of these exogenous factors that can cause depots to depart from theoretically optimal locations.

Factors affecting the siting of depots

The availability of sites

Storage premises can either be acquired *user ready* or *purpose built.* The former can be more rapidly brought into service and, being of standard size and design, can usually be more easily sold if necessary (Ogden, 1979). Purpose-built premises, on the other hand, can be tailored to a firm's particular storage, handling and transport requirements, and consequently operated more efficiently.

In the UK, user-ready premises fall into two broad categories: older, multi-storey warehouses mainly in inner urban locations and modern single-storey units on industrial estates that can be used interchangeably for storage or light manufacturing. Warehouses of the former type are expensive to operate, unsuited to the installation of modern handling equipment and inaccessible to goods traffic. As there is little demand for storage space in these buildings, many have been demolished or converted to other uses. Many warehouse/factory units were constructed speculatively on industrial estates in the 1970s and these continue to represent a large proportion of the total amount of storage space available for purchase or lease. Despite the sharp increase in vacant warehouse space since 1979, firms can still experience difficulty in finding user-ready depots that meet their operational requirements in the right area at an acceptable price. Sokel (1987, p.75) indicates that in the south-east of England firms are having to 'settle for unsatisfactory locations in order to achieve accommodation and land at realistic price levels'.

A firm building a new depot on a greenfield site to its own specifications takes on the additional tasks of finding and acquiring the necessary land and obtaining planning permission. In the 1970s many local authorities, such as Hertfordshire County Council (Watts, 1977), adopted restrictive policies towards warehousing, principally on the grounds that it had a low employment density relative to manufacturing and generated large amounts of lorry traffic.

Studies have since shown that warehouses vary enormously in the amount of employment and traffic they create (McKinnon and Pratt, 1985; Buchanan and Partners, 1986). As a result of the sharp decline in manufacturing employment since 1979, local planning authorities have become less likely to reject a warehousing application on grounds of low employment density (McKinnon and Pratt, 1984). Furthermore, where depots are well sited with respect to the trunk-road network, high traffic generation need not be a problem. In many areas, planning restrictions on warehousing appear to have been relaxed and planners become more sympathetic to the needs of firms storing and distributing goods in their areas. Indeed, some local authorities and development agencies have been making positive efforts to attract distribution facilities.

Labour requirements

As most distribution depots have a relatively small and low-skilled workforce, labour availability is not usually a major factor in depot location decisions. There have been instances, however, of depot relocation being affected by a desire either to retain or shed staff (Loasby, 1973). Firms have also avoided certain areas because of their poor industrial relations record (Westwood, 1975). In the late 1970s, for example, several firms were deterred from setting up depots in the West Midlands by the militancy of the local branch of the Transport and General Workers' Union.

Road connections

Most depot location models are not network based, making it necessary at a later stage in the siting exercise to take account of the road network. Particular attention is given in the UK to motorway access, congestion problems and lorry routeing restrictions. Many of the districts in England and Wales experiencing high rates of warehouse growth between 1974 and 1984 lie along motorways or are adjacent to motorway intersections (Buchanan and Partners, 1986; McKinnon, 1987). Firms using warehouses as bases for regional or national distribution generally consider proximity to a motorway essential. The vast majority of retailers' central warehouses, for instance, are located within 30 km of a motorway (Figure 5.3 (a) (b)). Property developers have reinforced this locational tendency by establishing numerous trading estates specialising in warehousing and distribution at points of high accessibility on the motorway network. As predicted by Lichfield and Partners (1981), there is a heavy demand for warehouse sites along the M25, London's orbital motorway, some of it from firms wishing to relocate their distribution operations from inner urban areas where vehicle access is difficult and roads badly congested.

Modal interchange

Chentnik (1974) complains that locational models are insensitive to the choice of transport mode. Modal choice can be an important locational variable where different modes are used for trunk-haul and local delivery movements. Where, for instance, goods arrive in bulk by rail and are delivered to customers by lorry, it is desirable to locate the depot at a railhead and thereby economise on terminal and handling costs. Modal interchange, breaking of bulk and storage can then all be carried out at the same location.

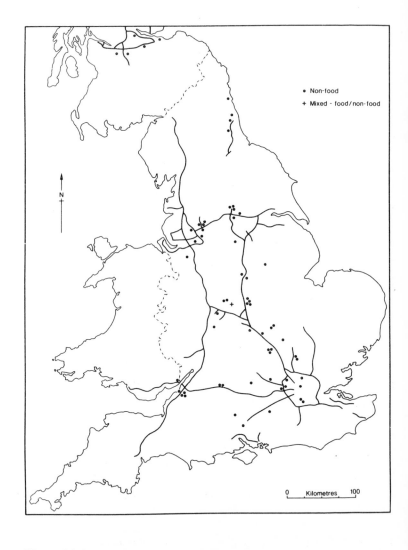

Figure 5.3 Spatial distribution of retailers' central warehouses:
(a) Non-food retailers
Source: McKinnon (1986a).

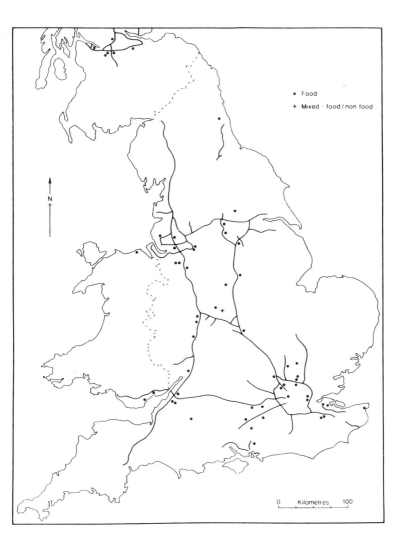

Figure 5.3 Spatial distribution of retailers' central warehouses
(b) Food retailers
Source: McKinnon (1986a).

Choice of contractor

In the case of those firms that contract out some or all of their distribution, stockholding locations are often determined by the choice of contractor. Firms employing a single contractor to handle their distribution over a wide area commit themselves to using its system of depots. Those that divide their distribution work geographically among a series of contractors can exercise greater control over the locations of depots they use in different areas. Usually, these firms select local contractors much more on the basis of their rates and quality of service than on the particular locations of their depots.

Area-specific grants and taxes

In some countries, such as the UK and Denmark, distribution depots can qualify for financial support as part of a programme of government assistance for poorer regions. Since 1984 in the UK, storage and distribution facilities have been eligible for regional development grants where their operators can prove that they have a genuine choice of location between an assisted area and the rest of the country. The peripherality of many of these areas, however, limits their suitability as bases for national distribution, while depots serving small areas seldom qualify for assistance as they are tied to particular localities. Firms are sometimes discouraged from establishing depots in an area by high local authority rates or, in the US, by state taxes on inventory.

Actual pattern of depot location

Clustering around strategic locations

Very little information is available on the actual locations of distribution depots. Official statistics on warehouse floorspace (Department of the Environment, 1986) fail to provide the necessary data because, first, they are based upon a very loose definition of warehousing that includes 'stores and workshops' and, second, they do not distinguish between different types of warehouse. One must, therefore, rely upon the limited amounts of geographical data collected in surveys of manufacturers and distributors, mainly in the food industry. These surveys have revealed a pronounced clustering of distribution depots around a small number of major centres. A survey of 67 food manufacturers and distributors commissioned by the Lorries and the Environment Committee (1979) found that roughly half the 652 depots operated by these firms were located either within

Figure 5.4 Spatial distribution of food manufacturers' stockholding points
Source: McKinnon (1983).

30 miles of London or within 10 miles of 13 other cities. A survey by the author of 306 depots employed by a sample of 29 large food manufacturers showed that 62% of these premises were within 20 miles of the centres of 9 cities (Figure 5.4). Distribution contractors serving the food industry, most of which have developed since the late 1960s, have also concentrated their operations around major population centres; roughly 40% of the depots they operate are in or around London, Manchester, Birmingham, Bristol and Glasgow (Institute of Grocery Distribution, 1986b). The results of these surveys confirm the view frequently expressed in the literature (Braithwaite and Dobbs, 1932; Sussams, 1969; Beattie, 1973; Coley, 1977) that there are several well recognised locations around the country to which distribution depots gravitate. Sussams (1971, p.92) contends that this concentration of depots in particular locations 'illustrates the fact that most traders have, over the years, arrived at good, if not optimal, solutions by a process of trial and error and that a process akin to natural selection has removed most of the errors'.

While the information presented above may be used to assess the overall popularity of a particular location as a centre for intermediate storage and distribution, it gives little indication of the chances of an individual firm establishing a base there, because this would also depend on the number of depots the firm employed and the locations of its other depots. It is not possible, therefore, to make a direct comparison of firms' choices of depot locations. One must instead explore the relationship between depot numbers and locations, to see if there is any regularity in the sequence in which depots are added to a distribution system and in the progressive subdivision of the market area as depot numbers increase.

Generalised sequence of depot locations

Very little information is available on the historical development of manufacturers' depot systems (McKinnon, 1981b). In the case of Cadbury's depot system, set up during the inter-war period, there was a close correlation between the date on which a town or city received a depot and its population size (Watts, 1975). In the absence of similar data for other firms, it is not possible to generalise about the chronological sequence in which depot locations were added to distribution systems. One can, however, establish a generalised succession of depot locations by means of a cross-sectional analysis of the existing distribution systems of a sample of firms varying widely in the number of depots they employ. This inductive approach to the derivation of a locational sequence should be contrasted with the essentially intuitive approach of Sussams (1969) and theoretical

Table 5.1 Towns and cities with three or more food stockholding points.

Aberdeen	Inverness	Northampton
Birmingham	Leeds	Norwich
Bolton	Liverpool	Nottingham
Bristol	London	Plymouth
Cardiff	Maidstone	Southampton
Colchester	Manchester	Spennymoor
Edinburgh	Montrose	Swansea
Exeter	Newcastle upon Tyne	Welshpool
Glasgow	Newport	

modelling work on the subject by Stoker (1978). The objective here is to examine regularities in the existing pattern of stock location rather than to theorise about the way in which such patterns should evolve. The exercise begins by identifying zones with a preponderance of stockholding points and then investigates the relationship between the total number of stock locations in a firm's distribution system and the likelihood of it holding stock in each of the identified zones. Not all the stockholding points surveyed were depots dedicated to a single manufacturer. In some cases, manufacturers held stock in a common storage area in a contractor's depot. To simplify the exposition, though, the terms 'stockholding point' and 'depot' will be used interchangeably.

The initial zonation was carried out as follows:

1. A list was drawn up of all the urban areas in which three or more manufacturers held stock. Three was chosen as an arbitrary cut-off value. The list contained 26 towns (Table 5.1).
2. The total number of stockholding points within 30 miles of the centre of each town was enumerated and assigned to that town. This choice of a 30 mile radius can be justified partly by the fact that the search for a suitable depot site typically extends over this range. It also makes allowance for the fact that many depots are today found in peripheral locations beyond the boundary of the urban district and, particularly in the case of conurbations, at a considerable distance from the centre.
3. Several towns were then removed from the list because of their close proximity to other larger depot concentrations. Towns within 30-40 miles of each other would tend, after all, to be regarded as possible alternative locations.
4. The remaining 18 settlements were plotted on a map and lines interpolated midway between them (Figure 5.5). These lines then served as idealised zonal boundaries. It was recognised that the results of the analysis would depend to some extent on the

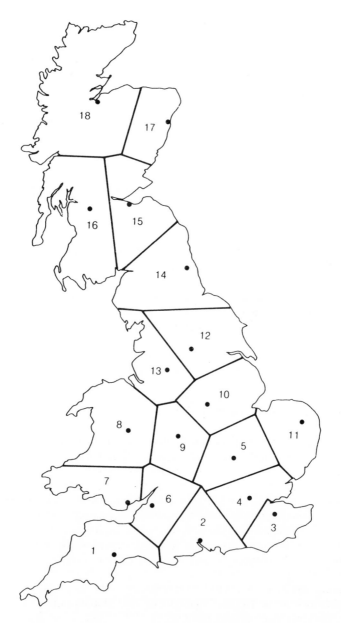

Figure 5.5 Zones used in the sequential analysis of stock locations

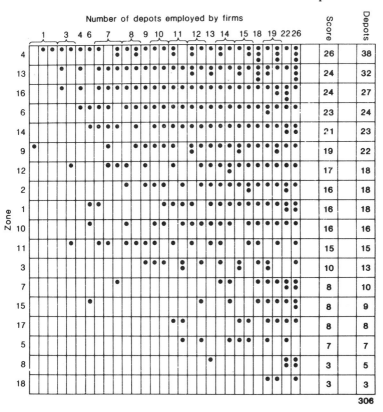

Figure 5.6 Zonal disaggregation of stock location data

configuration of these boundaries. To give some indication of the
likely sensitivity of the analysis to boundary alignment, a count
was made of depots lying within 10 miles of the boundaries.
These 'marginal' depots represented only 6% of the total number
of depots, reflecting the high degree of concentration around the
'nuclei' of the 18 zones. Given the comparatively small
proportion of depots in the vicinity of boundaries, it was
concluded that marginal changes in the alignment of these
boundaries would probably have little effect on the final
outcome.

5. Each zone was given a score of one for every food manufacturer
that held stock there. The total numbers of stockholding points in
each zone were added up separately.

6. All the stock location data are presented in Figure 5.6. Each black
dot represents a stockholding point. The zones were ranked in

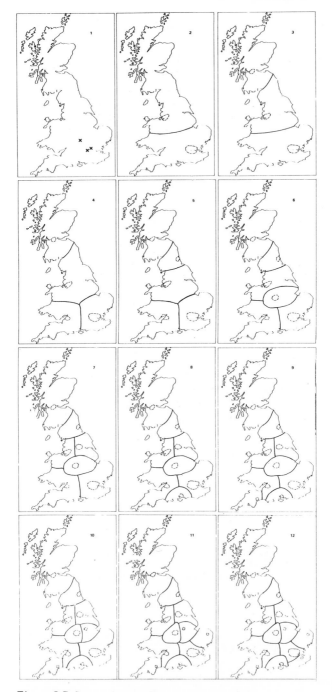

Figure 5.7 Successive subdivision of Great Britain into depot hinterlands
Note: The crosses on map 1 indicate the locations of the warehouses operated by the three manufacturers with fully centralised systems.

relation to their scores and arranged in descending order of magnitude along the vertical axis. Where two or more zones had the same scores, they were ranked in relation to the number of depots they contained. In the one instance where two zones had identical scores and depot numbers, the tie was broken arbitrarily. The 29 firms were arranged horizontally, in ascending order, by their total number of stockholding points. Where firms had the same numbers of depots, ordering was arbitrary. On the basis of this ranking, the country was successively subdivided into idealised depot hinterlands. Figure 5.7 shows the first twelve stages of this zonal breakdown and indicates the 'core area' within each zone where the stockholding points tend to cluster. The zonal boundaries have been generalised with respect to the actual pattern of depot area boundaries.

Under ideal conditions, where there was a clear ranking of zones in terms of their popularity as depot locations and where the number of depots used by firms increased by a uniform interval along the horizontal axis, a perfect succession of locations would produce a regular pattern in which every cell above and to the right of the leading diagonal would be occupied by a single depot symbol, and the leading diagonal would form a straight edge. In practice, there are numerous deviations from this ideal pattern. The boundary between the areas of occupied and unoccupied cells is ragged and several cells have more than one depot. These deviations are partly attributable to defects in the data set and method of analysis, particularly:

1. imperfections in the zoning scheme;
2. uneven intervals between the numbers of depots firms employ;
3. the arbitrary ranking of zones with similar scores and firms with similar numbers of depots;
4. the limited number of zones.

Table 5.2 Generalised sequences of stock locations

No. of stock locations in distribution system	Present study	Cumulative locations Sussams (1969)
2	South East, North West	London, Manchester
3	West Central Scotland	Glasgow
4	Avon	Bristol
5	Tyneside	Newcastle
6	West Midlands	Birmingham
7	West Yorkshire	Southampton
8	Hampshire	Leeds
9	Devon	
10	East Midlands	
11	East Anglia	
12	Kent	

When one allows for these various shortcomings, it appears that there is still considerable regularity in the succession of depot locations. Over the first seven rankings, this sequence very closely resembles that postulated by Sussams (1969) for the multiple location of production plants, though applicable also to distribution depots (Table 5.2). Eight of the first ten locations are included in the list of the ten best locations from which to distribute to England, Wales and southern Scotland compiled by Stoker (1978) using a profit-maximising multiple-location model. His model suggested Hull in preference to Leeds and placed Norwich within the first ten, whereas, in the empirically derived ranking, Norwich came eleventh.

As explained earlier in this chapter, it is not necessary to restructure an existing distribution system each time a depot location is added. Stoker (1978) established that multiple-location solutions are additive as the number of depots increases, and this seems to be borne out in practice. He largely attributes the stability of multiple-location solutions to the uneven distribution of population, arguing that the major population centres to which depots gravitate in the early stages of the sequence remain efficient and profitable. The only exception is the transition from a completely centralised system to one comprising two depots. Sussams (1969) identifies Birmingham as the optimum location for a single facility, but splits national distribution between two depots in London and Manchester. Of the three manufacturers in the empirical study which concentrated finished stock at a single point, two had depots in London and one in Banbury. Each of these depots was at or near a factory, suggesting that the location of centralised stockholding facilities is indirectly affected by the factors influencing the location of production.

Approximately two-thirds of the depots used by the sample of manufacturers were located in accordance with the generalised sequence. The deviation of the remaining depots may, in part, be attributable to variations in the spatial distribution of firms' sales and to geographical variations in their relative dependence on different distribution channels. Plant location can also distort the pattern of depot location. Approximately 13% of all the depots surveyed were located at a factory site. Firms can derive several benefits from locating a depot adjacent to a factory. It effectively eliminates a trunk movement, facilitates and accelerates the replenishment of the depot's stock and permits a sharing of various overhead costs. The establishment of depots beside factories appears, nevertheless, to have caused little deviation from the general pattern; of the 41 factory-based depots, only 8 were in locations that departed markedly from the generalised sequence of locations. Finally, there were several instances of firms deviating from the generalised locational sequence

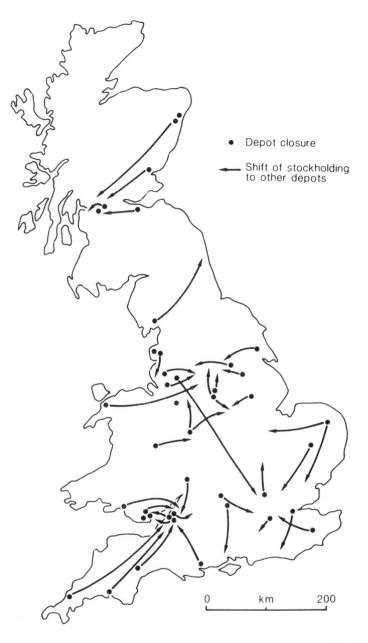

● Depot closure

⟵ Shift of stockholding
to other depots

0   km   200

Figure 5.8 Closure of food manufacturers' distribution depots: 1975–9
Source: Department of Transport (1986a).

by distributing their products in a particular zone via a 'satellite' break-bulk point rather than a stockholding depot.

Most of the manufacturers surveyed had reduced their number of stockholding points over the previous ten years. From this, one may infer that the generalised sequence has been operating in reverse. These firms closed a total of 42 stockholding depots between 1975 and 1979 and, in most cases, this resulted in a transfer of stockholding and distribution responsibilities to depots in more highly ranked locations (Figure 5.8). The withdrawal of stock from peripheral regions, such as the north-east of Scotland, south-west England, south Wales and Humberside, was made possible by the penetration of these areas by extensions to the motorway network during the 1970s. The convergence of stockholding and associated distribution functions on a few strategic locations is intensifying competition for sites. In some areas, most notably around London, this has inflated land values and led planning authorities to impose restrictions on the development of large warehouses/distribution centres. It is not known to what extent these economic and regulatory pressures are constraining the centralisation of inventory or diverting centralised facilities into suboptimal locations.

Chapter six

Choice of transport mode

The allocation of freight traffic among transport modes, often called the modal split, has been one of the most controversial topics in the field of transport. Allegations are often made that a particular mode is carrying too much or too little traffic and that, as a consequence, some freight is being transported inefficiently and/or in a manner that is excessively detrimental to the environment. The way in which road and rail 'track costs' are assessed and assigned to different types of traffic has been a major source of contention. Political debate on the subject has stimulated a good deal of research into factors influencing modal choice and the nature of the selection process. These studies have revealed that many modal choice decisions are not based upon a full and rational appraisal of the options available, suggesting that this is an area in which firms may be able to improve the efficiency of their distribution operations. They have also given credence to claims that, at the national level, freight traffic is misallocated between modes. It is extremely difficult, however, to define an optimum modal allocation, given the range of criteria involved and disagreement over the weighting that each criterion should receive (Sharp, 1971).

Freight modal split is usually measured with respect to tonnes lifted or tonne-kilometres. As the average length of haul differs markedly between modes, the tonne-km is generally considered to provide a fairer basis for intermodal comparison (St Seidenfus, 1985). Long-haul modes such as rail and waterway have a larger share of tonne-km than tonnes lifted. This is reflected in the UK modal split statistics presented in Table 6.1. These show that British industry is very heavily dependent on road transport and sends a minority of its freight by other modes, even when measured in tonne-km. It is not possible, under the system of commodity classification employed by the Department of Transport, to calculate separately the modal split for finished goods *en route* to retail outlets, though it can be confidently asserted that all but a tiny fraction of this traffic travels by lorry. As

Table 6.1   UK freight modal split,[a] 1986

	Tonnes lifted (million)	%	Tonne-kilometres (billion)	%
Road	1455	81	104.1	57
Rail	140	8	16.5	9
Water[b]	133	7	51.4	28
Pipeline[c]	79	4	10.4	6
	1807	100	182.4	100

Notes: a. Internal air cargo accounted for only 66,000 tonnes lifted and 22 million tonne-km in 1986.
  b. Includes inland waterways and coastal shipping.
  c. Oil pipelines only.

Source: Department of Transport, 1987.

Cooper (1987, p.7) observes, 'road transport's cheapness and flexibility have made it popular amongst companies as the prime distribution mode'. Nevertheless, by comparison with other developed countries, the UK appears to send an exceptionally large proportion of its internal freight by road (Figure 6.1). A country's freight modal split can be influenced by a range of factors, such as its size and topography, the spatial distribution of its population and industry, the relative density of its transport networks, the structure of its economy and government policies on transport regulation, investment and taxation (Pike, 1982).

The first part of this chapter will review the main characteristics of the road and rail modes, which are responsible for the movement of most finished goods. Later sections will consider how firms decide which mode(s) to use.

Modal characteristics

Freight modal split is frequently discussed in terms of the primary modes of road, rail and waterway, each with its own network. This modal classification is very crude, however, as it fails to distinguish the different types of service operating on the same network and largely ignores *intermodal* (or *combined transport*) *systems*. This section examines in greater detail the road and rail modes, which together carry almost all the traffic in finished, manufactured goods.

Freight transport operations can be divided into three categories:

1. Consolidation (or concentration): where goods are collected in small quantities from many locations and assembled into bulk loads;
2. Trunk haulage: movement of bulk loads between two points;

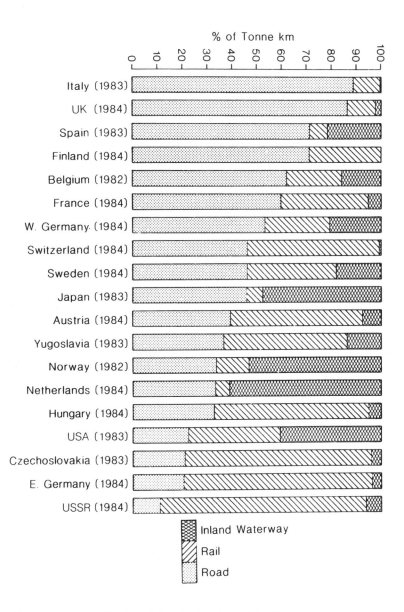

Figure 6.1 International variations in freight modal split
Source: Department of Transport, 1986a.

3. Distribution (or dispersion): disaggregation of bulk loads into smaller consignments and their delivery to numerous locations.

Some firms provide 'composite' freight services (Rimmer and Hicks, 1979) that combine all these operations. A parcels carrier, for example, picks up small consignments, consolidates them into viably sized loads for trunking and then disaggregates them again into individual consignments for final delivery. The great flexibility of road transport stems from its ability to undertake all three types of movement. The railway on its own can only offer a trunk-haul service, though in partnership with road-freight operators can market a wider range of consolidation and distribution services.

Road transport

A fundamental distinction can be drawn between hire and reward and own-account road-freight operations. *Hire and reward* (or *for hire*) services are provided on a 'third-party' basis by outside contractors. Many manufacturers, wholesalers and retailers prefer to internalise the transport function by acquiring and operating fleets of *own-account* vehicles. In 1986, approximately 96,000 firms operated lorries (MIL Research Ltd, 1986), 60% of them on an own-account basis. Own-account operations were exempt from the quantitative controls imposed on the hire and reward sector in 1933. Following the introduction of this road-freight regulation, there was a sharp increase in the number of lorries operated on an own-account basis and in the proportion of freight they carried. By 1964, 58% of all road-freight tonnage was carried in own-account vehicles. Since 1970, the proportion has fluctuated between 43 and 52%, though its decline from 49.7% in 1982 to 44.5% in 1986 is widely seen as part of a longer-term trend away from own-account operations (Department of Transport, 1987). Hire and reward vehicles have traditionally accounted for a significantly larger share of tonne-km, as they tend to be used for longer-distance movements. In 1986, their average length of haul was 89 kilometres as opposed to 52 kilometres for own-account vehicles.

Own-account and hire and reward operations are usually depicted as being quite separate, whereas, in practice, they are often complementary. In 1977, 66% of own-account operators made some use of haulage contractors and 41% employed them on a regular basis (Foster Committee, 1978). A more recent survey of 82 firms in the grocery, confectionery, drink, pharmaceutical and household goods trades found that 49% of manufacturers and 54% of multiple retailers supplemented their in-house distribution operations with some use of

Table 6.2 Relative dependence on own-account and third-party distribution systems

	Manufacturers	Multiple retailers
Total dependence on own account	12%	23%
Total dependence on third party	39%	15%
Mixed own account/third party	49%	54%
All goods delivered by supplier	—	8%

Note: Based on survey conducted by Kae Development Ltd for Lowfield of eighty-two firms in the grocery, confectionery, drink, pharmaceutical and household goods trades.

Source: The Grocer, 19 July 1986.

contractors (*The Grocer,* 19 July 1986) (Table 6.2). Only a small minority of manufacturers and multiple retailers were totally reliant on own-account systems.

Firms can derive numerous benefits from supplementing an own-account system with some use of contractors. It reduces the need for capital investment in distribution facilities and the risk of the distribution operation being totally paralysed by, for example, labour disputes. Some multiple retailers employ contractors to provide a parallel distribution service to ensure that the supply of goods to their shops is not disrupted (Barber and Payne, 1976). Firms geographically expanding their markets often find that contractors can provide the necessary logistical support more economically than in-house systems, at least in the early stages when sales in the new areas are low. Diversification into products with different handling and marketing characteristics can also require the use of specialist contractors possessing equipment and expertise lacking in the own-account system. Firms whose sales fluctuate widely throughout the year often employ contractors to accommodate seasonal peaks, allowing them to operate their own distribution systems more efficiently on a stable base load (Buck, 1985). Harris (1987) advocates the partial use of contractors as a means of establishing a 'benchmark' against which the performance of an own-account system can be judged.

Some contractors provide only a basic haulage service, while others also engage in consolidation and distribution, altering the size and composition of loads. Firms that 'make- or break-bulk' generally require depots, whereas the 'operating centres' of those specialising in trunk haulage can simply be garages or even private homes. There are few general statistics available on the structure of the British road haulage industry, and none of them differentiate operators in terms of the range of services they offer. It was estimated in 1977 that there were 46,400 haulage firms in the UK, 54% of which operated only one lorry and 85% fewer than five lorries (Foster Committee, 1978). By

1985, the number of operators had declined to around 37,000 (*British Business*, 17 July 1987), though the industry remains highly fragmented. Most of the smaller firms engage in general haulage, providing a trunk-haul service for a wide range of merchandise. The capital cost of entering this section of the market is low and operators' licences quite easily obtained. The general haulage sector is therefore highly competitive and characterised by high rates of entry and exit. Between January 1981 and January 1987, haulage rates increased, on average, by a much smaller proportion (14.5%) than vehicle operating costs (31.5% for a 32 tonne lorry) (Warner, 1987). Most hauliers have been able to absorb some of the cost increase by improving productivity. To hold down costs, some hauliers have infringed regulations on vehicle weight, maintenance standards and drivers' hours. Surveys in 1985, for instance, revealed that around 19% of lorries were overloaded (National Audit Office, 1987).

Many of the larger firms have moved out of general haulage in an effort to improve their profitability and return on assets. Some have specialised in particular types of haulage, while others have extended the range of services they offer, supplementing the basic transport service with storage, consolidation, breaking-of-bulk and order processing. The provision of an integrated distribution service increases the value added to the product by the contractor. This makes contract distribution more lucrative than general haulage and more likely to secure a long-term commitment from clients. The large capital investment required to set up a third-party distribution system also restricts entry to this sector. Firms offering ancillary sorting and handling can be divided into two broad categories.

1. Distribution contractors

These firms provide a combination of transport, storage and handling services. Not all distribution contractors have their roots in general haulage (Firth, 1976). Many were public warehousing firms which diversified into transport. Roughly half the members of the National Association of Warehouse Keepers offer distribution as well as storage services. Several contract distribution operations are based on what were formerly the in-house systems of manufacturers or retailers. As early as 1919, Unilever ran its distribution system (known as SPD) as a separate profit centre, carrying hire and reward traffic for other firms as well as its own products (Reader, 1969). Between 1933 and 1970, when quantitative licensing was in force, own-account operators were mostly debarred from 'carrying for others'. The 1968 Transport Act granted own-account operators freedom to carry traffic for others. Overall, few firms have taken advantage of this situation. Cooper (1978) estimated that only 2.7% of own-account tonnage was transported on a hire and reward basis, while the Foster Committee reckoned that own-account operators derived only about 4-6% of their turnover from this traffic. Several firms, however, such as Imperial Foods, Tate and Lyle, and United Biscuits, have built up successful third-party businesses on the basis of their original in-house distribution systems. This was regarded initially as a means of spreading the overhead cost of an own-account operation (Centre for Transport Studies, 1977), but some firms have been so successful in attracting third-party traffic that they have transformed their distribution department into an independent subsidiary. Of thirty distribution contractors listed in a directory published by the IGD (1986b), eight were owned by manufacturers, while the remainder had varied origins in general haulage, public warehousing, wholesaling, parcels carriage and even shipping.

Distribution contractors differ widely in the range of services they offer, the types of product they handle, their geographical coverage and the extent to which their operations are dedicated to particular clients. Product specialisation allows contractors to concentrate their delivery operations on particular types of outlet and adapt their depots, vehicles and handling equipment to the physical characteristics of specific product groups. All contractors offer a minimum range of storage, break-bulk and local delivery services, but some supplement this with trunk haulage, order processing, order picking and telephone sales. Most of the large distribution contractors in the grocery trade serve the whole country, though from varying numbers of depots. Many manufacturers do not entrust their national distribution to a single contractor, preferring instead to use different agencies in different regions. This reduces their dependence on individual contractors and enables them to compare the cost and quality of distribution services. Much of the competition between contractors is, therefore, conducted at the regional rather than national level.

When contracting out its distribution in a particular area, a manufacturer can either let the contractor group its traffic with that of other consignors or request the exclusive use of storage and transport facilities. Some contractors are heavily involved in providing dedicated services, while others derive most of their income from groupage traffic.

2. Parcels carriers

These firms collect, trunk and deliver small consignments, generally weighing less than 25 kg. Almost all parcels traffic in the UK is today carried by road. British Rail (BR) withdrew from the general parcels business in 1981, confining its operations thereafter to the express movement of Red Star parcels by passenger train between stations.

The Post Office continued to trunk around 40% of its parcels by rail until 1986, when this traffic was transferred to the road network.

Many new firms have entered the parcels business over the past ten years attracted partly by a growth in demand and partly by a desire to capture traffic relinquished by BR. The growth of parcel traffic is attributable mainly to the expansion of mail-order business and the increasing tendency for firms to reduce stock levels by obtaining spare parts and components in small quantities at small notice.

Parcels carriers differ in several respects:

1. Type of premises served: Most private carriers restrict the collection and delivery of parcels to business premises, leaving home deliveries mainly to the Post Office and the own-account systems of the larger mail-order firms. Most carriers have found home delivery unprofitable partly because of the vast number of possible delivery points (in 1986/7, the Post Office served 23.7 million points in the UK) and the practice of mail-order firms only to contract out deliveries that cannot be undertaken economically on an own-account basis.
2. Size of consignment: Most small parcels, weighing less than 5 kg are destined for private homes and handled by the Post Office. Other carriers transport parcels within the weight range 5-25 kg. As competition in the parcels market has intensified, carriers have widened the weight range of parcels they will accept. Some firms offer to transport 'maxi-parcels' weighing between 100 kg and several tonnes and falling into the intermediate-size range between the traffic typically handled by parcels carriers and general hauliers.
3. Geographical coverage: Only about 20 parcels carriers provide an integrated national collection and delivery service in the UK (Robinson, 1987). The majority of parcels carriers concentrate their operations in particular regions, though in co-operation with other regional carriers can offer national coverage.
4. Trunking system: The traditional trunking network comprised direct links between all depots (Figure 6.2). Every depot then sorted incoming parcels for forwarding in bulk loads to the depot nearest their final destination. Some firms continue to operate this system, but an increasing number have recently adopted an alternative *hub and satellite trunking system* in which all but local traffic passes through a centralised sorting point (or hub) (Scott and Cooper, 1985). Relieved of their sorting function, the satellite depots are downgraded to collection and distribution points. Complex networks of inter-depot links are replaced by a series of radial routes focusing on the hub. This makes the

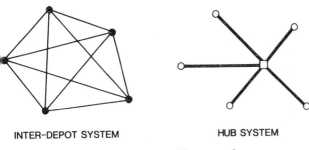

INTER-DEPOT SYSTEM   HUB SYSTEM

Figure 6.2 Inter-depot and hub-satellite networks

routeing of parcels traffic more circuitous but yields cost savings
through the improved utilisation of trunk vehicles and the greater
efficiency of centralised sorting. There has been a strong
technological pressure for this centralisation of the sorting
function because the installation of highly mechanised handling
systems is only justified in depots with a large throughput. By
moving over to a hub system, some firms have also been able to
accelerate the movement of parcels and compete more effectively
on the basis of delivery times.

Own account versus hire and reward

In advertising their services, contractors frequently claim to have a
cost advantage over in-house systems. Some own-account operators
dispute this; Bass (UK), for example, contends that the unit cost of
distributing beer through its in-house system is roughly 20% less than
the lowest charge quoted by outside contractors (McBeath, 1985).
Surveys by Cook (1967) and Westwood (1985) have established,
though, that firms justify operating their own vehicles mainly on the
grounds that this allows them to control the quality of service and that
cost reduction is, at best, a secondary objective. Any cost comparison
must recognise that the efficiency of the two types of operation is
likely to vary and that some cost variations will reflect differences in
service quality. There are, nevertheless, some fundamental differences
in the cost structures of own-account and contract operations.

Conventional own-account systems require the injection of capital.
The own-account operator can purchase vehicles either with funds
generated internally within the business or borrowed from a financial
institution. Self-financing has the disadvantage of diverting resources
from other activities where they could have earned a higher rate of
return. On the other hand, borrowing money to finance vehicle
acquisition can reduce a firm's ability to raise loan capital for other
more profitable initiatives. Up until 1984, owner operators were able

159

to write off the total cost of new vehicles against tax in the year of purchase. Between 1984 and 1987, these capital allowances were phased out and replaced, in 1985, by a much less generous annual writing down allowance of 25%. This has effectively reduced firms' cash flow and increased the capital cost of vehicle acquisition. Jones (1986) estimates that, as a result of these changes, the real value of tax relief on vehicle purchases fell between 1982 and 1987 from 46% to 24% of their cost. Partly to compensate for the loss of capital allowance, the government reduced the level of corporation tax paid on profits from 50% in 1984 to 35% in 1987. The combined effect of these measures has been to redirect tax incentives away from simply owning assets towards maximising the amount of profit they earn. In deciding whether to acquire their own vehicles firms must now evaluate more carefully their likely contribution to profitability. In particular, they must establish whether it is more profitable to operate their own vehicles or use a contractor. This is very difficult to judge, however, as transport is only one of many factors affecting profitability and as the relationship between the quality of a transport service and revenue generation is uncertain.

When comparing own-account and hire and reward operations it is important to distinguish contract hire, where vehicles and often depots are dedicated to a particular client, and common-user or groupage services, where several firms' traffic shares the same facilities.

Contract hire

Under contract hire arrangements, a firm can obtain the exclusive use of vehicles and exert a similar degree of control over their operation as in an own-account system. On the road they can even look like the client's own vehicles, bearing its name, corporate colour scheme and advertisements. The contractor, nevertheless, retains ownership of the vehicles and generally licenses, insures, maintains and, where necessary, replaces them. In most cases, it also employs the drivers and manages the transport operation.

Contract hire can prove a more economical option than outright purchase for several reasons. First, as contract hire firms have much larger vehicle fleets than most own-account operators, they can generally purchase and maintain them more cheaply (Harris, 1987). Second, their large fleet size enables them to respond flexibly to clients' requirements, tailoring vehicle size to the nature of the delivery, varying vehicle capacity during the year in line with traffic volumes and providing additional or replacement vehicles in an emergency. By balancing the varying requirements of numerous clients, contract hire firms can generally operate vehicles at a higher level of utilisation than individual own-account firms. Third, they can also spread administrative overheads across a much larger transport operation, further reducing unit costs. Unlike most in-house transport systems, however, contract hire agencies must incur the additional cost of marketing their services and must generate a margin of profit. These cost increments can, nevertheless, be more than outweighed by the other cost advantages of contract hire. Furthermore, as there is no evidence to show that the quality of transport service provided by contract hire firms is inferior to that of own-account operators, these cost advantages do not appear to be offset by poorer revenue-generating performance.

Common-user services

The provision of distribution services by contractors on a common-user basis offers several advantages over own-account systems. By combining several firms' traffic, contractors generate a larger volume of throughput and can thereby achieve greater economies of scale. Groupage also enables them to even out fluctuations in flow volumes, helping them to maintain the average utilisation of vehicles and depots throughout the year at a higher level than an individual in-house system. Where contractors specialise in the distribution of particular types of merchandise, however, there is a danger that clients' traffic levels will rise and fall in harmony, accentuating peaks and troughs and lowering average load factors.

Contractors claim to be able to mount a more efficient local delivery service than own-account operators. They base their argument on the fact that the unit cost of local deliveries is inversely proportional to drop density and drop size, both of which are likely to be greater in the case of common-user services. Contractors generally deliver to many more outlets than individual own-account operators. As a result, their vehicles travel shorter distances between outlets and their drivers make more productive use of their time actually offloading goods. The consolidation of orders destined for the same outlet increases average drop size and this further enhances the efficiency of the operation. Jobson (1976) suggests, however, that these local delivery advantages are exaggerated. He concedes that contractors usually serve more outlets, but argues that own-account operators can still achieve a similar drop density by adopting a 'nominated-day' delivery system and confining their delivery operations to specified areas on particular days. As contractors must satisfy the lead time requirements of many different clients they are unable to rationalise their delivery operations in the same way or to the same extent. It should be noted, though, that only a minority of own-account operators currently organise local deliveries on a nominated-day basis.

Jobson also contends that the savings resulting from consolidation are less than generally supposed. The degree of consolidation depends on the coincidence of drops at particular outlets. Jobson found that, in the case of the grocery delivery systems of three Cadbury-Schweppes subsidiaries, only a third of the total number of outlets served were common to two or more systems.

By matching randomly generated orders from these outlets, within the normal service level requirements, he estimated that consolidation would reduce the number of drops by only 9%. When other non-grocery outlets were included in the analysis, the 'levels of commonality and coincidence' were even lower. Two confidential studies of drop coincidence cited by Rushton (1979) yielded slightly higher *consolidation factors*, within the range 10-15%. Rushton also, however, quotes the case of a contractor specialising in grocery distribution which recorded consolidation factors of between 30 and 80% for the products it handled. Clearly, drop coincidence will depend on the product range and the number and types of outlets served, making it difficult to generalise across whole industrial or trade sectors. It is generally acknowledged, though, that groupage services have a significant cost advantage in peripheral and sparsely populated areas.

Common-user services are inferior to dedicated own-account and contract hire operations in several respects. As they generally employ standardised vehicles, handling equipment, operating procedures and delivery schedules to cater for the needs of a range of firms, they cannot easily accommodate the special requirements of individual firms. The system of average pricing that many contractors employ can disadvantage those firms whose products are relatively cheap to deliver by virtue of their handling characteristics, large order size and high drop density. Firms' main objection to common-user services, however, is their inability to exercise direct control over the movement of their goods and to use transport effectively as an instrument of marketing. Many own-account operators feel that by having dedicated vehicles readily at hand they can respond more flexibly to changing traffic demands. Some contend that carrying goods in these vehicles also reduces the risk of loss and damage. It is very difficult to check the accuracy of these claims as there have been no objective comparisons of the quality of service provided by dedicated and common-user operations.

Rail services

In terms of direct line-haul costs, trains are a much more efficient means of transporting freight than lorries, mainly because they consume less energy per tonne-kilometre and achieve much higher levels of labour productivity. This cost advantage is eroded, however, by higher terminal costs, the low accessibility of the rail network and the large element of fixed cost in rail- freight operations. These three factors seriously constrain the railway's ability to compete with road haulage and strongly influence the composition of rail-freight traffic. In an effort to overcome these handicaps, or at least mitigate their effect, new freight services and operating practices have been developed. In Britain, as in other countries, these developments have effectively transformed the railway freight business over the past 30 years. To appreciate the significance of these changes, it is necessary to consider in more detail how high terminal costs, low accessibility and high fixed costs inhibit the attraction of freight onto the rail network.

Terminal costs

These costs are usually regarded simply as the costs of loading and unloading freight on and off a vehicle. In the case of the railway, they also include the cost of assembling wagons into trains for the trunk movement. The unit of freight movement on the rail network is, after all, the trainload, and it is to this that the favourable line-haul costs relate. Thus defined, rail-terminal costs far exceed the cost of handling goods at either end of a road journey and, over short distances, more than offset the railway's line-haul cost advantage. The spreading of terminal costs over greater distances enables the railway to offer more competitive rates for longer hauls. As a large proportion of freight traffic moves relatively short distances, efforts have been made to reduce the distances over which rail can effectively compete with road. These efforts have concentrated on lowering the terminal costs incurred both in the physical handling of the goods and in the marshalling of rail wagons. One of the most successful innovations, the so-called merry-go-round (MGR) principle, has greatly facilitated the former and eliminated the latter. MGR trains offer a 'conveyor belt' service between coal mines and power stations. They are run as 'block trains' continuously around a circuit and use cheap, gravity-feed loading and unloading systems.

There are many other examples of block trains on the BR network travelling directly between sidings and without need of marshalling. Most of these are company trains commissioned by a single firm and usually consisting of rolling stock which it privately owns or leases. Apart from coal and coke, company trains carry iron and steel, cement, earth and stone, cars, petroleum products and chemicals. The Beeching Report argued strongly that BR should concentrate its efforts on developing its trainload business (British Railways Board,

1963). In the early 1970s BR management seriously considered shedding all its wagonload traffic and confining its freight operations thereafter to trainload movements (Ford, 1980). Complete withdrawal from the wagonload business would, however, have left BR overly dependent on the bulk transport of a limited range of primary commodities for a few large industrial customers. Moreover, demand for some of these commodities, such as coal, iron, steel and building materials, was particularly sensitive to short-term variations in the level of economic activity and subject to longer-term decline. There was felt to be a need, therefore, to diversify rail-freight traffic and to attract onto the rail network products with superior growth prospects. Such traffic was generally tendered in wagonload rather than trainload consignments.

The traditional wagonload operation made heavy use of marshalling yards. In addition to being assembled and dispersed at either end of the line-haul, most wagons were remarshalled several times *en route*. This inflated terminal costs, lengthened transit times and seriously reduced reliability. In 1977, BR established a new network of wagonload services, called Speedlink, that provided direct links between major industrial centres. By eliminating the need for intermediate marshalling, using larger air-braked wagons capable of higher speeds and adhering to fixed timetables, Speedlink offered a cheaper, faster and more reliable wagonload service. Although the Speedlink network has been greatly expanded over the past ten years, it still concentrates wagonload flows on a relatively small number of routes. Furthermore, the catchment area of each Speedlink terminal is limited by the high cost of 'trip-working' wagons to and from rail sidings. The cost and service advantages of the Speedlink service have, therefore, been won at the expense of the freedom of movement afforded by the traditional wagonload system. This traditional system has now been phased out with the closure of all BR's marshalling yards and the scrapping of its large fleet of 'unfitted' and vacuum-braked wagons. Partly as a result of these organisational changes, BR was able to reduce freight-train operating costs by 16%, in real terms, between 1978 and 1987 (*Motor Transport*, 4 June 1987).

Accessibility

Reference has so far been made only to the movement of freight between rail sidings and terminals. The majority of freight consignments travel between premises that do not have a direct rail connection. Before the Second World War, when the railways were the dominant mode of long-distance transport in the UK, firms distributing their products over a wide area had little choice but to locate their factories and warehouses beside railway lines. Over the

Table 6.3   Contraction of the British Rail network, 1962-86

	1962	1986
Approximate route length (km)	28,000	16,700
No. of private sidings	6,000	1,140
No. of freight depots	570	123

Sources: British Railways Board, 1963; Department of Transport, 1987.

past 40 years, as the economy has become much more dependent on road haulage, there has been a major realignment of its manufacturing and storage capacity towards the road network, leaving only a small minority of industrial premises in railside locations. A 'bandwagon effect' has developed because 'as the proportion of factories linked to the railways has fallen, the incentive for their suppliers and customers to remain directly connected to the rail system has progressively fallen' (Armitage, 1980, p.15). The widespread closure of railway lines, freight depots and private sidings since the early 1960s has compounded the railway's problem of low accessibility by reducing the number of points at which freight can enter and leave the network (Table 6.3). Fewer than a fifth of the factories surveyed by Bayliss and Edwards (1970) had a rail siding, while in 1983 only 6% of public warehousing in the UK was rail connected. When the origin and destination of a freight consignment are not on the rail network, the goods must be transported by road to and from railheads and transhipped between lorries and rail wagons. The additional cost and time involved in these operations generally render the rail service uncompetitive, except where the rail trunk haul is very long and road feeder movements very short. Low accessibility therefore seriously constrains BR's ability to attract freight traffic and this is reflected by the fact that less than 10% of BR's freight tonnage either starts or finishes its journey at premises without a rail siding.

Various measures have been adopted to ease this constraint:

1. Installation of rail sidings: Where industrial premises lie within about 400 metres of a railway line it is generally possible to install a rail siding. Under Section 8 of the 1974 Railways Act, government grants are available to cover up to 60% of the capital cost of installing sidings (and acquiring ancillary handling equipment and wagons) where it can be demonstrated that the resulting transfer of freight to rail will yield environmental benefits. By the end of 1986, 170 of these grants had been awarded in the expectation that they would enable BR to secure or retain a total of 35.5 million tonnes of freight per annum (British Railways Board, 1987). It has, nevertheless, been argued

that this scheme could be greatly extended and planning approval for industrial premises made conditional on the installation of a rail link (Association of Metropolitan Authorities, 1980). At present, if planning authorities impose such a requirement, the firm no longer qualifies for a Section 8 grant. The main limitation on this scheme, however, is that most existing premises are too far from the nearest railway line to be directly connected. A survey of 450 firms in West Yorkshire in 1979 found that fewer than a quarter either had a rail siding or were in a position to obtain one. Alternative methods have, therefore, had to be used to secure traffic from premises lacking a direct rail link.

2. Improved modal interchange: Various methods have been devised to facilitate the transfer of freight in unitised loads between road and rail. In each case the freight remains in a sealed box, removing the need for loose handling. In the first two systems shown in Figure 6.3, the unit is a road trailer. This is driven onto a railway flatcar and then trunked by rail usually on its own but sometimes accompanied by a tractor unit. The latter arrangement is less economical as the gross weight of the train is increased and the tractor unit is redundant for the duration of the rail journey. There are extensive networks of these *piggyback* (or *trailer on flatcar*) services on the European mainland and in North America. The development of such systems in the UK has been constrained by the small loading gauge of the BR network. It would be prohibitively expensive to increase the clearance of tunnels, bridges and stations by the necessary amount to accommodate conventional piggyback vehicles comparable to those in the French Kangarou and German Huckepack systems. Two new piggyback systems have recently been test marketed in the UK, however, which are capable of carrying road trailers within existing height restrictions. The French Ferdon system differs from the conventional piggyback arrangement by transferring rail wagons rather than road trailers between the two networks. The loading of rail wagons onto road transporters is a cumbersome and costly operation and, given the heavy weight of the combined vehicle, road feeder movements are only possible on particular roads and only economical over very short distances. New intermodal systems dispense with the railway flatcar and either have the trailer carry separate sets of road and rail wheels, one of which is always retracted when not in use (US Railroader system), or suspend the trailers between railway bogies (British TrailerTrain system). The latter system has the advantage of reducing the trailer's tare weight when travelling on

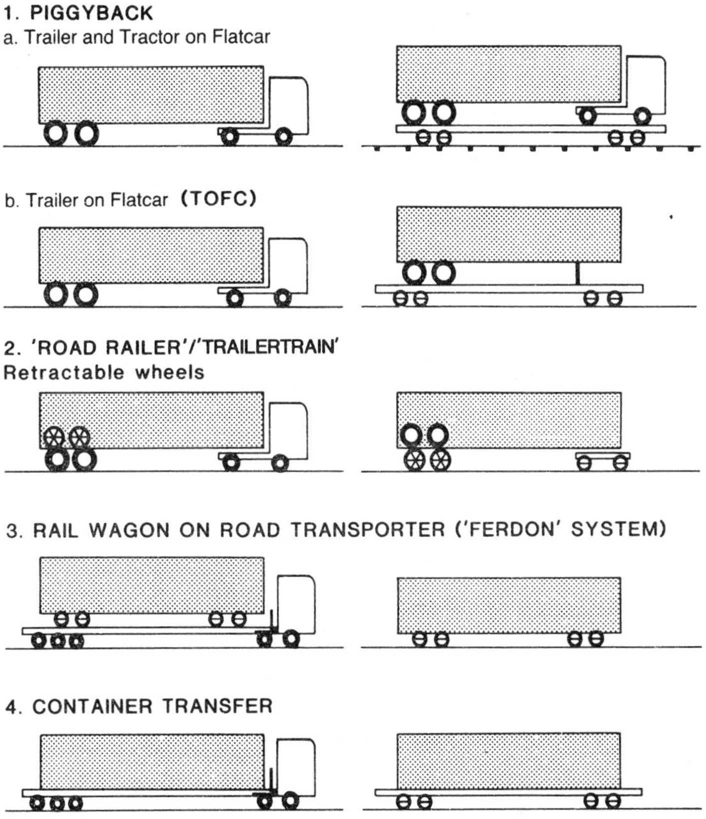

1. PIGGYBACK
a. Trailer and Tractor on Flatcar

b. Trailer on Flatcar **(TOFC)**

2. 'ROAD RAILER'/'TRAILERTRAIN'
Retractable wheels

3. RAIL WAGON ON ROAD TRANSPORTER ('FERDON' SYSTEM)

4. CONTAINER TRANSFER

Figure 6.3 Systems of road-rail interchange

the road network and enabling it to carry heavier payloads.

Partly to compensate for its inability to adopt the piggyback system of modal interchange, BR developed the Freightliner network of containerised services. Despite early optimism about the ability of Freightliner to capture freight traffic from the road network, even on hauls as short as 90 miles, Freightliner has never been responsible for more than 5-6% of BR's total freight tonnage. Its failure to meet original expectations can be attributed partly to the high capital cost of Freightliner terminals. Unlike drive-on drive-off piggyback services, the transfer of containers requires expensive handling equipment which can only be provided economically at relatively few locations. These terminals consequently have large hinterlands and relatively long road feeder movements. Moreover, the accessibility of the

Freightliner network has declined in recent years with the reduction in the number of terminals from a maximum of 40 in 1980 to 26 in 1987. Freightliner now specialises in the movement of traffic over distances greater than 250 miles, most of it with an origin or destination at a seaport, where modal interchange is required anyway. Maritime traffic has increased its share of total Freightliner business from around 50% in 1980 to over 80% in 1987.

3. Rail-based distribution system: It was established in Chapter 3 that most goods pass through at least one intervening stockholding point between factory and shop. Where these intermediate nodes lack a direct rail link, diverting freight onto the rail network entails additional handling and more circuitous routeing via rail terminals. If, however, the warehouses are sited at railheads, storage and intermodal transfer can be combined at the same location, eliminating the need for an extra freight journey and handling operation (McKinnon, 1982). BR's Speedlink distribution system exploits this situation by encouraging firms to channel their goods through rail-connected warehouses, operated in most cases by road hauliers. In 1986, there were approximately 100 such warehouses strategically located around the country and served by Speedlink services (*Freight*, 1985). In collaboration with the haulage and storage contractors operating these premises, BR now offers clients a complete door-to-door distribution service, comprising rail trunk haul, local collection and delivery by road, storage, breaking-of-bulk and associated information processing.

4. Attracting industrial premises to railside locations: In France and West Germany, railway management has for many years actively encouraged firms to locate or relocate factories and warehouses beside railway lines (Wardroper, 1981). In 1985 BR launched a scheme to promote industrial development on disused land adjacent to railway lines. It compiled, with the assistance of the Association of District Councils, a computerised listing, known as the Landbank, of 740 railside sites suitable for development. Although firms setting up factories and warehouses on these sites are under no obligation to use rail, their transport plans are taken into account at the time when the property deal is being negotiated. Even if they do not initially send goods by rail, proximity to the rail network widens their future modal options.

Fixed costs

Railway companies are usually responsible for the maintenance of track, signalling and terminals, and this encumbers their operations with a heavy burden of fixed cost. It is impossible for them, in the short term, to vary the capacity, and hence cost, of their infrastructure in line with fluctuations in traffic levels. A much larger proportion of road hauliers' costs are variable as they can decommission lorries during periods of low demand, suspending payment of road tax and insurance. Slater (1982) estimates that around 34% of the total cost of operating a freight train (comprising 12 ton wagons) is fixed whereas the corresponding figure for a 12 ton lorry is only 4%. It has been argued, nevertheless, that track maintenance standards on the BR network could be tailored more closely to traffic requirements (Department of Transport, 1983), reducing the fixed cost element. Furthermore, as much of the railway route mileage is shared by passenger and freight services, freight traffic often makes a relatively small contribution to the upkeep of track. Indeed, the development of company trains, Freightliner and Speedlink over the past 20 years has tended to consolidate freight flows on the major intercity passenger routes, helping to spread track costs over a larger traffic volume (Pitfield and Whiteing, 1985).

Modal selection process

There is general agreement in the logistics literature that, in deciding which mode or carrier to use, firms should observe the following general principles:

1. Compare the available alternatives.
2. Undertake this comparison at regular intervals.
3. Base the evaluation on a broad range of criteria.
4. Employ a rigorous selection procedure.

Evidence collected in a series of studies over the past 20 years suggests that these principles are not widely applied in practice. In this section we shall examine each of these principles in turn, assessing their significance and asking why some firms choose to ignore them.

Comparison of alternatives

Several modal split studies have revealed that many firms opt for a particular mode without fully considering the alternatives. Bayliss and Edwards (1970), for example, found that only in the case of 26% of the consignments surveyed was the consignor aware of the cost of sending the goods by alternative modes. Pike (1982, p.21) investigated the modal choice decisions of 34 producers of bulk commodities and discovered 'a lack of knowledge about available services, particularly rail freight'. It has also been established that some firms do not adequately evaluate modes they actually use and, therefore, have no basis for comparison with alternative modes. Sharp (1970, p.29) found that only 17.7% of own-account operators had 'detailed and up-to-date knowledge of fleet operating costs' leading him to suggest that the absence of such knowledge was 'the single most important reason for possible traffic misallocations'. A more recent survey of 497 transport operators suggests that detailed costing of in-house operations is now much more widespread, but own-account operators still do not appear to disaggregate these costs to the same extent as hauliers (Hallett and Gray, 1987). In the absence of rigorous cost analysis, the cross-subsidisation of own-account transport operations by other company activities can go unnoticed. The cost of using third-party carriers can be more easily ascertained, though some consignors still obtain very few quotations from these agencies. Saleh and La Londe (1972) found that roughly half the sample of 448 consignors they consulted chose a particular carrier without assessing the alternatives.

Firms may not only lack information about the cost of the available transport services — they also, in many cases, have scant knowledge of how the various modes perform in terms of speed and reliability. Where a consignor does not use a particular mode, an impression of its performance can be gained from past experience or the reports of current users, though neither provide a reliable basis for an evaluation. Where firms have had poor service from a particular mode in the past they are often reluctant to accept that the standard of service may since have improved. Surveys of modal preferences in the UK, for example, have revealed that many transport managers are prejudiced against BR, partly as a result of its past reputation. As Pike (1982, p.27) notes, 'Many potential customers still perceive the rail service as that which existed 10-15 years ago. This user-resistance is a serious impediment to expanding the effective area in which modal alternatives can be assessed'.

Even where firms use a particular mode, their perception of the quality of service is often inaccurate. None of the firms consulted by Sharp (1970) undertook quantitative monitoring of the speed and reliability of deliveries. Bruning and Lynagh (1984) found that while the majority of consignors claimed to evaluate carriers' performance, only 25% of them attempted to quantify the results. Many consignors' perceptions of performance levels are, therefore, likely to be ill founded. This was illustrated by Miklius and Casavant (1975) in a survey of the movement of cherries in the US. They compared the actual reliability of approximately 2,000 road and 1,000 rail shipments, measured in terms of variations in delivery times, with consignors' perceptions of this reliability, and discovered that consignors substantially underestimated the quality of service. This underestimation also exhibited a modal bias as it was much greater for rail than for road. Evidence such as this strengthens the case for a perceptual approach to the study of freight modal split, which relaxes the assumptions, commonly made in deterministic studies, that the decision makers have an accurate and detailed knowledge of all the available options (Gray, 1982). In an effort to improve consignors' awareness of the quality of service they provide, many carriers now offer potential customers a trial at discounted rates. Some try to build confidence in the reliability of their services by guaranteeing not to charge clients for consignments delivered late.

There are some circumstances under which a detailed comparison of all the available modes may be inappropriate. In the case of some freight movements, only one mode may meet all the technical requirements (Bayliss, 1973). Even where these requirements do not preclude the use of alternative modes, a consignor may still find, on the basis of a preliminary assessment, that the technical and economic advantages of one mode are so great as to render a full intermodal comparison unnecessary. This implies that modes have markedly different attributes and are not, therefore, easily substitutable. An analysis of the characteristics of seven transport modes in the US by McGinnis and Corsi (1979, p.40) showed that, 'Each mode offers a unique array of attributes not duplicated by any other mode'. From this they deduced that competition between transport modes is much more limited than is generally supposed. Similar reasoning underlay the claim by the British Department of the Environment in 1973 that effective competition between road and rail was confined to approximately 12% of the total freight market. The remaining traffic, it was argued, had a clear affinity for a particular mode, by virtue of its product type, consignment size and length of haul. Consignors may then be justified in rejecting some modes without fully assessing their cost and performance.

Frequency of re-evaluation

It would seem desirable for firms to review their modal choices at regular intervals to ensure that the mode they are using continues to offer the best combination of cost and quality of service for their particular pattern of traffic flow. In practice, few firms reassess their modal choice at short and regular intervals. Most do so only in response to pronounced changes in the internal organisation of their distribution system or in the cost and performance of externally provided transport services (Sharp, 1970). Marginal changes usually do not justify the diversion of traffic to alternative modes, especially

171

where the firm's distribution system is adapted to the use of a particular mode. In recent years there have been instances in the UK of firms being compelled to use alternative modes because their normal transport service has been disrupted by industrial action. This occurred in 1979 during the lorry drivers' strike and in 1982 and 1984/5 when many rail-freight services were suspended. Having experienced alternative modes under these exceptional circumstances, some firms have decided not simply to revert to their previous pattern of modal usage.

A firm's adherence to a particular mode need not indicate complacency on the part of its transport management. The decision to set up an in-house distribution system, for example, is essentially a long-term decision that subsequently constrains modal options. Once a firm possesses such a system, it will naturally seek to maximise its throughput and minimise its use of outside contractors. Where it has invested heavily in an own-account system, the high cost of disposing of vehicles, and perhaps depots, and of making staff redundant would often outweigh the benefits of externalising the distribution function. Some of the larger contractors, however, now offer to buy out firms' own-account operations and re-employ staff previously engaged in these in-house systems. A 'fleet takeover' eases the transition from an own-account to a contract operation and allows the client firm to release capital tied up in distribution facilities (Buck, 1985). Such buy-outs do not greatly enhance the flexibility of future modal selection, though, as they tend to replace one long-term commitment with another.

An increasing proportion of hire and reward work is being conducted on the basis of contracts of several years' duration. This partly reflects the growth of contract services dedicated to particular clients. A carrier naturally requires a longer-term commitment from a client before investing in vehicles and depots for its exclusive use. Where the carrier provides an integrated distribution service, the client is often bound as much by operational ties as by a legal contract. A consignor can find it difficult to extricate himself from a contract operation when delivery schedules, depots, handling equipment and computer systems are all geared to his particular needs.

Even consignors that are not under such obligations usually change carriers infrequently. Cunningham and Kettlewood (1976) define as 'source loyalty' a consignor's attachment to a particular carrier and, in a survey of 43 consignors in Scotland, found this to be very strong. The firms consulted had used 'the same principal source and mode of transport' (p.77) for an average of eleven years.

It appears, therefore, that the traditional view that modal selection is made on the basis of individual consignments is grossly misleading.

Table 6.4 Factors affecting freight modal choice

Traffic-related
length of haul
consignment weight
dimensions
value
value density (value:weight ratio)
urgency
regularity of shipment
fragility
toxicity
perishability
type of packaging
special handling characteristics

Consignor-related
size of firm
investment priorities
marketing strategy
spatial structure of production and
    logistical systems
availability of rail siding
stockholding policy
management structure
system of modal/carrier evaluation

Service-related
speed (transit time)
reliability
cost
product care
customer relations
geographical coverage
accessibility
availability of special vehicles/handling
    equipment
monitoring goods in transit (progress
    information)
unitisation
provision of ancillary services
    (e.g. storage, breaking of bulk)
computing facilities/compatibility
accuracy of documentation

Very few firms have this degree of flexibility. For many, modal choice is a strategic decision taken at the time when the distribution, and perhaps production, system is being restructured (Van Rens, 1985). Once factory and depot locations, stock management systems and marketing policies have been determined, modal choice can thereafter be tightly restricted. On the one hand, this weakens the case for reassessing modal choice at short intervals, but, on the other, it makes modal selection all the more critical as it cannot be easily altered.

Physical distribution systems

Selection criteria

Numerous attempts have been made to identify the factors that influence modal choice (e.g. Bayliss and Edwards, 1970; Sharp, 1970; Slater, 1982; St Seidenfus, 1985). These studies differ in their methodology, in the range of factors they consider important and in the manner in which they classify them. Table 6.4 presents a consolidated listing of the factors examined in these modal split studies and classifies them as being consignor, traffic and service related. Recent research (Pike, 1982; Van Rens, 1985) has highlighted the importance of consignor characteristics, many of which define the logistical framework within which modes and carriers are selected.

Superficially, the large number of factors appears to make modal selection a very complex, multivariate exercise. In practice, however, modal choice decisions tend to be dominated by a few key variables. Several studies have rank-ordered variables in relation to the number of firms deeming them to be significant. Others have asked firms to indicate on a numerical scale the amount of weight they attach to particular factors in deciding which mode to use. Both types of study have consistently accorded high ratings to factors such as consignment size, length of haul, transit time and cost. The practice of ranking factors can be criticised, though, for not taking account of the fact that they are often inter-related (Bayliss, 1973). In making modal choices, firms usually trade off one factor against another, rather than consider each separately in an ordered sequence. Furthermore, a simple ranking sheds no light on the way in which these factors, individually or collectively, condition modal preferences.

Selection procedure

It is unusual for consignor- and traffic-related factors to be so restrictive that they require the use of a particular mode. Normally, it is technically and economically feasible to use one of several modes. Each mode will have strengths and weaknesses in meeting a particular set of traffic requirements. In essence, the modal allocation problem involves finding the mode which, on balance, makes the greatest contribution to profitability. It need not be the cheapest mode, because this mode may be so slow, unreliable and insecure that the low price is more than offset by high inventory and wastage costs. Few firms therefore aim to minimise costs in isolation.

It is common, nevertheless, for transport managers to be instructed to find the cheapest transport mode (or carrier) capable of meeting a series of service requirements specified by higher management in accordance with production and marketing strategies. A preferable

174

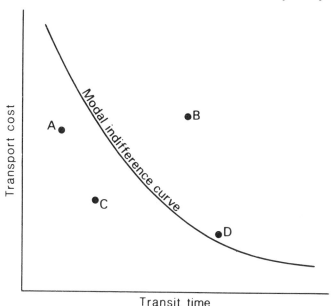

Figure 6.4 Differentiating modes on the basis of transport cost and transit time
Source: Baumol and Vinod, 1970.

approach is to allow the modal decision maker to vary both cost and quality of service and, thereby, establish the optimum trade-off. Trade-off analysis is, nevertheless, complicated in this context by the large number of relevant variables, many of which are difficult to quantify. Fowkes *et al.* (1987) note that 'there has been little attempt to quantify the trade-off between rates and quality of service features' in modal split studies. Several theoretical frameworks have, nevertheless, been proposed for such trade-off analysis. Pike (1982), for example, has suggested that quality of service variables, mainly speed, punctuality and liability to loss or damage, be assigned monetary values and combined with freight rates to produce an overall estimate of *generalised cost*. Sales lost as a result of delivery delays could be incorporated as an opportunity cost, giving modal choice decisions the sole objective of minimising generalised cost.

The three elements likely to figure most prominently in the generalised cost calculation, namely cost, speed and reliability, form the basis of the *inventory-theoretic model* of freight transport demand devised by Baumol and Vinod (1970). This model was originally designed to help explain consignors' modal choices, but it can also be used as a management tool to analyse the trade-off between these three

175

variables. To simplify the explanation, attention will focus here on the relationship between the cost and speed of transport services. As speed determines the size of in-transit inventories and influences the amount of stock held by the consignee, it can be expressed in terms of inventory carrying costs. Baumol and Vinod depict the trade-off between transport and inventory carrying costs for a particular consignor as an indifference curve whose configuration they establish with reference to standard inventory theory (Figure 6.4). Points A, B and C represent different modes, their x and y co-ordinates corresponding to particular combinations of freight charges and transit times. Consignors would have a preference for modes above the indifference curve to those below. Where two modes lay on or close to this curve, other criteria, such as reliability and liability to loss and damage, would have to be taken into account to determine modal preferences. By allowing for all possible combinations of cost and transit time, this model adopts the *abstract mode* approach first proposed by Quandt and Baumol (1966) to introduce greater flexibility into modal split analysis. Treating a transport mode as a continuous variable makes it easier to accommodate changes in modal characteristics, the emergence of new transport services and marginal intramodal differences in carrier cost and performance.

The main shortcomings of the Baumol and Vinod model are its neglect of service criteria unrelated to transit time and the unrealistic monetary evaluation of this time. Das (1974) argues that to calculate inventory carrying costs accurately one requires more information about stock control policies and the nature of demand. Empirical estimates of the value of time in long-distance freight transport also indicate that the true value of transit time far exceeds the opportunity cost of capital tied up in in-transit inventory (Hodgkin and Starkie, 1979). It appears from this work that consignors attach high monetary value to the prompt delivery of goods to customers, in the expectation that this will help to generate or maintain sales. Whatever grounds firms have for believing that sales are sensitive to order lead times, this belief clearly has a major impact on modal selection. McGinnis (1979, p.32) notes that such 'market considerations may be as important to transportation choice as inventory levels' and yet have received little attention in modal split research.

Distribution system modelling affords the most comprehensive assessment of modal options (Slater, 1982). Where a firm has developed a model capable of simulating its distribution operation accurately, this can be used to forecast the wide-ranging effects of choosing particular modes.

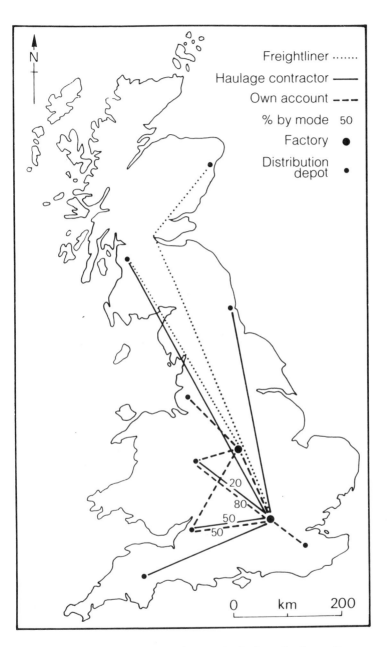

Figure 6.5 Modal split in the trunk network of a large food manufacturer

Multimodal strategies

Firms often find it advantageous to employ more than one mode. They can combine transport modes in three ways:

1. where more than one mode is used on a single journey, as in the case of road-rail container and piggyback movements. As many of these intermodal systems are today fully integrated, costed on a 'throughout' basis and under the control of a single agency, they can be regarded as a single, composite mode.
2. where different modes are regularly used for different products, regions and types of customer. Figure 6.5 shows how one food manufacturer uses own-account, road haulage and rail services for factory to depot movements, confining own-account vehicles to shorter hauls and employing Freightliner for long-distance movements.
3. where contingency plans allow for the use of additional modes to accommodate peak traffic volumes or to provide a more rapid delivery service in an emergency. The replenishment of cycle stock may be assigned to surface modes, and supplemented, when necessary, by top-up orders sent more rapidly at short notice by air. The high premium rates charged by the airlines then apply only to a small proportion of total output and can be more than offset by savings accruing from the centralisation of safety stock (Jackson and Brackenbridge, 1971).

Several developments have promoted the adoption of multimodal distribution strategies. These include the diversification of product ranges, the extension of market areas, company mergers, the desire to reduce the vulnerability of distribution to industrial disputes, the pressure to reduce inventories and the introduction of new improved systems of modal interchange. The range of transport options has consequently expanded and the emphasis shifted from choosing a single mode to deciding upon the optimum allocation of traffic among modes.

Chapter seven

Routeing of freight flows

In this chapter we shall examine the physical flow of finished goods through a distribution system. The first part examines the bulk movement of primary flows outward from factories to distribution depots and large customers. The remainder is concerned with local deliveries from depots to shops.

Pattern of bulk flow

Firms manufacturing their entire product range at a single plant generate a simple, radial pattern of bulk flow supplying distribution depots and large customers directly. The dispersal of manufacturing among several factories gives rise to a much more complex flow pattern. Firms that produce goods at more than one location can be divided into two categories: those that make the same products at each factory (homogeneous production) and those that have factories specialising in particular products (heterogeneous production).

Homogeneous production

In this situation, the allocation of bulk flows between factories and distribution depots largely depends on the production capacity of each factory, the requirements of each depot and the transport cost on each factory-depot link. In attempting to find the allocation that minimises total transport costs, within supply and demand constraints, firms encounter the classical *transportation problem* (Hitchcock, 1941). This problem can be solved by linear programming. Willis (1977) and Hay (1977) outline simple manual methods of obtaining good, if not optimal, solutions to smaller-scale transportation problems. The practical application of linear programming in this context can be frustrated, however, by three factors:

179

1. Non-linearities in the transport cost function: As explained in earlier chapters, the unit costs of transport seldom increase as a linear function of the size of consignment and distance travelled. This infringes the main assumption underlying the application of linear programming, namely that the functions are linear.
2. The desire to maximise return loading: To take advantage of back-hauls, firms may route products indirectly via factories or depots. Merchant and Calcis (1974) have devised a form of linear programming that can make allowance for indirect routeing, though their model lacks realism as it neglects terminal costs and treats vehicle capacity as a continuous variable.
3. The combination in the same vehicle of bulk supplies for depots and orders for direct delivery to customers: This introduces a combinatorial element into the transport cost function which is difficult to incorporate within a linear programming framework.

Heterogeneous production

Some firms in this category do not mix stocks prior to bulk delivery and thus require customers seeking bulk consignments to place large orders with each factory separately.

There are advantages, however, in consolidating mixed loads for bulk distribution. It raises the efficiency of direct distribution by increasing the average size of bulk drops and reducing the number of separate deliveries each customer receives. The order cycle time for individual products can be reduced, improving customer service and possibly generating additional sales. Even allowing for the extra cost of bulk mixing, direct deliveries are generally cheaper per unit of sales than the distribution of small consignments via depots. Product ranges can be consolidated either by interplant transfers or by assembling the output of different factories at a central mixing point.

1. Interfactory transfers (or 'cross-shipment'). This allows all or some of the factories to hold mixed stocks and permits the distribution of mixed bulk loads directly to customers, usually from the nearest factory (Magee, 1968). Mixed stocks tend to be concentrated at factories with the greatest output, largest storage capacity and/or most central location.

   Cross-shipment inflates the cost of bulk deliveries in several ways. By dispersing bulk stocks of each product, it increases the total volume of stock in the system. In addition to increasing the financial costs of stockholding, this also creates a greater demand for storage space at each of the factories. Cross-shipment also adds another transport link to the logistical channel with

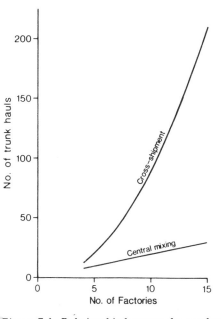

Figure 7.1 Relationship between the number of trunk hauls and the dispersal of production: Cross-shipment and Central mixing strategies

additional handling at either end. To the extra handling costs must be added the difference in movement costs between the delivery of unmixed orders direct from each factory and the more circuitous, indirect delivery of a proportion of the mixed orders. Where a firm operates many factories, cross-shipment can give rise to a complex network of trunk movements. A complete system of interhauls among X factories generates a network of $(X^2 - X)$ trunk movements (allowing for movement in both directions on each interfactory link). Figure 7.1 shows how the number of trunk hauls rises sharply as production becomes more dispersed. This can create a large demand for heavy goods transport and prove difficult to organise efficiently, especially where directional imbalance in interfactory flows makes it necessary to run vehicles on some journeys well below capacity. The movement of raw materials and semi-finished products between factories can in some cases redress this imbalance.

Over the past twenty years the demand for cross-shipment has been subject to two opposing forces. On the one hand, the formation of manufacturing conglomerates has absorbed plants making diverse products into the same logistical system.

181

Cross-shipment networks have been extended to incorporate these acquired factories. The demand for cross-shipment has been further strengthened by the desire of large retail and wholesale customers to receive their supplies more economically in direct, bulk deliveries. On the other hand, the amount of cross-shipment is likely to have been reduced by the spatial concentration of production. There have been many instances of firms closing smaller, often more specialist, plants and integrating their production in larger units. By concentrating the manufacture of more of their product range in fewer locations, firms have reduced the number of nodes in their cross-shipment networks.

2. Mixing bulk stock at a central depot. The centralisation of bulk stock at a single location permits a reduction in inventory levels and streamlines the network of trunk movements. Where production is highly dispersed, the consolidation of product ranges at a single location generates many fewer trunk hauls than a cross-shipment system (Figure 7.1).

There are, nevertheless, some disadvantages in adopting a central mixing strategy. As there is little or no reverse flow of goods from the mixing point to the factories, this arrangement offers less opportunity for back-haulage than a system of inter-plant transfers. It is often possible, though, for lorries on their return journeys to the factories to deliver bulk orders from the mixing point to major customers. The use of a separate mixing point can also result in a net increase in the amount of handling and transport required, because the proportion of each factory's production that would otherwise have been consolidated into mixed loads *in situ* must now be loaded onto vehicles and transported to the mixing point.

The extent to which the use of a central mixing point can improve the efficiency of the bulk delivery system largely depends upon its location. Ideally, it should be located centrally with respect both to the firm's factories and to customers receiving mixed bulk orders. Even so, the routeing of bulk supplies through a central mixing point can be long and circuitous. This is exemplified by a producer of canned fruit which assembled output from plants in Scotland and East Anglia at a central mixing depot in Spalding, Lincolnshire. Some of the canned fruit originating at a factory in Scotland was transported roughly 600 kilometres south to Spalding and then shipped back to large customers in Scotland in consolidated bulk loads. Although the use of a central mixing point can significantly increase the distances that products travel from factory to

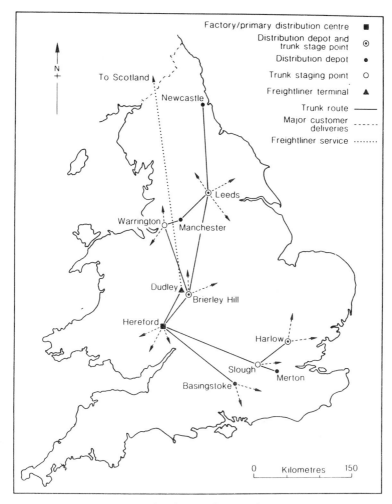

Figure 7.2 Use of staging points in a trunk network
Source: Joyce, 1982.

customer, it allows them to be transported in larger loads at a lower cost per tonne-kilometre.

The spatial distribution of a firm's storage space can affect the way in which it organises its bulk distribution. Some firms, for example, have little bulk storage space at their factories and must, therefore, disperse their output almost immediately to stockholding depots. Others have enough storage capacity at the factory site to retain larger

183

volumes of finished stock, but insufficient to permit the mixing of ranges or to accommodate the volumes of stock that would be necessary to support an extensive system of direct distribution.

Once the pattern of primary flow has been established, firms must design a trunk network capable of transporting bulk loads efficiently within service level and operating constraints. As most trunk vehicles carry a full load to a single destination, their routes can be planned more easily than multiple-drop rounds at the local delivery level. In the planning of trunk networks, greater emphasis is placed on obtaining back-loads, mainly because journeys are much longer and the vehicles larger and more expensive to operate. Legal and operational restrictions on drivers' hours also bear more heavily on trunk haulage, limiting the distance a single driver can travel in a working day. Joyce (1982) describes how, partly by inserting a series of 'staging bases' in their trunk network, H. P. Bulmer, the cider producer, were able to improve vehicle utilisation and labour productivity (Figure 7.2). Drivers based at the firm's plant at Hereford take trailers to strategically located staging points from which they are moved to their final destinations by outbased drivers.

Although devised originally to cope with tighter EC restrictions on drivers' hours, the staging of longer-distance trunk movements has proved more efficient, more flexible and capable of providing customers with a better service.

Delimitation of depot hinterlands

Before one can consider the routeing of local deliveries from depots to retail (and small wholesale) outlets, one must examine the way in which customers are assigned to depots. This assignment is simplified by the fact that customers almost always receive their supplies of a particular manufacturer's products from a single depot, usually the nearest. They can, therefore, be allocated to depots by dividing the market area into separate depot service areas (or hinterlands).

Generally speaking, three factors affect the delimitation of depot hinterlands. The first is the logistical constraint imposed by restrictions on drivers' hours. As most firms' local delivery operations are characterised by high drop densities and comparatively short *stem* and *intercall* distances, the daily range of their delivery vehicles is constrained much more by the length of the driver's shift than by legal limits on driving hours. Whatever the nature of the restriction, it is possible to draw a *time-constraint boundary* around each depot. The extension of deliveries beyond this boundary requires arrangements, such as the outbasing of drivers and the use of transhipment facilities, which add substantially to transport costs and delivery times

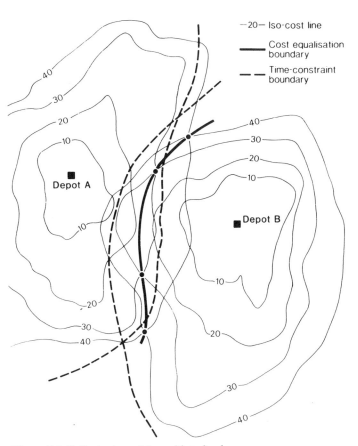

Figure 7.3 Delimitation of depot hinterlands

(Attwood, 1971). The time-constraint boundaries of neighbouring depots normally intersect, in which case the area of overlap is usually divided in relation to the capacities of the two depots and to their outward delivery costs. Given a uniform density of demand, the depot with the larger amount of storage and delivery capacity could serve a wider area. Where two neighbouring depots have adequate capacity to serve the areas enclosed by their respective time-constraint boundaries, the intervening area is likely to be divided on the basis of relative delivery costs. For this purpose, a *cost-equalisation boundary* can be drawn between the two depots using a method devised by Weber (1909) and later refined by Lösch (1954). Iso-cost lines are drawn around each depot, connecting up points of equal delivery cost (Figure 7.3). The cost-equalisation boundary is then interpolated between the

185

points at which the iso-cost lines encircling neighbouring depots intersect. It is often found in practice that the two sets of iso-cost lines are widely spaced. This means that total delivery costs are relatively insensitive to changes in the configuration of depot boundaries (Murphy, 1978). Firms often take advantage of this flexibility to make allowance for indivisibilities in the delivery operation, thereby ensuring that each depot is assigned a whole number of vehicles and drivers and that both are fully utilised (Sussams, 1969; Attwood, 1971).

There are numerous instances of delivery area boundaries coinciding with the boundaries delimiting salesmen's territories (Magee, 1968). This is largely due to the fact that distribution policy is often 'dictated by the need, or convenience, of the sales force' (Smith, 1979a, p.46). Many firms clearly prefer to have each salesman channel all his orders through a single depot and indeed often use depots as bases for local sales operations. There is evidence, however, of this practice impairing the efficiency of depot deliveries. NEDO (1967) cites the case of a manufacturer of 'tinned products' which was able to reduce its delivery costs by severing the spatial relationship between distribution and sales, and allowing the size and configuration of depot areas to be determined mainly by the economics of the delivery operation.

In theory, the redrawing of depot boundaries offers a means of adjusting a distribution system to short-term changes in the patterns of demand and accessibility, while the number, location and capacity of depots remain constant (Beattie, 1973). In practice, however, firms tend only to revise these boundaries in the event of a major reorganisation of their depot system. Many distribution managers admit that they would like to redraw boundaries more frequently, but claim that they lack the resources to do so and, in some cases, are constrained by working practices and trade union agreements.

Variations in the size and shape of depot hinterlands

In the analysis of the sequence of depot locations in Chapter 5, an attempt was made to idealise the pattern of zonal subdivision. The pattern that emerged was highly generalised and, even in the case of firms operating similar numbers of depots in similar locations, concealed wide differences in the sizes and shapes of hinterlands in some parts of the country.

In zoning their market areas for distribution purposes, firms do not attempt to equalise the population served by each depot. The logistics and economics of the delivery operation make it much more efficient to vary hinterland size and depot throughput in relation to population

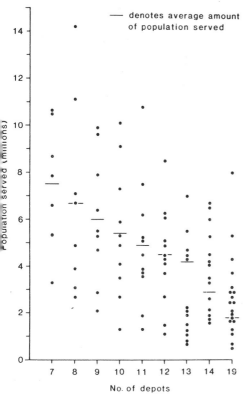

Figure 7.4 Populations served by the depots of nine food manufacturers

density and accessibility. Figure 7.4 shows how 103 food distribution depots operated by a sample of 9 food manufacturers varied enormously in the amounts of population they served.

Depots in close proximity can have hinterlands that differ markedly in size and shape. Table 7.1 and Figure 7.5 relate to 8 food manufacturers that operated similar numbers of depots, within the range 10 to 14. It was found that these firms had depots within 30 miles of each other in three areas: the north-east, north-west and south-west of England. It can be seen that in each region there is a wide variation in the sizes and shapes of the areas served.

In practice, geographical subdivisions bear little resemblance to the ideal hexagonal pattern postulated by Sussams (1969). Irregularities in the configuration of depot boundaries can be attributed to several factors:

Table 7.1   Populations residing in depot service areas

Firm no.	No. of depots operated by firms	Depot location	population (m)	
North-east England:				
1	10	Spennymoor	3.5	
2	11	New Herrington	5.1	
3	11	Newcastle upon Tyne	3.2	Range = 3.2
4	12	Greatham	2.7	Mean = 3.3
5	13	Gateshead	1.9	
6	14	Durham	3.4	
North-west England:				
1	10	Haydock	7.2	
2	11	Eccles	10.9	
3	11	Kirkby	9.1	Range = 4.2
4	12	Middlewich	8.5	Mean = 8.2
5	13	Bolton	7.0	
6	14	Ashton	6.8	
South-west England:				
1	10	Bristol	4.0	
2	11	Caldicot	4.5	
3	11	Bristol	8.8	Range = 6.7
4	12	Yate	5.0	Mean = 4.8
5	13	Bristol	4.4	
6	14	Brislington	2.1	

1. Presence of physical barriers. The alignment of depot boundaries can be strongly influenced by poor road connections across upland areas and estuaries. Many firms, for example, have divided service areas in the north of England along the Pennines (Murphy, 1978). The bridging of the main estuaries has reduced their barrier effect, though it has generally taken firms several years to adjust their distribution systems to the resulting changes in accessibility (Cleary and Thomas, 1973).
2. Distribution of population. The drawing of depot boundaries is facilitated by the uneven distribution of population. Wherever possible, firms run depot boundaries across sparsely populated areas. It is, nevertheless, quite common for firms to split distribution to conurbations, particularly those of Greater London and the West Midlands, between several outlying depots, and draw hinterland boundaries through densely populated areas. This can be justified on several grounds:
    (i)   A single depot serving these areas would be too large.
    (ii) Employing several depots reduces the risk of deliveries to these crucial sales areas being totally disrupted.

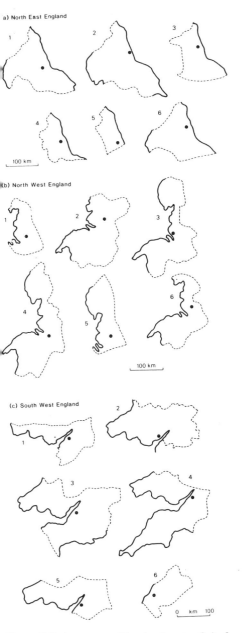

a) North East England

b) North West England

(c) South West England

Figure 7.5 Areas served by the depots of six food manufacturers in three regions

189

(iii) Road congestion on inner urban roads impedes movement across a conurbation. In the case of Greater London, the limited number of bridges on the Thames coupled with the high levels of congestion on their approach roads makes the river a natural dividing line for distribution purposes.

3. Trunk-road network. The pattern of depot boundaries can reflect differences in the ease of movement across the road network. Depot hinterlands are sometimes elongated along the line of major trunk routes, as a result of a corresponding distortion of iso-cost lines and time-constraint boundaries.

Routeing of delivery vehicles

Single- versus multiple-drop deliveries

The route a delivery vehicle follows and the distance it travels depends on the number and locations of the outlets it visits. Other things being equal, the larger the consignments, the smaller will be the number of drops per delivery. The limiting situation is where one consignment fills the vehicle and is delivered directly to a single outlet.

Eilon *et al.* (1971) have examined the relationship between direct radial distance and minimum delivery round distance, using random distributions of customers within an area of given extent. Multiple-drop journeys generate fewer vehicle kilometres than direct deliveries to each of the customers, and as the number of drops increases this differential widens. Although the multiple-drop journey is more devious than the direct route to each customer, it dispenses with the individual back-hauls associated with direct deliveries.

The multiple-drop delivery round and the direct radial delivery are not strictly comparable, though, as they differ in the sizes of consignment they can supply to each customer. A vehicle delivering to several customers *en route* supplies only a fraction of the full payload, whereas a direct delivery can supply a whole lorry load, perhaps meeting the customer's demands in full. It therefore requires several delivery rounds to distribute the same quantity of goods as a series of direct deliveries. In practice, the number of vehicle kilometres is usually minimised by direct single-drop deliveries. A system of direct deliveries is more efficient despite the fact that it usually entails more empty running by vehicles. In the course of multiple-drop rounds, lorries travel much longer distances only partly loaded.

Reducing the number of drops per delivery and increasing average drop size also permits the use of larger vehicles. Vehicle size is determined mainly by the volume (or weight) of goods that can be

Table 7.2 Effects of varying vehicle weight on a supermarket chain's delivery operation

Gross vehicle weight (tons)	No. of vehicles required	Total vehicle km per week (000)	Delivery cost per ton (£)	Ave. no. of visits/shop per week	Total fuel (gallons/ week)
8.5	135	184	6.60	23	7,700
16.0	72	88	4.30	11	4,900
24.0	53	59	3.95	8	4,200
32.0	45	48	3.80	6	4,200

Source: Margason and Corcoran, 1978.

delivered within a driver's shift. On rounds with numerous drops, so much of the driver's time is spent travelling between customers and offloading small consignments that only a relatively small payload can be distributed in the time available. Where few drops are made, particularly to customers in close proximity, much larger amounts can be delivered per trip. Margason and Corcoran (1978) have shown how a supermarket chain can substantially reduce unit delivery costs, fuel consumption and total vehicle kilometres by employing larger vehicles (Table 7.2). The arrival of supplies in large quantities also makes for much more efficient offloading, reduced paperwork, greater security and the alleviation of 'backdoor congestion'. As noted in Chapter 3, there is, overall, an inverse exponential relationship between drop size and delivery cost.

Load consolidation

Where the volume and spatial distribution of demand remains constant, firms can increase drop size and reduce the number of drops per delivery by consolidating orders. Consolidation can either be organised internally within a single firm or externally through interfirm collaboration or the use of a common carrier.

Internal consolidation

Rather than despatch a small quantity of supplies each time an order is received, a firm can hold back individual consignments until a larger, more economically sized load has accumulated. Various decision rules can be adopted to determine when a consolidated load should be forwarded. In a survey of 53 firms in the US, Jackson (1985) found four such rules (or 'shipment release policies') in common use:

All orders withheld until (a) minimum weight is accumulated.
                    or (b) the oldest order reaches a
                           predetermined age or minimum
                           weight accumulates.
All orders despatched on (a) a predetermined date whether
                          consolidated or not,
                      or (b) when minimum weight accumulates,
                           whichever is sooner.

This form of consolidation inevitably lengthens order lead times, increasing cycle stocks and making it necessary for customers to hold more safety stock to accommodate demand variations over the longer periods between deliveries. Burns *et al.* (1985) equate this type of consolidation with the direct 'shipment' of bulk orders and contrast it with the delivery of small consignments on multiple-drop rounds (or 'peddling'). The former offers lower transport costs at the expense of longer order lead times and higher inventory carrying costs. Burns *et al.* make a full cost comparison of the two delivery strategies and show how optimum load sizes can be determined in each case.

Marketing and sales staff often resist the implementation of this type of consolidation, fearing that the lengthening of order cycle times will result in a loss of sales. Cooper (1984), nevertheless, points out that the sensitivity of sales to order lead times is uncertain and suggests that customers would be more tolerant if they felt that they too were deriving benefit from consolidation.

Much of the modelling work that has been done on the effects of consolidation on the cost and quality of distribution services has been concerned only with this internal form of consolidation (e.g. Masters, 1980; Jackson, 1985).

External consolidation

This involves grouping different firms' products into combined orders for individual customers. It has been advocated as the most promising means of rationalising the movement of freight in urban areas. In the early 1970s, concern was expressed about the increasing private and social costs of urban freight deliveries. Research in several countries, such as the United Kingdom (Foulkes, 1979), the United States (McDermott, 1980), Canada (Wood, Suen and Ebrahim, 1982) and Japan (Toyota Transport Environment Committee, 1977), revealed that many of these deliveries were being organised very inefficiently, resulting in the gross underutilisation of resources and exacerbating problems of traffic congestion and environmental intrusion. A major cause of this inefficiency was the unco-ordinated delivery of small orders by a multitude of separate agencies. Studies revealed that large

Table 7.3 Potential benefits of consolidating urban goods deliveries: Columbus, Ohio

Performance index	Existing system	With full consolidation	% reduction
Number of vehicles	660	69	90
Distance travelled (km)	1,280	114	91
Transit time (hours)	244	22	91
Unloading time (hours)	392	186	53
Loading time (hours)	81	51	37
Queueing time (hours)	251	—	100
Annual cost (million $)	2.9	0.8	76

Source: McDermott, 1975.

benefits could be gained from consolidating small consignments bound for the same customer. A simulation model was developed to assess the effects of a comprehensive consolidation scheme in Columbus, Ohio. Under this scheme, all consignments of less than 5,000 lbs requiring collection or delivery within the city were to be aggregated at an 'urban consolidation terminal'. As shown in Table 7.3, if fully implemented, this system would have yielded enormous reductions in vehicle numbers, kilometres and operating costs.

A great deal of consolidation is already undertaken by wholesalers, multiple retailers and distribution contractors. On the basis of a survey of shop deliveries in Bradford, Rushton (1979) calculated that approximately 76% of retail supplies (by value) arrived in loads that had undergone some consolidation. More recent statistics suggest that around 82% of retail supplies in the UK are subject to consolidation (NEDO, 1985).

According to Rushton (1979), the proportion of consolidated deliveries rose sharply in the UK in the 1960s and 1970s, as a result of the following processes:

1. growth of multiple retailers and their increasing involvement in distribution upstream of the shop;
2. growth of distribution contractors providing groupage services to manufacturers and retailers;
3. contraction of manufacturers' retail delivery networks as a result of shop closures, the imposition of larger minimum-drop sizes and the growth of bulk deliveries to multiple retailers' central warehouses.
4. growth of voluntary group and cash and carry wholesaling.
5. company amalgamations resulting in the integration of own-account transport systems.
6. firms using own-account vehicles to carry traffic for others.

The main advantage of multifirm consolidation is the reduction of distribution costs. The community can also benefit from reductions in traffic levels, fuel consumption and environmental damage. The environmental implications of consolidation are discussed in Chapter 9. Several government-sponsored studies have extolled the virtues of consolidation and encouraged further rationalisation of freight deliveries by this means (Pettit, 1973; Roudier, 1976; Lorries and the Environment Committee, 1979; Armitage, 1980).

There are, however, numerous impediments to increased consolidation. These are fairly exhaustively listed by Rushton (1979). The main obstacle is the unwillingness of many manufacturers to relinquish control of distribution to 'consolidation agencies' such as distribution contractors and multiple retailers. Wilson (1979) contends that in some trades the scope for additional consolidation is limited. He found, for example, that in the furniture industry consolidation was inhibited by the bulky and fragile nature of the products, while in the case of confectionery and footwear, it was already nearing its maximum extent.

Although there has been a substantial increase in freight consolidation over the past 20 years, a large proportion of orders continue to be delivered on multiple-drop rounds. The following section will examine the way in which these rounds are planned.

Planning multiple-drop deliveries

In designing multiple-drop delivery routes, one encounters a variant of the *travelling salesman problem*, which has exercised the minds of mathematicians for over two centuries. In essence, this problem involves establishing the shortest route around a series of points. Dantzig and Ramser (1959) recast this problem within the context of freight distribution by imposing two constraints on route formation:

1. maximum distance a vehicle can travel on a single route;
2. maximum load the vehicle can carry.

Under normal circumstances, these constraints prevent a vehicle from delivering the required volume of supplies to all customers on a single journey, thereby creating the need for several separate routes. This complicates the problem by making it necessary to allocate customers to routes as well as decide in which order they are to be visited. The *vehicle despatching problem*, as it has become known, can be formally stated as follows:

> To design a set of routes serving a number of customers, with known locations and order requirements, which minimises

delivery costs within vehicle payload and distance (or travel time) constraints.

Numerous attempts have been made to develop and refine algorithms capable of solving this problem, though few of these techniques have been applied in practice. It appears that much of the academic work on the subject has been motivated more by the desire to solve an intriguing mathematical puzzle than to satisfy the needs of road transport operators. Much of industry can also be criticised, however, for adhering to fairly primitive methods of route planning and unfairly dismissing many of the recent technical advances in this field. The following section examines the main algorithms available and considers their practical shortcomings. For a fuller review of the literature on the vehicle despatching problem, most of it in operations research, readers should consult Eilon *et al.* (1971), Mole (1979) and Bott and Ballou (1986).

Vehicle routeing algorithms

A broad distinction can be drawn between algorithms that build all the routes needed to serve a set of customers concurrently and those which construct them one at a time. The former, known as *simultaneous methods*, generally minimise the distance travelled without giving due regard to the loading of vehicles and hence the total number of vehicles required. The latter, adopting a *sequential approach* to route building, take more account of vehicle utilisation and fleet size.

Simultaneous methods

The most straightforward way of solving the vehicle despatching problem is to generate all feasible routes and select the ones which, collectively, yield the lowest cost. A complete search through all the possibilities quickly becomes unmanageable, however, as the number of delivery points increases. There are, for example, 6.08×10^{16} different ways of routeing a vehicle around a set of 20 customers, though many of these routes would be likely to infringe distance and load size constraints. Where the scale of the problem permits a full enumeration of feasible routes, mathematical programming can be used to establish the optimum set of routes. Branch and bound methods can yield an exact solution by developing a 'tree' comprising all feasible routes and then searching along particular 'branches' to find the set of routes that minimises the distance travelled (Christofides and Eilon, 1969). All these methods, however, have relatively heavy computational demands and can only realistically be used to solve relatively small routeing problems.

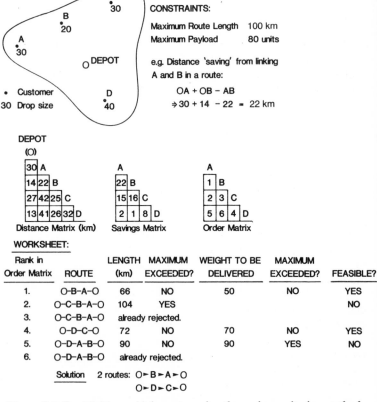

Figure 7.6 Establishing vehicle routes using the savings criterion method

Most research has concentrated on the development of heuristic algorithms that greatly reduce the amount of calculation, but do not guarantee optimality.

The most widely used of these algorithms employ a *savings criterion* to determine the order in which customers are connected to a route (Clarke and Wright, 1964). This method is outlined in Figure 7.6. The distribution of supplies from depot O to customers A and B can take the form of either two separate direct deliveries or a round trip. The latter yields a distance 'saving' of (OA + OB - AB), confirming that, *ceteris paribus*, multiple-drop rounds generate less vehicle kilometres than direct radial journeys. Distance savings are calculated for all pairs of customers and recorded in a savings matrix. These savings are then used to rank customer links in descending order, producing an order matrix. This ranking determines the sequence in which customers are added to emerging routes. In a manual application, the stages in the route-building exercise can be displayed on a worksheet. Each time a route is extended to connect an additional customer, a check is made to ensure that its length and vehicle loading do not exceed the specified maxima. This procedure continues until all customers are linked into feasible routes.

All algorithms can be judged by the compromise they strike between the amount of calculation required and the quality of the final solution. In this respect, the savings criterion method, as originally formulated, performs poorly. Compiling the savings matrix can prove very time consuming and require large amounts of computer storage space. The routes produced can, nevertheless, be markedly suboptimal. They tend to form broad arcs and often intersect. The inefficiency of the routes stems partly from the fact that once customers are added to a route their position on that route remains fixed. This ignores the fact that by altering, at a later stage, the sequence in which customers are visited, it may be possible to reduce the route length. Mole (1979) thus considers the savings criterion method to be 'myopic'.

The 3-optimal method, devised by Christofides and Eilon (1969), does not suffer from these failings and generally yields superior results. The term r-optimal was first used by Lin (1965) in his work on the travelling salesman problem. It refers to a route whose length cannot be reduced by replacing any set of up to r links with an equivalent number of other links. In their application of this principle to the vehicle despatching problem, Christofides and Eilon start with a series of feasible routes and upgrade them to 3-optimal status, ensuring throughout that the vehicle capacity and distance constraints are not violated. They use a random process to generate the initial set of feasible routes, though the savings criterion method could also have been used for this purpose. The removal of three links from each route leaves three disconnected route segments which can be reconnected in eight different ways. Every possible set of three links is systematically removed and all the possible reconnected routes evaluated and compared. The 3-optimal route is the one which yields the lowest cost. This is seldom the true optimum, but is usually only marginally suboptimal. Full optimality would be defined by the n-optimal route, where n is the total number of customers to be supplied, and would require a complete evaluation of all possible routes. Christofides and Eilon discovered that increasing the optimality rating beyond three substantially inflated the computing demands, yet only slightly improved the final solution.

Sequential methods

The simultaneous methods outlined above have two major disadvantages. In the first place, building up a complete set of routes at the same time makes the calculation very cumbersome. Second, both methods assume that there is no limit to the number of vehicles available and tend, as a result, to be prodigal in their use of vehicle capacity. Sequential methods try to overcome these problems by decomposing the route-building exercise. This is done either by dividing the depot hinterland into separate delivery areas or by confining attention to the formation of one route at a time.

The first approach is adopted by Gillett and Miller (1974), who effectively divide the depot hinterland into a series of wedge-shaped zones, each containing a set of customers that can be connected in a feasible route. The alignment of these wedges is determined by the position of a radial axis drawn from the depot through a randomly selected customer location. A travelling salesman algorithm is used to calculate the length of the shortest route around each set of customers. This minimum distance and the sum of the customer orders must be less than maximum values specified at the outset. Having grouped customers on the basis of radial contiguity, Gillett and Miller then apply a 'refine' procedure which reallocates them between routes and resequences them within routes wherever this reduces journey length. The resulting route structure is then evaluated in terms of the total distance travelled. This evaluation can also take account of vehicle requirements. The radial axis is then moved in a clockwise direction until it passes through the second customer location and the same procedure followed as before to build up a second set of routes. Thereafter the axis is rotated into alignment with each customer location in turn and each time a new route structure formed and evaluated. The axis then sweeps round in an anticlockwise direction, generating another series of route structures. Finally, all the sets of routes are compared, to establish the minimum cost solution.

This algorithm has three shortcomings. First, wedge-shaped zones do not necessarily constitute the best framework within which to cluster customers prior to routeing. Daganzo (1984) outlines a method of grouping customers in areas of different shapes which provides a superior basis for route building. Second, the sweep mechanism makes it difficult to apply the algorithm in situations where a firm operates vehicles of differing capacity. Third, computing demands quickly become extravagant as the number of customers per route increases.

The route-building algorithm devised by Mole and Jameson (1976) does not suffer from these drawbacks. It employs the savings criterion method to construct routes one at a time, adding contiguous links to a single route until distance and payload constraints are reached. The algorithm overcomes the three major disadvantages of the savings criterion method outlined earlier. It relaxes the assumption that customers are only added to routes at either end (i.e. between the depot and the first or last customer) and regularly resequences customers within an evolving route using a 2-optimal approach. Routes are, therefore, restructured as customers are added and the possibility of intersections occurring thus eliminated. Mole and Jameson also follow the example set by Gaskell (1967) and Webb (1972) by modifying the savings criterion in such a way as to generate routes that are more radial and less circumferential, exhibiting a petal rather than an arc shape. Their algorithm does not zone customers prior to route building and allows the user to specify different capacity constraints for each vehicle and to allocate the same vehicle to more than one route. While improving the quality of the final solution, Mole and Jameson have reduced computing requirements by considering only small subsets of the total customer array at any given time, thus removing the need to compile and store the complete savings matrix for all possible intercustomer links.

Conventional methods of vehicle scheduling

Waters (1987) reckons that 'many hundreds of man years' of work has gone into the development and refinement of vehicle routeing algorithms. Despite this, the vast majority of firms continue to employ intuitive or 'rule of thumb' methods of route planning. Their reluctance to put these algorithms into practice can be attributed to several factors. Most transport managers are daunted by their mathematical complexity and naturally prefer procedures that can be more easily understood. Many transport departments also lack the necessary computing facilities to cope with the large amounts of calculation the algorithms require. Underlying user resistance, too, is a general feeling that these algorithms produce unrealistic solutions that do not take adequate account of the range of special circumstances that affect local delivery operations.

Over the past decade or so, an increasing number of constraints have been imposed on the movement of delivery vehicles. They have had to contend with an increasing number of route and access restrictions imposed by local authorities for environmental reasons. Where the timing and duration of access restrictions vary between neighbouring towns, their combined impact on vehicle routeing can be particularly severe (Chapman, 1980). Meanwhile, many retailers and wholesalers have reduced the number of hours during the day when they are prepared to receive deliveries (i.e. the *delivery window*) and implemented booking-in systems. There has been a growth in the

199

number of *refusals* (i.e. occasions when delivery vehicles are turned away) and this has forced route planners to devote much more attention to the timing of deliveries. Mounting road congestion is, however, making it harder for vehicles to adhere to strict timetables, particularly as much urban delivery work is done during periods of heavy traffic flow, such as between 08.00 and 12.00 (Robson, 1982). Efforts to reschedule deliveries to take place in the evening ('Operation Moondrop') or very early in the morning ('Operation Dawndrop'), when traffic flows are much lighter, have met with little success (Collins and Pharoah, 1974).

Another major criticism of routeing algorithms is that they attach undue importance to the minimisation of distance. This in itself would be an acceptable objective if delivery costs were a direct function of distance. A large proportion of delivery costs, however, relating mainly to vehicle acquisition, taxation and insurance, are insensitive to distance. These 'standing costs' are affected much more by the number of vehicles than by the distances they travel. More efficient routeing can reduce the time taken to complete delivery rounds, thereby making it possible for a smaller number of lorries to make the required deliveries within the time available. Fleet size is much more dependent, though, on the sizes of load the vehicles carry and this is determined by the assignment of customer orders. The assignment exercise is known as *vehicle scheduling* (or *load planning*) and must be distinguished from vehicle routeing. Cooper and Jessop (1983, p.1) define these terms as follows:

> vehicle scheduling: 'selection of customer drops to be made by a single vehicle and its driver';
>
> vehicle routeing: 'establishing the sequence in which the drops are made by the vehicle on the road network'.

The algorithms outlined earlier effectively combine scheduling and routeing, whereas in practice firms generally handle each operation separately. Scheduling is undertaken at the depot by specialist clerical staff (known as load planners or despatch clerks), but much of the responsibility for routeing is devolved to the driver. Firms are much more concerned about the loading of vehicles than with their routeing between customers. There is a general belief that once customer orders have been allocated to vehicles, working out an efficient route is relatively straightforward. The allocation is usually made on a zonal basis and drivers given an indication of the order in which these zones should be visited. As each zone contains a comparatively small number of customers, routeing within them (sometimes called micro-routeing) is usually left to the driver's discretion, allowing him to exploit his detailed knowledge of local road conditions and

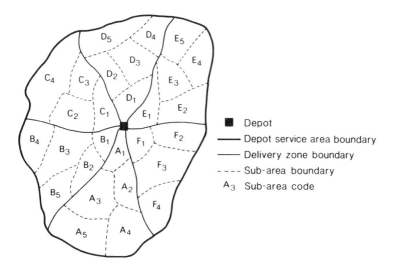

Figure 7.7 Subdivision of depot hinterland into delivery zones
Source: Slater, 1979.

customers' delivery preferences. A survey by the Transport and Road Research Laboratory (TRRL) found that in 80% of cases drivers decide which roads to take (Corcoran, Hitchcock and McMahon, 1980).

Routeing between and within delivery zones is generally much easier in practice than much of the theoretical literature suggests, because customers tend to be clustered in towns and cities. The standard algorithms plot routes around individual customer locations and, in many of the test problems used to evaluate their performance, these locations are randomly dispersed over a wide area. Clusters of customers can, however, be treated as single nodes, greatly reducing the scale of the problem and making it possible to obtain good solutions by subjective judgement.

The efficiency of the routes produced by manual planning methods is critically dependent on the subdivision of hinterlands into delivery zones. This subdivision can be done systematically on the basis of grid squares or more subjectively, taking account of variations in the density of demand and geographical barriers such as hills and estuaries. The latter method is more commonly used and well illustrated by the *simplified delivery system* (Slater, 1979). Under this system, the depot hinterland is divided into approximately wedge-shaped zones, each of which is capable of generating enough work for a single vehicle. These zones are further subdivided in

201

relation to customer groupings and topography. The delivery zones are usually given letter codes and the 'sub-areas' numbered in ascending order moving outwards from the depot (Figure 7.7). It is generally desirable to keep sub-areas quite small. Although this increases the number of sub-areas and makes the initial sorting of orders more laborious, it simplifies the subsequent load planning exercise and the routeing of vehicles within sub-areas. The pattern of sub-areas is physically represented by an array of pigeon holes in the traffic office. Each sub-area is given a separate pigeon hole whose position corresponds to its relative geographical location. Orders destined for customers in a particular sub-area are placed in the appropriate pigeon hole. The scheduler then takes each delivery zone in turn and builds up vehicle loads by working inwards from the most peripheral sub-area. The total weight (or volume) of orders to be delivered in a particular zone may exceed the capacity of a single vehicle, while in another zone a vehicle may be underutilised. To even out variations in vehicle payloads, load planners can have vehicles move between delivery zones in the vicinity of the depot. Additional flexibility is gained by having extra 'floating' vehicles available which are not committed to particular zones but move between them as required. Furthermore, as not all orders need to be delivered on the same day, those with lower priority can be held back to help balance daily workloads.

The main virtues of this method are its simplicity and its ability to ensure that loads are equitably distributed between vehicles. The efficiency of the schedules it produces largely depends on the skill and experience of the load planner and on the variability of the pattern of demand. The framework of delivery zones and sub-areas, within which vehicle scheduling is undertaken, generally remains fixed for many months or even years. The 'routes' formed by linking these sub-areas are, therefore, regarded as 'fixed'. This greatly facilitates the load planning operation, and can enable a driver assigned to a particular delivery zone to become familiar with its road network and to establish a good working relationship with customers. Adherence to fixed routes, however, severely restricts the extent to which the delivery system can be adjusted to accommodate day-to-day variations in the pattern of demand. Delivery zones are usually delimited with reference to the average level of sales in the past, with some allowance for future growth. This average sales pattern can conceal wide short-term variations in the spatial distribution of orders. In the absence of fixed delivery zones, loads can be planned more flexibly on a daily basis to accommodate these variations, with consequent improvements in vehicle utilisation and customer service levels. The adoption of flexible routeing greatly complicates the load planning exercise, though, and can only be carried out effectively with the assistance of a computer.

Computerised route planning

Computerised routeing packages have been available for almost 20 years, but are still used by only a small minority of firms. The 18 routeing and scheduling packages listed by Slater (1986a) in his comprehensive directory of physical distribution software, were used by a total of only 169 British firms. They account for only 6.6% of all commercial software applications in the field of physical distribution. Many firms were discouraged from computerising their route planning by the poor performance of the first generation of packages. The shortcomings of these early packages have been documented by Jones (1976), Menzies (1976) and Mercer *et al.* (1978). Most employed the savings criterion method and as a result produced oddly shaped routes that often made poor use of vehicle capacity. They also failed to take account of the host of special circumstances that, in practice, influence the configuration of a delivery route. The packages, nevertheless, required the use of large computers and often had a slow response time. They were too unwieldy to be used for day-to-day tactical routeing and were generally confined to the strategic planning of fixed routes. The introduction of computerised route planning was also resisted by many despatch clerks who believed that it would result in, at best, a deskilling of their jobs and, at worst, their elimination.

Since the late 1970s, many new routeing packages have been developed which are superior to their predecessors in several respects. Most run on microcomputers which can be acquired and operated much more cheaply than the computing hardware required by the first generation of packages. Their algorithms have also been modified to yield routes that make better use of vehicle capacity, even if this entails longer journeys. Most importantly, they have come to assume a new role in the route-planning operation. Previously, computerised vehicle routeing was promoted as an alternative to manual scheduling methods. It is now accepted that it should supplement rather than replace the load planner's judgement. As Robson (1982, p.19) points out, 'It would be a somewhat dangerous and rather naive approach to simply program the mathematical equations into the computer and expect optimised answers to be produced'. The new packages aim to exploit the load planner's intimate knowledge of the delivery system and practical experience in adjusting delivery arrangements at short notice to changing circumstances. To fulfil this new role, routeing packages have become much more user-friendly and now offer greater scope for altering delivery parameters. Almost all the packages developed since 1980 run interactively and have sufficiently short response times to permit their use for tactical routeing on a daily basis.

Several of the packages can also be used in association with road network data bases, such as Roadnet, so that they not only specify the sequence in which customers should be visited, but also the roads along which the vehicle should travel (Beasley, 1982). This can yield significant reductions in vehicle kilometres, as empirical studies have revealed that, without such guidance, lorry drivers frequently follow routes that are unnecessarily circuitous (Urquhart, 1976; Hasell and Christie, 1978).

It has been claimed that computerised routeing packages can reduce delivery costs by between 10 and 50% (Robson, 1982), though savings of 5-10% seem more credible (Peters, 1986). It is difficult to generalise about the scale of these benefits because they depend on the competence of the load planner, the number of customers to be served and the variability of their demand. Moreover, computer routeing is often introduced as part of a general reorganisation of the delivery system, making it difficult to assess its particular contribution to increased efficiency. In some cases, it has had little impact on delivery costs, but instead allowed firms to improve customer service levels within existing resources (Peters, 1986). The use of computers in this context can also reduce the amount of clerical work, facilitate the tracing of consignments and help managers monitor the performance of the delivery operation. Cooper and Jessop (1983) note that, in the field of route planning, computers are often used more for information management purposes than for problem solving. They relieve despatch clerks of the more tedious and time-consuming tasks of order sorting and arithmetical calculation, enabling them to concentrate on the more skilful job of scheduling. Route planning is, therefore, becoming computer assisted rather than fully computerised and is likely to remain heavily dependent on the judgement of load planners for the foreseeable future. The computer's role will expand, however, as vehicle scheduling becomes more closely integrated with order processing and as more firms are linked into EDI networks. In the longer term, the installation of microcomputers in lorry cabs should make it possible for drivers to replan routes actually during the journey in response to changing circumstances (Rushton, 1984).

Although computer packages have recently been tailored more closely to the practical needs of the load planner, they are still only used by a small minority of firms to plan tactical routes on a daily basis. Of the 30 firms sampled by Peters (1986), only 4 used them in this capacity. This may reflect an unwillingness to change operating practices rather than an aversion to new technology. To exploit the advantages of computerised routeing, firms must abandon fixed routeing and organise their delivery operations more flexibly. For most firms, this entails upsetting accepted working practices and renegotiating union agreements. Many have yet to be convinced that the likely benefits justify such reorganisation.

Nominated-day delivery schemes

All forms of route planning can be applied more easily and with better results where the pattern of demand remains stable. The most effective way of stabilising the demands on a local delivery system is by arranging to have vehicles visit individual customers only on nominated (or specified) days. Each customer is informed that he can receive a delivery only on a particular day within a weekly, fortnightly or monthly cycle, and that orders have to be submitted a certain period (say, 4-5 working days) in advance. At present, it is common practice in most trades for retailers' orders to be submitted at irregular intervals. As manufacturers promise to deliver the goods within a certain number of days of the order being received, the timing of the order will largely determine on which day of the week the delivery is made. Much of the day-to-day variation in the spatial distribution of delivery points therefore stems from customers submitting orders in an uncontrolled and irregular manner. In many cases, the irregularity of the inward flow of orders results from retailers postponing the replenishment of their stocks until supplies are almost exhausted, thereby minimising the amount of stock they need to hold. This, therefore, has the effect of transmitting fluctuations in the level of consumer demand back along the distribution channel and impairing the efficiency of shop deliveries.

By imposing more discipline on customers' ordering habits and making service level guarantees conditional on orders being submitted in accordance with a specified timetable, manufacturers can exert much greater control over the distribution of points requiring delivery on any given day. This produces a more stable framework within which vehicle routes can be planned (Bowersox, 1978). By implementing a system of specified-day deliveries, Cadbury-Schweppes were able to reduce the number of vehicle kilometres per case by 9.3% (Mercer *et al.*, 1978).

Despite these benefits, there is considerable resistance to the implementation of nominated-day delivery schemes. Much of it comes from marketing and sales staff who argue that, by forcing customers to accept a rigid timetabling of ordering and delivery, it weakens their company's competitive position and jeopardises sales (Christopher and Wills, 1974). In many firms where marketing considerations dominate distribution planning, the fear of losing sales usually outweighs the desire to improve the efficiency of the delivery system. Nominated-day schemes can, however, enhance the reliability of deliveries and, as explained in Chapter 5, this is often a critical factor in customers' evaluation of suppliers. These schemes can also lower unit delivery costs and thereby help support a more extensive network of shop delivery than would otherwise be economically feasible. The fears of sales staff can be partly allayed by the fact that firms, such as Cadbury-Schweppes, which have adopted such a scheme have been able to maintain or improve their trading position in highly competitive markets.

Changing pattern of local delivery

The nature of the vehicle routeing problem has changed in recent years as a result of structural change in the distributive system and increasing constraints on lorry movements. As reported in Chapter 2, there has been a sharp decline in the number of retail outlets in most trades since 1960, as sales have become concentrated in larger premises. At the same time, many manufacturers and wholesalers have curtailed deliveries to smaller customers unable to order goods in sufficiently large quantities. While these trends have reduced the total number of delivery points across the country, the spatial concentration of storage and distribution operations has resulted in these points being divided among fewer depots (Mole, 1979). It is likely, though, that on balance, the number of customers served by each depot has declined, reducing the complexity of vehicle scheduling problems. Route planning has been further simplified by the increase in drop size and consequent reduction in the number of drops per journey. This trend has been partly offset, though, by increases in vehicle size and the introduction of new handling systems, both of which have raised the number of drops that can be made within the constraints of a single journey. The consolidation of deliveries by wholesalers, multiple retailers and distribution contractors has greatly increased the proportion of supplies distributed directly to individual outlets on single-drop journeys. These journeys do not require route planning in the normal sense.

Ironically, while changes in the internal organisation of physical distribution have tended to simplify the routeing problem, external factors such as road congestion, access restrictions and booking-in schemes have had the opposite effect. For many firms, therefore, the delivery of goods to final point of sale remains a major source of inefficiency and frustration.

Chapter eight

International distribution

Manufacturers invariably find it more difficult to distribute their products to foreign customers than to supply their home markets. International freight movements are generally longer, often involve the use of more than one transport mode and are subject to delay at national borders. Special care must be taken to ensure that they conform to transport regulations in the countries through which they pass. To compensate for longer order lead times, international distribution channels generally contain more stock than their domestic counterparts. Exporting firms frequently encounter distribution channels in other countries that contrast with those to which they are accustomed in their home markets. Foreign wholesalers and retailers often have different service level expectations and purchasing behaviour (Stock and Lambert, 1982). Surrounding the whole operation is an enormous amount of paperwork. This is a reflection of the large number of agencies involved in international trading and a measure of the degree of detailed planning required. Much of this planning is complicated by the need to conduct business in foreign languages with foreign currencies in accordance with foreign laws and customs.

Given these difficulties, it is, perhaps, not surprising that many manufacturers do not attempt to enter foreign markets or avoid taking responsibility for international logistics by exporting goods on an *ex-works* or *free on board* (FOB) basis and having the foreign customer arrange the delivery. Other firms marketing their products abroad externalise the organisation of the distribution function by employing freight forwarders or export agencies. Many fail, however, to evaluate the quality and cost of these external services, and to enquire if they could be provided more cheaply and effectively on an own-account basis. In many exporting firms, international physical distribution has not received the attention it deserves. The staff responsible are often inadequately trained and lack managerial clout.

The management of national and international distribution is usually divided between different departments, limiting opportunities for co-ordinating the two operations and for imposing similar cost and performance standards. This partly explains why it is only recently that the principles of physical distribution management, which were developed and refined mainly with respect to distribution in a single national market, have been applied in an international context. Giving them an international dimension has proved difficult as there are many more cost and service elements to be considered. In adopting a Total Cost approach to international distribution, firms must make more complex trade-offs, not only between the 'functional' costs of transport, stockholding, handling and packaging, but also with various 'trade barrier' costs (Cook and Burley, 1985). The low managerial status of international physical distribution has impeded higher-level trade-offs with export marketing and production functions. Physical distribution is often seen, unfortunately, in a supportive role and not regarded as a key element in the export marketing mix (Slater, 1980). As in the case of domestic distribution in the 1960s and 1970s, though, the importance of international logistics is gradually being recognised.

International logistics has expanded in line with the growth of world trade and in the number and scale of multinational companies. It is of particular importance to countries, such as the UK, that are heavily dependent on international trade. The competitiveness of British manufactured goods in overseas markets has, nevertheless, been impaired by long and uncertain delivery times. A study of firms selling British goods in Europe identified poor delivery as the main factor limiting their sales of these products (Christopher, 1981). When Turnbull (1985) invited 416 purchasing executives in France, Germany, Italy, Sweden and the UK to rate suppliers in terms of five delivery criteria (speed, reliability, degree of integration with buyers' operations, availability of local stocks and the monitoring of goods in transit) he found general dissatisfaction with the standard of delivery in all the countries surveyed, but the most serious criticism was levelled at British suppliers. He concluded that:

> The level of delivery service of British suppliers on four of the five factors can only be described as appalling. It is on delivery speed and reliability, which are perhaps the most important features of delivery service, where the UK reputation is worst (p.45).

Efforts have been made by NEDO (1977) and the British Overseas Trade Board to encourage British exporters to improve the marketing and distribution of their products in other countries, though the UK government, like most other Western governments (Czinkota, 1982), provides them with very little practical assistance in the field of international logistics. It is very difficult to assess quantitatively the loss of export revenue resulting from poor delivery performance, though, in many cases, it is likely to exceed the cost of overcoming deficiencies in international distribution operations.

In the remainder of this chapter, we shall review the options open to firms marketing their products in other countries. A similar framework will be adopted to that applied in the previous six chapters to distribution within a single market. The export of unitised traffic from Britain to other European countries will be used to exemplify the decisions firms must make in the field of international distribution.

Export marketing

It is important to distinguish the way in which a firm gains access to a foreign market from its subsequent use of distribution channels within that market. This is not to deny that these two aspects of export marketing are closely inter-related.

Market penetration

Five methods of market entry are commonly used in the export of consumer goods:

Indirect exporting

This essentially involves selling goods in the home country to agencies which then market them abroad. Two major types of agency fulfilling this role are the buying offices of foreign wholesale/retail organisations and international trading companies (Terpstra, 1978). The best examples of the latter are the Japanese trading companies, such as Mitsubishi, which today handle a large proportion of Japanese exports, and European trading companies, mostly of colonial origin, which still have a major presence in Third World countries. By indirectly exporting, manufacturers are relieved of the effort, expense and worry of international distribution, but must often accept lower prices and smaller sales than could be obtained by direct export, and forego the experience they could have gained in overseas markets.

Piggyback schemes

It has become increasingly common for manufacturers to channel non-competing products through the foreign distribution systems of other manufacturers. The so-called 'rider' in such piggyback arrangements gets ready access to foreign markets along established distribution channels, while the 'carrier' is able to spread the overhead costs of its marketing operations and to tempt distributors with a wider product range and larger sales volume. Many British electrical manufacturers, for example, now supplement their own product ranges with imported goods and market them under their trade names. In 1984, 43% of small electrical appliances imported into the UK were 'badged' with British manufacturers' trade marks and channelled through their distribution systems (Euromonitor, 1986).

Contracting out the export marketing function to specialist agencies

These agencies are known by various names, such as export management companies (EMCs) or export brokers, and differ in the range of services they offer. Most take full responsibility for organising the marketing and distribution of clients' products in particular countries. Unlike trading companies, they tend not to assume ownership of the goods and instead charge a percentage commission on sales. They, therefore, act as brokers rather than merchant wholesalers. From the client's standpoint they provide a superior service to trading companies in that they generally give the client greater say in how and where the products are marketed, relay more information about foreign sales and do not handle competing products. By undertaking export marketing for several firms, they can perform the task more economically than individual in-house export departments, particularly those of smaller firms. Many EMCs have, nevertheless, been criticised for being too small and too limited in their penetration of foreign markets. Ironically, their growth can be inhibited by success, because once a client's foreign sales reach a certain level, it often feels justified in mounting its own export marketing operation thus depriving the EMC of further business (Terpstra, 1978).

In the early stages of international marketing, most firms seek to minimise management effort, capital investment and risk by adopting one of the previous three strategies. Keegan (1980) suggested that once the annual value of exports exceeded between $200,000 and $500,000, a company could justify the establishment of its own export management department. Czinkota (1982) set this threshold level of exports at 7.5% of total turnover or $100,000 per annum. Internalisation of the export management function gives firms much greater control over the marketing mix and closer communication with foreign customers. Having established an export department, a firm must still decide if it wishes to use foreign distributors or to extend its control still further by setting up sales offices in other countries.

Use of foreign distributors

In most foreign markets there are many different types of agency available to organise the distribution of imported goods. Some take title to the goods, while others work on a sale and commission basis. Some only engage in promotion and sales, leaving physical distribution to subcontractors, while others provide an integrated marketing and distribution service. Ross (1972) has compiled a fairly exhaustive list of the factors likely to influence the choice of foreign distributors, distinguishing those internal to the exporting firm, such as product design and marketing policy, from external factors such as the geography of the foreign country, its market size, retail structure and legal system. He presents an 'empirical framework' within which firms can systematically select foreign distributors by matching their requirements against the attributes of available distributors within external market constraints. Sometimes, manufacturers give a single agency exclusive distribution rights within a country. It is often advantageous, though, to divide responsibility among several agencies on a regional or channel basis (McKinnon, 1986c). This can increase market exposure and avoid over-reliance on a single distributor.

Establishment of foreign sales offices

Firms can either build up a foreign sales operation from scratch or acquire a ready-made sales network by buying out a distributor. Sales offices organise marketing and distribution in one or more foreign markets, forging direct links with wholesalers and retailers. Exporters vary in the extent to which they decentralise marketing and logistical functions to foreign sales offices. Some grant them the freedom to decide marketing policy and to distribute other manufacturers' products on a third-party basis. As foreign sales expand, sales offices generally become more autonomous, often acquiring the status of independent subsidiaries. Eventually, the growth of export sales may justify the establishment of a production facility in the foreign market.

Choice of foreign marketing channels

The selection of an EMC, piggyback manufacturer or foreign distributor can largely determine through which foreign marketing channels a firm's products flow. Channel preferences must, therefore, be taken into account in formulating a market entry strategy. The establishment of a sales office in a foreign market confers greater control over the choice and manipulation of marketing channels.

Keegan (1980, p.331) contends that, 'As distribution channels in markets around the world are among the most highly differentiated aspects of national marketing systems...channels strategy is one of the most challenging and difficult components of an international marketing program'. A firm importing goods finds it most cost-effective to use channels in which direct links with a few intermediaries afford extensive retail exposure. The UK market is generally considered very permeable to imported goods as, in most consumer goods trades, distribution channels are short and characterised by a high degree of concentration at the retail level. In many sectors of the market, such as footwear, electrical goods, photographic equipment and cosmetics, the ten largest retailers account for over 50% of total sales (Business Statistics Office, 1986), and, in many cases, these firms deal directly with foreign suppliers. In other countries, such as Italy and Japan, independent stores hold a much larger share of the retail market and receive most of their supplies via wholesalers.

Manufacturers accustomed to dealing directly with retailers in their home markets are often averse to using foreign wholesalers. Establishing direct links with foreign retailers is often unprofitable, though, especially where sales volumes are low and the retail system highly fragmented. Moreover, in some countries, wholesalers refuse to handle the products of manufacturers that sell directly to retailers, preventing foreign suppliers from combining the use of direct and indirect channels.

The concentration of sales at the retail and wholesale levels tends to increase with economic development, while the use of intermediaries gradually diminishes. Terpstra (1978, p.366), in fact, argues that, 'Since the nature of wholesaling and retailing is related to economic growth, the marketer can follow economic growth in the world markets as a rough guide to predict distribution changes'. The main exception to this relationship has been Japan, which, despite its impressive industrial achievements, retains a very complex distribution system that 'seems by Western standards archaic, inefficient and wasteful' (Adams and Kobayashi, quoted in Shimaguchi, 1978, p.1). This system is characterised by a multitude of small wholesale and retail outlets and heavy reliance on indirect channels comprising two or more wholesale intermediaries (Ikeda, 1974). Relative to their Western counterparts, Japanese distributors hold small stocks, partly because they lack working capital, but also because high land values severely restrict the amount of storage space they can afford. They, therefore, require frequent deliveries of small quantities and expect suppliers to grant them long repayment periods. This makes it very expensive for foreign manufacturers to attempt to streamline the distribution of their products by bypassing one or more of the wholesale levels (Ross, 1983). The use of existing indirect channels can also prove unsatisfactory as they are often closely aligned with large Japanese manufacturing firms. Furthermore, Shimaguchi argues that, to market their goods effectively in Japan, foreign firms must appreciate the socio-cultural setting within which distribution takes place.

There are several examples of firms creating their own systems of distribution in export markets by setting up or acquiring wholesale and/or retail outlets. Singer, the American sewing machine company, for instance, established an overseas network of retail outlets, while Benetton, the Italian fashion clothing firm, has more recently pioneered a system of retail franchising throughout Europe and North America. Other multinationals, such as Avon Cosmetics, have extended their control over foreign distribution right to customers' homes and avoided using indigenous channels.

There is no single optimal strategy for marketing products in other countries. Exporters must adapt their marketing strategies to foreign commercial environments and resist the temptation simply to transplant practices that have proved successful in the home market.

Pricing schemes

The division of responsibility for international physical distribution between exporter and foreign distributor/customer is largely determined by the terms on which products are sold. The main international terms of trade were originally defined by the International Chamber of Commerce in 1936 and are widely known as *Incoterms*. These terms differ in the degree to which they incorporate distribution costs. Where the exporter quotes an *ex-works* price, the foreign customer must bear the freight and insurance costs. Some exporters charging *ex-works* prices are, nevertheless, prepared to organise delivery at the customers' expense. *Delivered* or *franco domicile* prices, on the other hand, include all distribution costs to a point in the foreign market specified by the customer. Most exports of manufactured goods are sold on terms that fall between these two extremes. *Free-on-board* (FOB) pricing generally results in responsibility being shared between exporter and customer. The term free on board should be accompanied by a location, such as 'inland port', indicating the point to which the seller's responsibility extends. Where this point is a port, the FOB price includes stevedoring; *free alongside ship* (FAS) indicates that the price only includes delivery to the quayside. *Free carrier* (FRC), another variant of FOB, is being used increasingly when the seller pays for transport to a carrier's depot. *Free-frontier* pricing applies to overland movements between adjoining states, where responsibility for transport transfers from

Table 8.1   Export pricing schemes used by British manufacturers

| | Gumbrell survey[a] | | CPDM survey[b] | |
	% consignments	% export value	% firms[c]	% firms
Ex-works	17.5	11.5	18	26
FOB	30.0	29.0	35	27
C and F	15.5	10.5	13	7
CIF	26.0	38.5	23	22
Delivered	8.0	10.5	10	18
Other	3.0	—	5[d]	—

Notes: a. Results quoted in Davies, 1984, p.144.
  b. Based on survey of British firms exporting to north-west Europe.
  c. Most frequently used terms.
  d. No dominant terms.

Sources: Davies, 1984; CPDM, 1984b.

seller to buyer at the international border. The use of the word 'free' in these terms is, of course, misleading as the exporter's share of the transport cost is simply absorbed in the selling price. Where an exporter pays for the movement of his goods by sea or air to a foreign port or airport, the term *cost, insurance, freight* (CIF) is commonly used or *cost and freight* (C and F) where the buyer incurs the cost of insurance.

Gumbrell measured the relative importance of different pricing schemes by asking a sample of 97 British exporters which they used most frequently (Davies, 1984). Just over half used mainly *ex-works* or FOB, while only 10% charged delivered prices for the bulk of their foreign sales (Table 8.1). *Ex-works* and FOB were found to be less important in terms of the numbers of export consignments and their aggregate value. Roughly 60% of the firms' exports (by value) were transported at least as far as the foreign port of entry at the exporter's expense. A more narrowly focused survey by the CPDM (1984b) of British firms exporting to north-west Europe revealed slightly greater use of delivered pricing but an almost identical dependence on *ex-works* and FOB pricing (Table 8.1). The CPDM argued that too few exporters quote delivered prices. Similar opinions were expressed by NEDO (1977).

Delivered pricing yields numerous benefits, both for the exporting firm and its national economy:

1. The exporter gains control over international distribution and can use it as an instrument of marketing, ensuring that the level of customer service and final selling price are competitive. Knowledge of distribution possibilities and costs strengthens the exporter's hand in negotiations with foreign distributors and customers.

2. Exports are traded on the same basis as goods manufactured within the foreign market, which are usually sold at delivered prices.
3. Most customers have a preference for delivered pricing and this can influence their purchasing behaviour. For example, in a survey of firms in the American babywear industry, Gill (1979) found that 86.2% of buyers preferred to purchase goods at delivered prices.
4. The exporter may be able to obtain bulk or loyalty discounts from freight forwarders, carriers or shipping lines and, hence, provide cheaper transport than the foreign customer can obtain. This effectively reduces the final selling price of its products. The vast majority of buyers consulted by Gill associated delivered prices with lower freight rates.
5. Delivered pricing overcomes the problem of carriers abusing FRC arrangements, either by distributing costs unfairly between exporter and foreign buyer or overcharging both (Walker, 1986).
6. The exporting nation's balance of payments can benefit through increased foreign sales, the greater use of domestic carriers and the purchase of international distribution services in its currency.

Walker describes how, partly by switching to a system of delivered pricing, Thorn-EMI were able to increase their sales of electrical appliances in Belgium by 50%, while reducing transport costs by 48%. A survey by TNT-IPEC of firms changing over to delivered pricing found that on average their level of sales or orders rose by 19% (Cooper, Browne and Gretton, 1987).

Many manufacturers are, nevertheless, still reluctant to use delivered pricing. Some do not wish to take on new managerial commitments in the complicated field of international logistics. Calculating international distribution costs can be a very difficult task, while quoting prices in other currencies makes the profitability of foreign sales sensitive to exchange rate variations. In trades where it is customary for all suppliers to sell *ex-works* or FOB, individual firms are unwilling to switch unilaterally to delivered pricing. In some cases, such a move would be resisted by customers, because the choice of selling terms does not always rest with the exporter. Foreign customers can stipulate that they want to purchase goods *ex-works* or FOB and thereby assume responsibility for all or part of the delivery. This represents an extension of their control back along the international distribution channel, enabling them to demand larger discounts and to improve the reliability of incoming deliveries.

The export strategy of many British manufacturing firms is a hangover from the days when most of their sales were to distant overseas markets, whose remoteness and often primitive distribution systems discouraged the use of delivered pricing. Since the UK joined the European Community (EC) in 1973, there has been a steady increase in its exports to other member countries. The proximity of these foreign markets, the removal of tariff barriers and the availability of unitised through-transport services ought to have promoted greater use of delivered pricing. It appears, however, that firms have been slow to adjust their pricing schemes to the new international trading conditions, and that few have come to regard the 'common market' simply as an extension of their home market. This may be partly attributed to Britain's island status and colonial past.

Heavy reliance on *ex-works* and FOB pricing may not, however, be placing British manufacturers at such a competitive disadvantage as is often claimed. Many firms that quote FOB terms in their standard international price list in fact offer 'FOB plus services', meaning that they will organise full delivery for an additional charge. Furthermore, the limited survey evidence available suggests that exporters in some other European countries are, if anything, less likely to use delivered or CIF pricing (Davies, 1984). It is estimated, for example, that 60-65% of French exports and 40% of Italian exports are sold *ex-works* (Cooper *et al.*, 1987).

Freight forwarding

It is possible for exporters quoting delivered or CIF prices to avoid becoming directly involved in international distribution by employing freight forwarders. These agencies vary enormously in the range of services they offer, making freight forwarding a notoriously difficult activity to define. In essence, they act as brokers, purchasing and booking transport services on exporters' behalf and preparing the necessary documentation. Some can also provide road transport, storage, groupage and packaging services, blurring the distinction between freight forwarding, road haulage and public warehousing. Many forwarders specialise in the use of either air-freight or surface modes. They also differ in the range of commodities they handle and in the geographical extent of their operations.

Estimates of the number of freight forwarding firms in the UK range from 'over a thousand' to 2,725 (Davies, 1984, p.167). Their size distribution appears highly skewed, with the 40 largest firms handling around 80% of the UK forwarding business (Highsted, 1980). It is relatively easy to set up a freight forwarding operation in the UK as the initial capital outlay is small and entry into the industry is neither regulated, as in the US, nor restricted to those with professional qualifications, as in some other European countries. Consequently, the freight forwarding industry is one of intense competition, relatively low profitability and a high turnover of firms.

The use of freight forwarders carries several advantages. It allows the exporting firm to concentrate its management resources on 'mainstream' activities, such as production and marketing. Forwarders often have greater accumulated knowledge and expertise in export distribution than exists in-house. By consolidating the transport demands of several clients, they can obtain larger discounts and rebates from hauliers, shipping companies and airlines. Those providing a groupage service assemble several exporters' traffic into more economically sized trailer or container loads.

The greatest disadvantage of using a freight forwarder is loss of control. Exporters have difficulty co-ordinating the international logistics function with their other activities when it is under the control of an outside agency. As Davies (1984, p.38) points out, freight forwarders have traditionally been 'dealt with at arms' length'. Some forwarders have, nevertheless, adopted what he calls a *reverse integration strategy* forming much closer relationships with exporters and having their staff actually work within the client firm. This enables them to respond more effectively to internal pressures, though many exporters will not accept such intrusion. A more common strategy has been that of *forward integration*, where the exporter bypasses the forwarder to deal directly with transport operators. Soorikan (1974, p.36) argues that exporters have been slow to take this initiative. He believes that the existence of a 'vast freight forwarding operation' is the result of exporters' 'unwillingness, particularly outside the United States, to face the challenge of physical distribution system analysis'. Slater (1980), too, contends that manufacturers have traditionally been overdependent on freight forwarders. The propensity of exporters to internalise the forwarding operation is, however, largely a function of size. As manufacturers expand their export sales they tend to reduce their reliance on forwarders. This tendency, combined with the increasing concentration of export business in the hands of fewer, larger firms, has reduced the demand for forwarders' traditional brokerage services. Some forwarders have responded by adopting a forward integration strategy themselves and diversifying into road haulage and storage.

Some exporters have expressed dissatisfaction with freight forwarding services and, in some cases, this is likely to have reinforced the decision to internalise the international distribution function. A common complaint is that forwarders misrepresent the transport service they arrange by failing to reveal the degree of subcontracting and underestimating delivery times (Highsted, 1980).

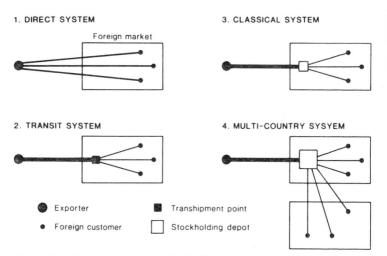

Figure 8.1 International physical distribution systems
Adapted from Schary, 1984

Some also have a poor record on documentation and on providing progress information about consignments in transit.

Despite these criticisms, freight forwarders still handle a large proportion of UK exports. Davies (1984) estimated that forwarders were responsible for between 80 and 95% of air freight and around 50% of export traffic travelling by surface modes. This gives freight forwarders a dominant role in international logistics and, as Highsted (1980, p.19) observes, 'The efficiency and cost effectiveness of a chosen freight agent must, in the end, reflect on the esteem of British exporters and their competitiveness abroad'.

International physical distribution systems

Exporters controlling the movement of their goods to foreign distributors and customers must establish an international system of physical distribution. The structure of this system, like its domestic counterpart, is largely determined by the spatial organisation of the stockholding and break-bulk functions. On this basis, Picard (1982) has differentiated four systems (Figure 8.1):

1. Direct system

Stocks are centralised in the home country and deliveries made directly to foreign agencies and final customers. This is the international equivalent of Bowersox's direct system of distribution in

218

a single national market. Its main advantages are that it obviates the need for foreign warehousing and permits greater centralisation of inventory. Supplying goods directly from the factory, though, results in long order lead times. Transit times can be reduced by using faster transport services, but these are more expensive, particularly as the urgency of deliveries limits the scope for consolidating orders into larger loads. The length of the supply line makes the delivery vulnerable to disruption and delay. The packaging and documentation costs of this system can also be significantly higher than those of alternative systems.

2. Transit system

Exports are channelled through a non-stockholding, break-bulk point in a foreign market. Freight can then be transported more economically in greater bulk to the foreign market and disaggregated into individual orders much closer to the foreign customer. Depending on the pattern of flow, the resulting transport cost savings can more than offset the additional terminal and handling costs. Otherwise, the transit system has similar advantages and disadvantages to the direct system.

3. Classical system:

Stocks are dispersed to depots in foreign markets. This corresponds to Bowersox's echelon system and yields similar benefits:

(i) Orders can be delivered more rapidly from the foreign warehouse than the factory, helping to generate additional sales.
(ii) The presence of readily available stocks in the foreign market can be reassuring for distributors and customers.
(iii) Freight can be despatched to the foreign market with less urgency, permitting the use of cheaper transport modes and offering greater scope for load consolidation.
(iv) As the international movement of stock is an intracompany transfer less documentation is required and smaller import duties payable.

The classical system's main shortcoming is the expense of acquiring or renting storage space abroad and of maintaining the higher level of stock required by a decentralised system. Handling and local delivery costs are also higher than in a direct system.

4. Multi-country system

A single foreign warehouse supplies customers in several countries. By centralising the foreign stockholding operation in fewer locations,

Table 8.2   Factors influencing the choice of international physical
             distribution system

Product-related	Exporter-related
value density	location of plants
perishability	firm size
length of product life cycle	investment priorities
product range	export marketing strategy
turnover rate	corporate structure
Market-related	*Environment-related*
no. of distributors/customers	standard of infrastructure
size of distributors/customers	political/economic stability
level of customer service	government regulations
volume of sales	customs constraints
quality of distributors	availability, cost and quality of
growth prospects	distribution contractors

exporters can reduce inventory costs, partially overcoming the inherent weakness of the classical system. This is achieved, however, at the expense of making the routeing of international deliveries much more circuitous and significantly increasing transport costs outward from the foreign warehouse. Long transit times to peripheral parts of the international hinterland may jeopardise sales. Difficulties can also arise in co-ordinating the activities and finances of foreign sales offices drawing supplies from a single multi-country warehouse. Ideally, such a warehouse should be located in a free trade zone, so that exports destined for customers in other countries are exempt from local taxes and duties.

Table 8.2 groups under four headings the numerous factors likely to affect the choice of international physical distribution system. As many of the factors vary between foreign markets, it is common for firms to employ different systems in different countries. Several systems can be used in parallel to serve a single foreign market, with, for instance, large customers receiving bulk deliveries directly from centrally held stocks in the home country and smaller outlets obtaining supplies from a local warehouse. As foreign sales grow, emphasis generally shifts from direct and transit systems to more decentralised systems capable of supporting denser delivery networks and providing a higher level of customer service.

Modal options

Exporters who retain control of the transport function have a wide range of modal options. Many international movements involve the

Table 8.3 Relative importance of different forms of unitised traffic[a] between the UK and other European Community countries, 1985

	Exports		Imports	
	% value	% tonnage	% value	% tonnage
Road trailer (RoRo)				
Powered:	49.0 ⎫	34.0 ⎫	48.9 ⎫	33.6 ⎫
	⎬ 73.1	⎬ 77.3	⎬ 78.6	⎬ 73.1
Unaccompanied:	24.1 ⎭	43.3 ⎭	29.7 ⎭	39.5 ⎭
Containers (LoLo)	9.8	19.4	12.1	24.1
Rail Wagons	0.6	1.9	0.1	2.6
Air	16.3	0.6	8.3	0.2

Note: a. Excludes post, tax-free cars, continental shelf and Irish land boundary traffic.

Adapted from Cooper *et al.*, 1987, p.7.

use of more than one transport mode: this is almost inevitable where the foreign market is 'overseas'. Choices must then be made between:

1. sea and air as the international/intercontinental medium;
2. road, rail and canal networks for inland feeder services;
3. numerous systems of intermodal transfer.

Given the abundance of possible modal permutations, each with its individual cost and performance characteristics, it is difficult for an exporting firm to establish which is best suited to its particular transport requirement. Many firms, therefore, delegate responsibility for modal selection to freight forwarders. As many of these agencies specialise in the use of certain modes, consignors often exhibit a modal preference in their choice of forwarder. Forwarders can still, nevertheless, provide valuable advice on the selection of specific carriers and services.

The vast majority of manufactured goods are today exported in unitised loads. This means that they are transported and transhipped in sealed, rigid boxes either with wheels (e.g. road trailers, rail wagons) or without (e.g. ISO containers). Unitisation offers major advantages over the loose handling of individual packages (Goertz, 1976). It facilitates intermodal transfer and removes the need for enclosed storage space at ports and other freight terminals. It also reduces the risk of the goods being damaged or stolen while in transit. In 1985, about 27% of the freight tonnage passing between the UK and other EC countries was unitised, but this represented 71% of Britain's visible trade with the EC in terms of value (Cooper *et al.*, 1987). Non-unitised traffic, carried by general cargo vessels, comprised mainly bulk products of low-value density, such as raw materials and fuel. We shall confine our attention here to the modes of unitised transport.

Table 8.3 shows the relative importance of the different types of unitised traffic in UK trade with other EC countries. Between 1975 and 1985, the amount of freight carried by road trailer rose by 160%, increasing its share of unitised traffic from 54 to 75%. Over the same period, the amount of trade handled by containers fell by 7%, leaving them with only around 22% of unitised freight. Only a tiny proportion of UK-EC trade crosses the Channel in rail wagons, though the railways have a much greater role in moving international traffic to and from the ports. The airlines too carry a very small quantity of freight, but its high-value density gives them a significant share of total trade when measured by value.

The two most popular units of international freight movement, containers and road trailers, have very different operational characteristics and cost structures (PSERC, 1981). Containers have to be lifted on and off vessels by a gantry crane (LoLo system), whereas trailers can roll on and off ferries along ramps (RoRo system). LoLo ships have a lower capital cost than RoRo ferries of similar capacity. They can be operated at lower cost per unit kilometre, partly because containers can be stacked and thereby make more efficient use of hold space. LoLo vessels can also achieve higher load factors, because, unlike RoRo ferries, they do not have to adhere to fixed schedules and can have their sailing times adjusted to match incoming traffic flows. LoLo terminals, however, are more expensive to construct, equip and operate. Loading and unloading containers is much slower than driving trailers on and off RoRo vessels. RoRo ramps can carry up to 50 trailers per hour, whereas gantry cranes at LoLo ports seldom handle more than 20-25 units per hour. RoRo ferries can, therefore, achieve a much faster turnaround, spending more time at sea and compensating for their lower load factors. Indeed, even allowing for their poorer space utilisation, RoRo ferries can achieve twice the productivity of container vessels on voyages of less than 100-200 miles. LoLo systems have a comparative advantage over longer distances, where vessel operating costs are not only lower than those of RoRo ferries, but low enough to offset their higher terminal costs. Both types of operation yield economies of scale, principally as a result of the spreading of fixed terminal costs over larger traffic volumes. Scale economies are greater in the case of RoRo terminals. For example, a berth for RoRo traffic capable of handling 150-200,000 trailers per annum can have a lower capital cost than and similar labour costs to a LoLo container terminal with only a quarter of this capacity (Garratt, 1981). As the volume of road trailer traffic has expanded, RoRo ferries have increased their cost advantage, particularly on shorter sea routes. The growth of private car traffic on the Channel and North Sea routes has also helped RoRo ferry operators capture a larger share of the freight market. It has enabled them to increase the frequency of sailings and, as the marginal cost of providing extra capacity for road trailers on car ferries is small, to offer more competitive freight rates.

Containers

By comparison with other forms of unitisation, the container's main advantages are its multimodal compatibility and its ability to be efficiently stowed in ships and stacked at terminals. The use of containers has, nevertheless, several drawbacks (Allcock, 1980). Reference has already been made to their relatively high handling costs. They are also subject to longer delays at ports than road trailers. To help them withstand rough handling, they are constructed of thick metal, but this raises their tare weight and reduces their maximum payload. ISO containers also have less cubic capacity than road trailers of similar length, reducing their relative suitability for low-density products. They are also too narrow to take a full complement of European-standard (or Euro-) pallets.

Containers can be moved to and from LoLo ports by road or rail. British Rail has developed a much more extensive container system than its European counterparts, largely because its network cannot accommodate conventional piggyback services. Container movements to and from continental Europe and Ireland account for approximately 20% of BR's Freightliner business and exceed its volume of internal UK traffic. A comparable rail-based container delivery system is operated on the European mainland by Intercontainer, an agency jointly sponsored by eleven national railway administrations.

Road trailers

Road trailers crossing between Britain and the European mainland can either be accompanied by a tractor unit and driver (known as a 'powered' unit) or shipped unaccompanied. In the latter case, the ferry operator generally takes responsibility for towing the trailer on and off the vessel. The trailer is then forwarded to its final destination either by a foreign haulier or on a rail piggyback service. In 1986, 54.6% of trailers moving between Britain and the European mainland were powered, the ratio of accompanied to unaccompanied having remained fairly stable for over a decade (Department of Transport, 1987).

Accompanied services are more easily organised, as the driver can control the movement of the export consignment from door to door. He can usually accelerate its passage through customs, get the trailer

Table 8.4 Road trailer traffic on sea routes between Britain and the European mainland, 1986

	% Powered	% Unaccompanied
Straits of Dover	84.2	15.8
English Channel	63.6	36.4
North Sea	18.4	81.6
All routes	54.6	45.6

Source: Department of Transport, 1987.

onto an earlier ferry sailing and reduce the waiting time at the foreign port. Accompanied deliveries are therefore faster, reducing order lead times while improving the utilisation of trailer units (Hayter, 1980). Express services are invariably accompanied. With the driver present throughout the journey, there is less risk of the load being damaged or stolen and greater opportunity for making multiple drops and collecting return loads. The main disadvantage of an accompanied delivery is the high fixed cost involved in having the driver and tractor unit make the sea crossing. This inflates the ferry charges and represents an unproductive use of driver and vehicle time. Firms operating accompanied services are, therefore, under strong pressure to maximise the utilisation of their vehicles by achieving rapid turnaround. This is reflected by the heavy concentration of powered units on the Channel routes, particularly out of Dover, on which sailings are very frequent and crossing times short (Table 8.4).

Unaccompanied services are generally inferior in terms of transit time, trailer utilisation and consignment care, but are more economical, especially on the longer North Sea routes. Cooper *et al.* (1987) observe that they tend to be used for lower-value products requiring less urgent delivery. Their operational requirements are quite different from those of driver-accompanied deliveries. They need fewer tractor units and drivers, but more trailers. Although turnaround time is less critical for unaccompanied trailers, firms, nevertheless, aim to minimise their stock of trailers by retrieving them from foreign carriers as quickly as possible. They must also ensure that the tractors and drivers which shuttle trailers to and from the ports are fully utilised. This often entails deploying them part of the time in domestic haulage. Firms operating unaccompanied services must also arrange the collection and delivery of their trailers in foreign territory and establish an overseas communication network through which information can be relayed on their progress.

Altogether, the international movement of unaccompanied trailers demands a higher level of organisation and, consequently, tends to be handled by larger firms, many of which are vertically integrated with

224

freight forwarders, domestic haulage contractors or shipping lines. In contrast, many of the international hauliers providing accompanied services operate few vehicles and have very limited managerial resources. As there are few economies of scale in accompanied international haulage, these small carriers can compete successfully with larger operators.

Until recently, the growth of accompanied services outwards from the UK was inhibited by a lack of international haulage permits. Most European countries only grant entry to foreign hauliers in possession of either a *bilateral* or *multilateral permit*. (These permits are not required by own-account operators moving their own traffic.) Each bilateral permit enables a haulier to make a single journey from his home country to, or through, one other country, while a multilateral one allows him to make an unlimited number of journeys between his home country and any other EC country during a twelve-month period. Bilateral permits are more freely available for movements to some countries than to others. The supply of permits for West Germany, Italy and Spain, for example, has fallen well short of British hauliers' demands. This has impeded the growth of accompanied haulage to these countries and favoured the movement of unaccompanied trailers, which do not require permits. This distortion of the haulage market has become less acute in recent years as the numbers of both bilateral and multilateral permits has increased in line with the EC policy of road-freight liberalisation (Cooper *et al.*, 1987).

A target date of 1992 has been set for the full liberalisation of international road-freight movement in the EC. Thereafter, hauliers will not only be granted freedom to transport goods from their home country to, or through, any other member state, but will also be allowed to engage in *cabotage*, a practice that is currently forbidden in the EC. In this context, cabotage can be defined as domestic haulage work undertaken by a foreign carrier. For example, a British haulier on a return journey from Marseilles might transport a consignment entirely within France, say from Lyon to Paris. If he transported it from Lyon to Brussels, thereby crossing an international border into another country in which he was not registered, he would be '*cross-trading*'. This is currently permissible where the operator holds a multilateral permit, but because these permits are difficult to obtain, it is a comparatively rare occurrence. The legalisation of cabotage and liberalisation of cross-trading will intensify competition in both international and domestic haulage markets. For this competition to be fair, it will be necessary to achieve greater uniformity between member states in the way they regulate and tax road-freight transport. At present, for instance, there are marked differences in the nature and extent of quantitative controls on national haulage industries, in vehicle size and weight restrictions and in levels of vehicle taxation. Attempts to harmonise road-freight policies have in the past, however, proved highly contentious.

Own-account operators are exempt from European permit restrictions. They require special authorisation to transport goods between countries, but, unlike third-party haulage permits, this is not subject to quota restriction. Very little freight is exported from the UK in driver-accompanied own-account vehicles, though, principally because it is difficult, and in some cases illegal, for these vehicles to obtain return loads. In some countries, road-freight regulations prohibit the carriage of third-party traffic in own-account vehicles, while others require their operators to obtain bilateral permits for this work. Back-loads can also be difficult to find, particularly as they must originate close to the return route, so as not to lengthen turnaround times excessively. Given these constraints, international own-account operations tend to be confined to firms operating plants and warehouses in several countries and, therefore, capable of balancing traffic flows internally.

In theory, there should be no shortage of back-loads for British hauliers returning from the European mainland, because approximately twice as much unitised freight flows into the UK from other EC countries as flows in the opposite direction. The ratio of imports to exports is even higher at regional and county levels (Hayter, 1980). The trade imbalance, however, makes it more difficult for British hauliers to secure outward loads at profitable rates. Foreign firms exporting goods to the UK naturally tend to use carriers of the same nationality. This creates a healthy demand for the services of continental-based carriers and enables them to charge relatively high rates on the journey to the UK. In an effort to obtain back-loads out of the smaller pool of UK exports, foreign hauliers charge much lower rates for the return journey. British hauliers consequently suffer a loss of traffic to foreign carriers and are forced to operate on slimmer margins. The deterioration of the UK's trade imbalance with the EC contributed to the decline in British hauliers' share of RoRo traffic from 58% in 1980 to 40% in 1985 (Cooper *et al.*, 1987).

Rail wagons

Cross-Channel rail services are used much more for the movement of fruit and vegetables, chemicals, timber, iron and steel than for the distribution of manufactured consumer goods. Traffic volumes have been constrained by a combination of high costs and poor service. Terminal costs are higher than those of road-based RoRo operations, and wagons much less intensively used than road trailers. Poor wagon utilisation results from slow turnaround and the sizeable imbalance in traffic flows to and from Europe (Highsted, 1981). Many wagons are returned empty to the European mainland because of a lack of export traffic from the UK. Rail ferries on the cross-Channel routes have also been considerably smaller than their road vehicle counterparts and had higher unit costs. These cost disadvantages can be more than offset by lower trunk-haul costs where goods are being moved in large consignments over long distances between rail-connected premises. Even so, many shippers are still reluctant to use rail services between Britain and Europe because of their poor record on speed and reliability. Long rail transit times are partly attributable to operational shortcomings, often leading to the formation of bottlenecks at the ports, but also to excessive delays at frontiers, where official checks generally take longer than for road vehicles. Efforts are currently being made to reduce the cost of cross-Channel rail services by concentrating traffic on the Dover-Dunkirk route and commissioning larger vessels. Service quality is also being enhanced by accelerating through-movements and subjecting them to closer computerised monitoring. In the longer term, the construction of the Channel Tunnel will help the railways to capture a larger share of cross-Channel freight traffic. BR has predicted that there will be a three-fold increase in the amount of freight passing between Britain and the European mainland in rail wagons when the Channel Tunnel opens in 1993. Steer, Davies and Gleave Ltd (1987) forecast that, if the constraints imposed by BR's low loading gauge can be successfully overcome using new intermodal systems, there will be a substantial diversion of high-value traffic onto direct cross-Channel rail services.

Air freight

Airlines have traditionally specialised in the carriage of products of high-value density, which derive great benefit from rapid delivery. For these products, high air-freight rates are more than offset by savings in inventory costs, yielding lower total distribution costs than movement by slower modes. Wider application of the Total Cost approach has enabled airlines to secure traffic of lower value where consignors move different categories of stock by different modes. According to the *differentiated distribution* or *multiple-mode principle*, cycle stocks should be transported in large quantities by slower, cheaper modes, while small orders withdrawn at short notice from centrally held safety stocks can be more quickly delivered by express air, or road, services (Sletmo and Picard, 1985). The use of air services can thereby help firms to reconcile the conflicting objectives of centralising safety stocks in the home country and minimising the risk of stock-outs in foreign markets. Higher transport costs can easily be justified where the consequences of such contingencies are the disruption of overseas production for want of a spare part, or, in the case of finished goods, the erosion of customer loyalty. Air freight is often the preferred mode for what Gray (1981, p.52) calls 'critical consignments', that is consignments 'likely to influence the reputation of the exporting company or country at the point when the level of delivery reliability becomes critical', such as in the early stages of the product life cycle or when a competitor is gaining a service level advantage.

Aircraft exploit their speed advantage most fully on long-distance intercontinental hauls. Consignments transported by air within Europe often spend as much as 90% of their transit time on the ground, travelling to and from airports or awaiting customs clearance, handling and forwarding at air cargo terminals. Premium services exist for the very rapid movement of individual consignments, but most air freight is consolidated by forwarders into more economically sized loads. The consolidation operation causes further delays. Following improvements to European road networks and ferry services, international express haulage services can now achieve similar transit times to air-freight operators on many intra-European routes at lower cost. In recent years, they have been increasing their share of the express freight market at the expense of the airlines. Davies (1984) contends that many shippers continue to use air-freight services because they perceive them to be faster, when, in reality, this is no longer so. Even the airlines themselves are expanding their use of express road feeder services within Europe as part of a policy of concentrating long-haul air-freight operations on fewer airports.

Routeing of international flows

The routeing of export consignments is seldom the manufacturer's direct concern. The choice of route is typically delegated to freight forwarders or carriers. When goods are sold *ex-works* or FOB, the customer gives the exporter instructions, or *routeing orders*, indicating how he wants the goods transported. Only the small minority of manufacturers which organise international distribution on an own-account basis exercise full control over the route their exports follow.

For the 99% of all unit loads moving between Britain and the European mainland by sea, routeing is largely determined by the choice of port. There was a great proliferation of ports with RoRo and LoLo capability in the 1960s and early 1970s. The total number of unit load berths in the UK increased from 21 in 1962 to 166 in 1975, most of them located along the east and south coasts. Elliott and Fullerton (1977, p.411) observe that they were developed in a 'piece-meal,

Table 8.5 Sensitivity of total transport costs to ferry charges: accompanied road trailers, 1978

	Total cost (£)	Ferry charge (£)	%	% Reduction in total cost resulting from 30% ferry discount
Leicester to Brussels via:				
Dover – Calais	327	198	60.6	18.2
Harwich – Hoek van Holland	343	242	70.6	21.2
Edinburgh to Milan via:				
Dover – Boulogne	728	198	27.2	8.9
Hull – Zeebrugge	721	272	37.7	11.3

Source: Hayter, 1980.

unplanned and potentially wasteful fashion', with very little central government intervention. Over the past decade, there has been some rationalisation of port capacity, with both LoLo and RoRo operations becoming more spatially concentrated. At the same time, the ferry companies have consolidated their operations on a smaller number of routes.

Jones and North (1982, p.29) note that, with the development of unitised *through-transport*, 'the established function of many of our ports as distinct interfaces between land and sea transport has become increasingly obsolete'. Unit loading has transformed the port into 'little more than the transit point where documentary procedures and customs controls are carried out' (Slijper, 1977, p.15). Many traditional port functions, such as goods handling, load consolidation/disaggregation and customs clearance have shifted to *inland container depots* (ICDs) or other inland terminals. An increasing proportion of export traffic is now routed through these facilities, most of which are strategically located with respect to industrial centres and motorway links.

Unlike the previous generation of bulk-cargo ports, unit load ports tend not to have localised hinterlands. Indeed, ports like Dover and Felixstowe effectively serve the whole country. In pursuit of economies of scale, RoRo ferry companies compete nationally for freight traffic. Freight forwarders and hauliers are encouraged to place all or most of their traffic with a single ferry operator by the offer of handsome discounts, or *loyalty rebates*, which can represent savings of over 30% on the published tariffs. Through-movement costs can be highly sensitive to the level of discount (Table 8.5), making the choice of ferry company and port a critical decision, particularly in the case of shorter journeys (Hayter and Wingfield, 1981). As the rebate is calculated on the basis of throughput over a certain period of time, the choice is not made separately for each consignment. For example, a forwarder committed to a particular ferry company would channel traffic through the ports that company serves, regardless of its point of origin. The heavy concentration of RoRo capacity in the south-east of England results in export traffic from Scotland and the north of England travelling long distances to port. In 1978, unitised traffic bound for north-west Europe travelled on average 243 km to port (Garratt, 1984). If all this traffic had been exported through the nearest RoRo port, the average length of haul would have been only 98 km. This would generally have entailed a longer sea crossing, but, as Garratt points out, the cost per kilometre of transporting a trailer by sea is approximately half that by road. PSERC (1981) estimated that a policy of directing all unitised European traffic through the nearest port could reduce road transport costs by about 15%. There is no guarantee, however, that minimising the overland distance within the UK would also minimise total transport costs (Lösch, 1954), especially as some ports have difficult road access. The poor quality of road connections between the English Midlands and the east-coast ports of Felixstowe and Harwich, for instance, is likely to have caused the diversion of some export traffic onto longer, but easier, routes via the Channel ports.

Tookey (1971) asserts that 'real economies' can be made by improving the routeing of international freight movements. Having relinquished control of international physical distribution, however, many firms are unaware of the large savings that could be made by rerouteing export flows, or indeed restructuring the exporting operation in other ways.

Chapter nine

Environmental impact

Physical distribution imposes a greater burden on society than is reflected in the financial accounts of individual firms. It has a number of detrimental effects on the environment whose cost is borne by the community at large. The distribution of material goods throughout the population is inevitably intrusive in people's lives. This intrusion takes various forms. It is manifest in fixed facilities such as depots, freight terminals and lorry parks, which can be unsightly and, in some cases, noisy. Their effects are, nevertheless, localised and often confined to industrial estates. The movement of freight is much more pervasive, especially on the road network, and has caused much greater public resentment.

Although the total number of lorries has been declining, the amount of heavy lorry traffic has been increasing. Between 1973 and 1982, the number of lorries with unladen weights (ULW) of over 2 tons fell by 21%, but the number of vehicles in the heaviest weight class (over 10 tons ULW) approximately doubled (Newton, 1985), their share of road tonnes lifted and tonne-kilometres rising from 19.8% and 35.5% to 40.3% and 60.5% respectively. Between 1976 and 1986, the total distance travelled by lorries increased by around 10%, but in the case of heavy lorries with four or more axles it went up by 47% (Department of Transport, 1987). Heavy vehicles ran most of these additional kilometres on motorways and trunk/principal roads in non-built-up areas. They have also been increasingly deployed, however, in a shop delivery role, bringing them more often into the central areas of towns and cities.

This growth of heavy lorry traffic has occurred over a period of mounting environmental consciousness (Starkie, 1982) and become a central campaigning issue for many environmental pressure groups. In recognition of this public concern, central government has commissioned studies of the effects of lorries on the environment and taken various measures to alleviate them. Heavy lorries are, nevertheless, still widely perceived as posing a major environmental problem. This chapter will examine several aspects of this problem and seek answers to the following questions:

1. In what ways are lorries detrimental to the environment?
2. How many people are affected by lorry nuisance and to what extent?
3. What can be done to reduce the environmental costs of physical distribution?

The environmental effects of lorry traffic

Noise

Road traffic produces a very complex pattern of sound, varying in its frequency, intensity and duration. The main measure employed in traffic noise studies is a decibel index, dB(A), which emphasises the middle-range frequencies that are most audible to the human ear. In 1983, the maximum permitted noise levels for lorries in the UK were reduced from 89 dB(A) for lorries of under 200 brake horsepower and 91 dB(A) for more powerful vehicles to 86 and 88 respectively. Most cars generate noise within the range 77-80 dB(A). Wardroper (1981) argues that the dB(A) index underestimates the annoyance caused by heavy lorries as it largely ignores the low-frequency vibrations produced by diesel engines. These, he asserts, can easily penetrate walls and windows, even when double glazed.

Measurements of traffic noise on a particular stretch of road must take account of variations in noise levels throughout the day. In the UK, it is standard practice to measure the noise level (in dB(A)) that is exceeded for 10% of the time between 06.00 and 24.00. By focusing on peak noise levels, this index (known as L^{10}) is believed to give a good indication of the annoyance caused. Surveys by the Greater London Council (GLC), however, revealed that many people have their sleep disturbed by heavy lorries between 24.00 and 06.00 (Buchan, 1985). As heavy lorries tend to be much noisier than other classes of road vehicle, they are responsible for many of the individual noise peaks. This was demonstrated by a traffic survey in Putney High Street, in which vehicles producing noise peaks in excess of 85 dB(A) during sample periods were enumerated (Christie, Bartlett and Cundill, 1973). Although heavy lorries represented only 1.7% of the total traffic flow, they accounted for 31.3% of the noise peaks.

Objective measures of noise have been found to correlate poorly with the degree of irritation people experience (Kryter, 1970). People differ in their perception of noise and in their ability to tolerate noises of particular frequency and loudness. The annoyance caused by a given sound also depends on the ambient noise level to which the person is accustomed and their view of the importance of the activity generating the sound (Adams, 1981). There is therefore no general yardstick of noise irritation against which the contribution of heavy lorries to noise nuisance might be assessed.

The double glazing of buildings and erection of roadside barriers helps to reduce people's exposure to traffic noise. Burt (1972) argues, though, that, as far as heavy lorries are concerned, it would probably be more effective and economical to quieten the vehicles responsible for the noise. The Transport and Road Research Laboratory (TRRL), in association with Foden and Rolls Royce, has developed a 'quiet heavy vehicle' (QHV) that emits around 80 dB(A) and is only slightly noisier than a car. In a two-year trial with a typical haulier, this 38 tonne lorry was found to operate almost as efficiently as other conventional vehicles of its size (Nelson and Underwood, 1982). Its capital cost, however, is approximately 7.3% higher than comparable, unmodified vehicles and this is likely to deter its use. Only if the government lowers maximum noise levels or gives quieter vehicles special tax privileges will firms gradually replace their existing lorries with QHVs.

Vibration

Lorries cause both air-borne and ground-borne vibration. The former are emitted mainly by their engines and exhaust systems, and closely resemble the low-frequency sounds mentioned above. Some people hear low-frequency sound as a noise, while others sense them as a vibration (Civic Trust, 1979). These air-borne vibrations are irritating, but very seldom of sufficient magnitude to affect people's health or cause damage to property. Ground-borne vibration, although less perceptible, poses a more serious threat to roadside buildings. It results from the bumping of wheels over irregularities on the road surface. The force of this vibration depends mainly on the character of the road surface, the speed of the vehicle, the nature of its suspension and tyres and the loading on each axle (Armitage, 1980). The total weight of the vehicle may also be significant, as individual axle-load pressures can combine at a depth of 5-7 feet below the road surface to amplify the vibration (Wardroper, 1981).

Heavy lorries are blamed for much of the damage done to underground gas and water pipes, though their operators make no contribution to the cost of their repair. It is also believed that lorry-induced vibration can be one of several factors triggering superficial, 'architectural' damage to roadside premises, such as the cracking of plaster. Official reports deny that heavy lorries inflict serious 'structural' damage except in the case of very old buildings whose weak foundations make them especially vulnerable. A large body of circumstantial evidence implicating lorry traffic in the structural deterioration of buildings has, nevertheless, been collected by the Civic Trust (1979) and others. In an effort to resolve this controversy, the TRRL is currently undertaking a major study of the effects of ground-borne vibration.

The vibration problem could be alleviated in various ways. Some relevant measures, such as reducing lorry weights and diverting heavy lorries from routes flanked by more sensitive properties, offer wide-ranging environmental benefits and are more fully discussed later in this chapter. Two measures more specifically targeted on the vibration problem are the maintenance of a smooth road surface and the installation of more resilient vehicle suspension systems.

The condition of road surfaces in the UK has deteriorated over the past ten years principally as a result of public expenditure cuts, though the present government is committed to reducing the road maintenance backlog. Major improvements in vehicle suspension are technically possible, but at present economically unattractive. Moreover, as industry is under no pressure to curb lorry-induced vibration, it has little incentive to incur the extra cost of acquiring and operating vehicles with substantially improved suspension.

Air pollution

Lorries make only a small contribution to total atmospheric pollution. Armitage estimated that they were responsible for 8% of nitrogen oxides emissions, 3-4% of hydrocarbons, 2% of carbon monoxide and less than 1% of sulphur dioxide. Wardroper contends that these figures underestimate the nuisance caused, because, unlike emissions from the chimneys of industrial premises, lorry exhaust fumes are released and concentrate at street level in close proximity to the general public. Much more of the blame for air pollution at this level is, however, attributable to cars, whose petrol engines release a much higher proportion of noxious gases and which, of course, are much more numerous. Unlike cars, lorries' diesel engines often emit black smoke. Armitage estimated that lorries produced about 6% of all smoke emissions (by weight), though in urban areas this proportion can be several times higher. Sharp and Jennings (1976, p.84) note that 'a major technological problem in dealing with emissions is that reducing the emission of one substance may increase that of another'. They cite the example of a reduction in the fuel:air ratio inhibiting the production of smoke at the expense of increasing the proportion of unburnt hydrocarbons and nitrogen oxides. Improved vehicle maintenance can, nevertheless, yield significant reductions in all emissions, particularly of smoke (OECD, 1982).

Accidents

In the UK in 1985, heavy lorries were involved in 14,452 road accidents, resulting in the death of 811 people and serious injury to a further 4,331 (Department of Transport, 1986b). These lorries have a much lower rate of involvement in traffic accidents than cars; 67 per 100 million vehicle kilometres against a corresponding figure for cars of 121. This disparity is due mainly to the fact that HCVs travel much longer distances on motorways and other trunk roads whose accident rates are relatively low. Little comfort can be taken from the fact that lorries are less accident-prone than cars though, partly because car accident levels are deemed to be appallingly high, but also because accidents involving lorries result much more frequently in death or serious injury. In 1985 HCVs were involved in 3.7% of all road accidents, but 11% of fatal accidents. Lorries' fatal accident rate per million kilometres travelled is 73% higher than that of cars. The severity of lorry accidents is obviously a function of the greater size and momentum of these vehicles.

Various measures have been adopted both to cut lorries' rate of involvement in accidents and to reduce their seriousness. These include reductions in the 'driving day', tachographic monitoring of driver behaviour, improved vehicle design, mandatory installation of safety features such as under-run bumpers and anti-jack-knife devices and the raising of vehicle maintenance standards.

Visual intrusion

Some people feel that the mere presence of a large lorry can degrade an urban or rural landscape. It can appear out of proportion in an urban street or country road and intimidate pedestrians. A lorry's visual impact is clearly a matter of subjective judgement and likely to vary from person to person and between environments. Sharp (1973, p.22) concedes that little can be done to make lorries more aesthetically pleasing, but speculates that with time people may come to find similar 'beauty and romance' in lorries as in steam locomotives and tramcars! Reducing their size would make them less conspicuous, though this would entail an increase in their numbers and not necessarily reduce overall intrusiveness.

Overall assessment

Wardroper (1981) estimated that, in total, the environmental effects listed above represented an annual cost to the community, in 1980, of £790 million, or 57 pence for every tonne of freight transported by road (Table 9.1). His assignment of monetary values to essentially imponderable factors, such as noise irritation and visual intrusion, involved highly subjective, and often arbitrary, judgements. Button

Table 9.1   Evaluation of the environmental effects of lorry traffic, 1980

	£ million
Noise	300
Vibration	150
Air Pollution	150
Accidents	140
Intrusion	50
Total	790

Source: Wardroper, 1981.

and Pearman (1981, p.150) argue that the costing of such externalities rests on 'rather flimsy theoretical foundations' and employs data that are 'subject to considerable error and unreliability'.

Public attitudes

A more realistic assessment of the environmental impact of lorries has been made by Baugham, Hedges and Field (1983) using data collected in a survey of 2,198 people throughout Britain in 1978-9. These revealed that approximately 12% of the adult population were bothered 'very much' or 'quite a lot' by lorries while at home. 19% felt that the road in front of their home carried too much lorry traffic. Traffic counts, undertaken at the same time, showed that almost two-thirds of homes were on streets along which an average of 3 or fewer lorries passed during a 90 minute period. At the other extreme, 5% of houses were exposed to lorry traffic of between 64 and 500 vehicles over this period and 1% to even denser lorry flows (Table 9.2). The environmental impact on these houses was even more acute than the aggregate traffic figures suggest because the proportion of lorries in heavier weight classes tends to increase with the total volume of lorry traffic. The picture that emerged, therefore, was of a significant minority of homes experiencing a level of disturbance from lorries that their residents considered excessive. A much larger proportion of the population come into contact with lorries away from their homes, as pedestrians and occupants of other motor vehicles. 38% of respondents claimed that they were bothered by lorries while in cars or on motorcycles, while 14% felt that they were a source of difficulty or danger to them as pedestrians. It should be noted that the public attitudes investigated by this research would, in most cases, be based on direct observation and take little account of less visible effects, such as the emission of noxious gases, damage to property and traffic accidents. Overall, almost two-thirds of the people consulted believed that measures should be taken to reduce the amount of lorry traffic to which they were exposed. The remainder of this chapter will examine the ways in which this could be achieved.

Table 9.2   Exposure of residences to lorry traffic

No. of lorries passing in 90 minutes	% of homes exposed to this level of lorry traffic
> 500	1
64 – 500	5
32 – 63	5
16 – 31	8
8 – 15	8
4 – 7	11
2 – 3	13
0 – 1	49

Source: Baugham *et al.*, 1983.

Reducing the environmental impact of freight movement

Pettit (1973) argues that, as the lorry is an integral part of the modern economy, the only way of substantially reducing the volume of lorry traffic would be to suppress the level of economic activity. He doubts that the vast majority of the population would be prepared to accept the resulting cut in living standards and hence dismisses deliberate economic contraction as a practical solution to the lorry problem. This assumes, however, that there is a fixed relationship between GDP and the volume of freight traffic and that lorries will maintain their share of this traffic. We shall deal first with the latter assumption about modal split before going on to consider the broader issue of freight traffic generation.

Modal transfer

The railways, inland waterways, pipelines and coastal shipping are generally acknowledged to be less environmentally offensive than road transport (Nash, 1976). A diversion of freight traffic to these modes might, therefore, be expected to yield environmental benefits. Of the alternative modes, the railway is by far the most eligible candidate for a transfer of freight from road as it has the densest network and it alone can offer a comparable quality of service to road haulage for trunk movements. Attention will, therefore, focus on the environmental case for sending a greater proportion of the nation's freight by rail.

Armitage states that 'there can be little doubt that the overall impact of rail freight on the environment is substantially less than that of road freight, even when account is taken of the much greater amount of freight which road carries' (p.60). The much lower density of the rail network makes it less intrusive, while freight trains are inherently less polluting, less noisy and much safer than the lorries required to carry a comparable load. Much of the environmental impact of rail freight was felt in the vicinity of marshalling yards in urban areas, but these have been closed as BR has phased out its traditional wagonload service.

Pressure groups with a strong concern for the environment have long sought a substantial transfer of freight from road to rail. The official response has been somewhat dismissive. The Department of Transport has consistently argued that the modal imbalance between road and rail is so great that a large increase in rail-freight tonnage would only marginally reduce lorry traffic. In its evidence to the Armitage Inquiry, BR estimated that about 40 million tonnes of road freight were suitable for transfer to rail. This represented 20-25% of rail-freight tonnage at the time, but only 2.5% of road freight. If one assumes that this traffic had an average length of haul of 200 km, it would represent 40% and 8% respectively of rail and road tonne-kilometres. Wardroper (1981) argues, however, that it is unrealistic to use all road freight as a basis for these percentage calculations as this includes a large amount of local delivery work which the railways would be technically unable to handle. On the other hand, much of the long-haul traffic suitable for transfer to rail travels largely on the motorway network where its environmental impact is relatively low.

To increase their share of the freight market substantially, the railways would have to capture traffic moving between premises without a direct rail connection. This would create the need for road feeder movements which could cause nuisance and detract from the environmental benefit of using rail for the trunk haul. Sharp and Jennings (1976) compare the environmental implications of sending loads of 1-3 tons by road and rail on three hypothetical journeys from Leicester to Millwall Docks (London), Leicester to Croydon and north London to Loughborough. Their conclusion that the use of rail would offer little environmental advantage is questionable, however, as the examples chosen are unfavourable to rail. None of the origins or destinations are rail connected and most are on the urban periphery, from which they can gain much easier access to the motorway network than to terminals on the rail network. The decentralisation of industry has certainly left many inner urban rail depots and Freightliner terminals ill placed, from an economic and environmental standpoint. Nevertheless, substantial numbers of factories and warehouses are still to be found in inner suburbs and likely to be as far from a motorway junction as a rail terminal. Moreover, many of the new generation of railhead depots in the Speedlink distribution system are in peripheral or out-of-town locations.

By comparison with 10-20 years ago, BR today has much less spare capacity available with which to absorb traffic displaced from the road network. The amount of rolling stock has been drastically reduced and many sidings closed or shortened. Much new investment would be required if BR were now to try to accommodate an extra 40 million tonnes of freight per annum.

Armitage considered four general measures that the government might take to promote greater use of rail: legally compelling shippers to send goods by rail, reintroducing quantitative controls on the road haulage industry, imposing higher taxes on lorries and subsidising rail freight. Of these, he considered only the latter two justifiable and then only to a very limited extent. He recommended an increase in the taxation of heavy lorries 'on grounds of equity, the better allocation of resources and in respect of social and environmental costs', and conceded that this should help BR compete for long-haul traffic. He also endorsed the subsidisation of rail siding development under Section 8 of the 1974 Railways Act and recommended that the maximum level of financial support be raised from 50 to 60%. The virtue of the Section 8 grant scheme is that it targets state financial inducements on those traffic flows whose transfer from road to rail yields clear environmental benefits. As explained in Chapter 6, this scheme has enabled BR to secure a substantial amount of new freight business.

Finally, it should be noted that Britain sends a much larger proportion of freight by road than most other industrialised countries (Figure 6.1). The experience of other countries, such as West Germany and Japan, suggests that economies can thrive at much lower levels of dependence on road transport.

Rationalising the logistical system

For many years, there has been a close relationship between the volume of freight movement (measured by tonne-kilometres) and GDP in most developed countries (Adams, 1981). Up until the late 1970s, the correlation was considered, in the UK, to be sufficiently strong and stable to warrant its use as a basis for freight traffic forecasting. Quinet, Marche and Reynaud (1982) noted, however, that in France during the 1970s the relationship weakened, with tonne-kilometres increasing at a slower rate than GDP. In the UK, during the 1980-1 recession, tonne-kilometres dropped by a significantly greater margin than GDP, though in recent years these indices have again risen roughly in parallel (Warner, 1987).

In this section, we shall investigate the possibility of reducing the amount of freight traffic, measured in both tonne- and vehicle-kilometres, while maintaining or expanding economic output.

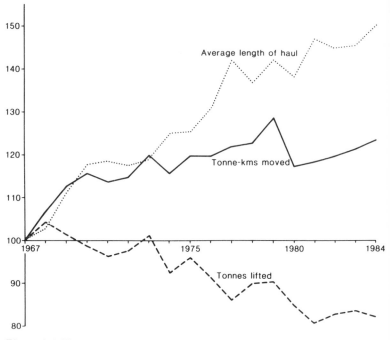

Figure 9.1 The movement of freight by road and rail in the UK: 1967–84
Source: Department of Transport, 1976, 1985.

Scope for reducing tonne-kilometres

The tonne-kilometre statistic is a composite measure of freight movement, incorporating two elements: tonnes lifted and average length of haul. Variations in the tonnes-lifted statistic can result from changes in either the mass of goods in the economy or the structure of the logistical system. Over the past 20 years, the number of tonnes lifted by surface modes in the UK has declined, though fairly erratically (Figure 9.1). The upward trend in tonne-kilometres has been due mainly to increases in the average length of haul. It appears that a diminishing amount of freight is being transported over greater distances.

Increasing average length of haul could result from changes in the composition of national output, if, for example, products typically transported over longer distances became relatively more important. Cundill and Shane (1980), however, show that variations in the commodity mix have had only a very marginal effect on average length of haul. Three other processes appear to have been responsible for most of the lengthening of hauls:

240

1. *Expansion of market areas.* This increases the average distance between the point of supply and the customer. Many large manufacturers of food and consumer durables achieved complete national coverage before 1960, but there have still been numerous instances of producers extending their market areas since then. Brewers, brick manufacturers and foreign producers of a range of consumer goods have more recently expanded the areas over which they distribute their products in the UK (Corcoran *et al.*, 1980). The growth of multiple retailers and their increasing involvement in centralised distribution has also made it easier for small producers to gain access to a wider market.

2. *Spatial concentration of production and stockholding.* The Department of Transport (1976, p.16) identified the 'growing concentration of industry' as 'probably the chief contributor' to the increase in average length of haul. Corcoran *et al.* (1980) and Armitage (1980) acknowledged that the spatial concentration of the storage function was also playing an important part in this process. Spatial concentration has occurred with respect to both the vertical and horizontal dimensions of the logistical system. 'Vertical' concentration has been achieved by the assembly at a single location of different stages in the productive process. In the case of stockholding, it has resulted from the closure of regional depots and centralisation of stock at the factory site. Both of these processes have the effect of eliminating intermediate nodes in the logistical channel and usually result in two freight journeys being replaced by one longer and more direct haul. The effect on the average length of haul depends on the geography of the production and stockholding operations. By reducing the number of separate links in the logistical channel, vertical concentration also reduces the tonnes-lifted statistic for a given mass of goods. It is, therefore, difficult to assess the net effect of this type of concentration on tonne-kilometres.

   The effect of 'horizontal' concentration is much more clear-cut. Reductions in the numbers of factories (or warehouses) at the same level in the logistical channel lengthen delivery distances to the premises they supply. An attempt was made by Saunders (1978) to relate the (horizontal) concentration of production in the brewing industry to the lengthening of beer deliveries. She found that, between 1957 and 1973, the number of breweries in England fell by 67% while the average length of haul for beer increased by a factor of between two and three. The effects of the centralisation of inventory on average length of haul are discussed in McKinnon (1986b). The factors promoting this centralisation were examined in Chapter 4.

3. *Relocation of production away from the main concentration of demand.* The main pressure for such relocation has been exerted by regional policy. The Department of Transport (1979) acknowledges that by inducing firms to locate factories in peripheral locations, regional policy has contributed to the lengthening of freight hauls. Much of the industry attracted to assisted areas, however, has been in the form of branch plants, and it is difficult to generalise about the effects of their development on average length of haul. This depends on where they obtain their supplies and on how widely they distribute their output.

Insufficient data are available to assess the relative contribution of these spatial processes to the lengthening of freight hauls and hence the growth of tonne-kilometres. One can, however, examine the possibility of them being arrested, or even reversed, in an effort to stabilise, or reduce, the amount of freight movement.

Restructuring the economy would prove a very clumsy and costly way of reducing the demand for freight transport. It is inconceivable that a government would try to control freight traffic growth by this means. It is equally unlikely that, in peacetime, a government would be prepared to restrict the area over which a firm markets its products. Where the market areas of competing firms overlap, *cross-haulage* results, with similar, but differently branded, products passing in opposite directions in the course of their distribution. From a transport standpoint, it would be much more efficient for each producer to have a separate territory over which it had exclusive distribution rights. This would eliminate cross-haulage and greatly reduce delivery distances. An attempt was made during the Second World War to rationalise the system of food distribution in the UK to ease congestion on the railway network, economise on fuel and reduce the vulnerability of supply lines to air attack. Between 1941 and 1945, 'zoning' schemes were introduced for many food products with the aim of subdividing the country into reasonably self-sufficient zones. Retailers and wholesalers were allowed to draw supplies only from producers within their zone. This programme required complex and detailed planning as a different zonal pattern had to be devised for each product type to take account of the particular geography of its production. Altogether, the zoning schemes reduced the volume of food movement by around 300 million ton-miles per annum. Hammond (1951, p.345), nevertheless, concludes that, in the light of this experience, 'it does not appear that vast economies could be made in food transport under peace-time conditions'. As these schemes were planned and implemented during a period of national crisis, they form a poor basis upon which to assess the present scope for rationalising the distribution of food and other products. Furthermore, since 1945, the amount of cross-haulage has greatly increased. It is doubtful, however, that many people would consider even a substantial reduction in freight traffic so desirable as to justify the high costs associated with the elimination of cross-haulage. These costs would stem mainly from the creation of spatial monopolies, the loss of economies of scale in production and the extensive bureaucracy needed to support the necessary system of trading restrictions. Consumer choice would also be severely constrained and living standards almost certainly lowered.

A stronger case could be made for discouraging the spatial concentration of production and stockholding, as it is a source of several disbenefits. Apart from making the logistical system more transport-intensive, it also drains more peripheral areas of employment (Botham, 1980) and creates land-use pressures in more central locations. It can be argued that, while the spatial concentration of production and stockholding raises the internal efficiency of these operations, the resulting externalities are largely ignored. If, for example, the external effects of the additional freight movement were fully costed and internalised in an environmental tax on transport operators, firms might not centralise their operations to the same extent (Plowden, 1985). Sharp (1977, p.79) examines the practical problems in introducing such a tax on lorries and concludes that its 'long term effects on industrial location' would be 'unpredictable'. Centralisation has now progressed so far that a return to more dispersed systems of production and storage would cause great economic dislocation and take many years. Ironically, regional policy, which is designed to counter the centralisation of economic activity in more prosperous areas, is itself responsible for some lengthening of hauls. As it has diverted only a small proportion of new industrial capacity to peripheral areas, however, its freight traffic generating effects are likely to have been small and, in most people's estimation, more than outweighed by regional development benefits.

Fairly radical measures would, therefore, have to be taken to reduce tonne-kilometres and, as they would have a detrimental effect on the economy, it is unlikely they would command much political support.

Scope for reducing vehicle kilometres

Vehicle kilometres can vary independently of tonne-kilometres. Between 1973 and 1979, for example, tonne-kilometres on the UK road network increased by 15.7% while the total distance travelled by lorries rose by only 1.5% (Armitage, 1980). In theory, therefore, it might be possible to reduce vehicle kilometres without effecting a parallel reduction in tonne-kilometres. To explore the feasibility of such a change, we must examine the factors affecting the relationship between tonne- and vehicle kilometres:

Vehicle size   The conventional wisdom is that the increased use of heavier lorries permits a reduction in vehicle kilometres. Armitage (1980), for example, predicted that raising the maximum lorry weight to 44 tonnes would lead to the consolidation of freight in fewer vehicles and cut the total distance travelled per annum by vehicles of over 25 tonnes GVW by 8.5%. This prediction rested on two assumptions: first, that the introduction of larger, more economical vehicles would in itself generate very little extra freight traffic, and, second, that past levels of vehicle utilisation would be maintained. Starkie (1982, p.17) regards the former assumption as 'probably the weakest element in Armitage's case'. In monitoring the effects of the introduction of 38 tonne lorries on British roads, Johnson and Wilding (1986) again assume that new traffic generation has been negligible and, on that basis, calculate that in 1984 they reduced the total distance travelled by lorries of 32.5 tonnes or above by 150 million kilometres. Until the traffic generative effect of lorry weight increases is empirically evaluated, such calculations must remain suspect. The second assumption, about vehicle utilisation, is much more credible for reasons outlined in the next section.

It is a moot point whether it is preferable, in environmental terms, to have freight consolidated in a few heavy lorries or carried by a larger number of small vehicles. The issue is complicated by the fact that some environmental costs are a function mainly of vehicle size, whereas others correlate more closely with vehicle numbers. Research by Smith (1977) suggests that the consolidation of freight in large vehicles increases noise peaks, smoke emissions and vibration-induced damage, but, at the same time, reduces the emissions of invisible air pollutants, accident levels and traffic congestion.

Deciding whether the consolidation of freight in large vehicles makes lorry traffic more or less visually intrusive is a matter of subjective judgement. Several surveys conducted by the TRRL have shed light on public preferences for different lorry size combinations. In the first, lorries of differing size were driven around circuits in Borehamwood and Marlow, and a total of 329 pedestrians and residents asked which size combinations bothered them most and least (Rosman, 1976). Each of the three size combinations tested had a total carrying capacity of 16 tonnes. This load could be carried in one 16 tonner, two 8 tonners or four 4 tonners. It was found that approximately equal numbers of interviewees regarded the heavy lorry as most and least bothersome. Slightly fewer expressed a strong opinion about the convoy of four small lorries, but, again, those who did divided fairly evenly between the most and least bothersome categories. The same division of opinion emerged over the two medium-sized lorries, though only about one person in six claimed they bothered them most or least. The inconclusiveness of these results can be partly attributed to the artificiality of the experiment and the requirement that respondents base their assessments on the transitory impact of the particular vehicles used in the experiment rather than general impressions of different sizes of lorry built up over a longer period. Baugham (1979) tried to examine these general impressions by showing a sample of 309 people in Nottingham photographs of the same three vehicle size combinations and again asking them to indicate which bothered them most and least. Respondents in this survey exhibited a much clearer order of preference. The two medium-sized lorries were ranked least bothersome, followed by the four small lorries and finally the single large one. Subsequent work by Baugham *et al.* (1983) showed, however, that people's responses to questions about lorry sizes are influenced by the range of options available. Where this includes medium-sized vehicles, they prove a popular compromise. If the choice is restricted to large and small vehicles, though, no clear preference emerges.

The trade-off between lorry numbers and sizes is in practice more complicated than these surveys suggest. They assume that all the combinations of vehicles run along the same roads and are seen by the same people (Baugham, 1979). This would apply in situations where the freight was destined for a single location. It would not apply in the case of multiple-drop deliveries, because instead of having a single large lorry make all the drops, they could be divided between several small vehicles. These small lorries could then travel more directly to the various delivery points. This means, first, that total vehicle kilometres would increase by less than the ratio of the carrying capacities of the large and small vehicles, and, second, that lorry nuisance would be more dispersed and affect more people less seriously. In judging the relative advantages of concentrating or dispersing lorry traffic, consideration must be given to the nature of the particular roads and roadside environments.

Vehicle utilisation   When assessing the environmental effect of lorry movement, the most relevant measure of utilisation is the average weight load factor. For a given vehicle stock, maximising average load factors has the effect of minimising vehicle kilometres. Between 1962 and 1977, average load factors declined across most vehicle size classes (Cundill and Shane, 1980). They then remained fairly stable between 1977 and 1983 (Newton, 1985). The overall utilisation of the lorry fleet is, nevertheless, likely to have improved over the whole 20 year period as heavier lorries increased their share of total freight tonnage. This is because the heavier the vehicle, the higher tends to be its load factor. As heavy lorries generally transport bulk loads over long distances often to a single destination, they travel a larger proportion of their annual kilometres fully laden than smaller delivery vehicles on multiple-drop rounds. The direct relationship between vehicle size and average load factor appears to extend to the new generation of 38 tonners, because they have been found to have significantly higher levels of utilisation than 32.5 tonne vehicles. It would seem, therefore, that operators are, as Armitage (1980) predicted, taking advantage of the higher weight limit to consolidate loads.

There are clearly some circumstances under which average weight load factors of 100% are technically unattainable. Many low-density loads, for example, fill the available space on a lorry long before the maximum weight limit is reached. In a survey of 9,004 loads carried by 1,533 maximum weight vehicles, Mackie and Harding (1982) found that 26.7% were volume constrained and a further 16.7% constrained by both volume and weight. Most underutilisation, though, results from the way in which road-freight operations are organised and managed. There are three ways in which their organisation could be improved to reduce the degree of underutilisation:

1. *Increase return loading.* On average, lorries travel approximately a third of their annual kilometres empty. Empty running reduces the average weight load factor of 32.5 and 38 tonne vehicles by almost 30% (Newton, 1985). On the basis of a series of 'fairly conservative assumptions', Cundill and Hull (1979) estimated that by increasing the return loading of platform vehicles it would be possible to reduce the amount of empty running by heavy lorries by 150 million vehicle kilometres per annum. This 3.5% cut in vehicle kilometres would have yielded a cost saving of £48 million at 1978 prices, and could have been augmented by the inclusion of box vehicles in the analysis. Cundill and Hull found that about 70% of the return journeys made by platform vehicles over distances greater than 50 kilometres were suitable for a return load, but only about half of them actually obtained one. To increase this proportion, they recommended that shippers and operators make greater use of clearing houses and adopt a code of practice protecting each party's interests. Since 1979 there has been a growth in clearing house activity and an

increased use of new information technology to facilitate the matching of shippers' demands with available back-haul capacity. The proportion of empty running has, nevertheless, remained fairly stable.

2. *Redefine service level standards.* Vehicles are often despatched partly loaded because particular customers must receive their orders within a specified time. If this time constraint were relaxed a fuller load could accumulate. As noted in Chapter 7, though, this 'temporal consolidation' is often opposed by marketing departments on the grounds that it jeopardises sales. Marketing policies can, therefore, result in the prodigal use of lorries and be indirectly responsible for some of the nuisance they cause. Nominated-day delivery schemes offer a means of reconciling marketing objectives with the desire, for economic as well an environmental reasons, to reduce vehicle kilometres.

3. *Improve load planning.* Even within service level constraints, it would be possible for many firms to plan loads more efficiently, particularly with the assistance of the computer software now available.

Unlike many of the other measures proposed to ease the burden of lorry traffic on the environment, these methods of enhancing vehicle utilisation would also yield commercial benefits. A general drive to make road transport more efficient could, therefore, reduce external as well as internal costs.

Vehicle routeing   Once a lorry's size and loading are determined, there remains the question of the route it should follow. On the majority of journeys, lorry drivers decide which roads to travel along. Limited survey evidence suggests that many of the resulting routes are unnecessarily circuitous, especially in the case of one-off or infrequent journeys (Corcoran *et al.*, 1980). In the short term, drivers could probably find more direct routes by referring more often to maps, while, in the longer term, computerised route guidance could further reduce the distance travelled.

The shortest path across the road network need not, of course, minimise social costs, as it may pass through areas that are especially sensitive to environmental disturbance. Simply minimising vehicle kilometres might, therefore, prove counter-productive. A preferable objective would be to minimise the distance lorries travel through these more vulnerable areas, even if this entails some circuity in their routeing. The next section reviews efforts by central and local government in the UK to control the routeing of lorries to improve amenity.

Lorry routeing schemes

Prior to 1973, county highway authorities had the power to prohibit large lorries from using particular stretches of road which, by virtue of limited load tolerance or clearance, were technically unable to accommodate them. The Heavy Commercial Vehicles (Control and Regulation) Act of 1973, more popularly known as the Dykes Act, empowered them also to restrict the movement of lorries of over 3 tonnes ULW for environmental reasons. It required these authorities, for the first time, to assess the environmental impact of lorry traffic and draw up plans for the control of lorry movement in their areas. Lorries over a particular weight could then be banned from environmentally sensitive roads and channelled along other more suitable roads which became designated *lorry routes.*

Local authorities varied enormously in their enthusiasm for lorry routeing. Some merely satisfied the minimum legal requirements of the Dykes Act, while others undertook detailed research and planned extensive lorry networks. By 1981, roughly 450 lorry routeing schemes were in operation, about ten per county, and many of these affected only short stretches of road (Christie, Prudhoe and Hornzee, 1982). In 1982, while trying to muster parliamentary support for an increase in maximum lorry weight to 38 tonnes, the Secretary of State for Transport issued a Guidance Note to local authorities reminding them of their statutory duties and powers under the Dykes Act. Central government has been criticised, however, for providing them with too little guidance and encouragement on lorry routeing (Buchan, 1978; Wardroper, 1981). Most counties, after all, experienced great difficulty in developing lorry routeing schemes.

The most serious problem was that of finding roads suitable for designation as lorry routes. Many roads were considered to carry an excessive burden of heavy lorry traffic, but often the alternative routes had little spare capacity and were already disturbing large numbers of people. There was a danger that lorry routeing would merely concentrate the lorry nuisance along particular corridors, displacing rather than alleviating the problem. This was illustrated by three studies undertaken by the TRRL of lorry routeing schemes in Windsor, Lymm and rural Hertfordshire. In each case, as one would expect, the reduction in HCV traffic past some dwellings resulted in an increase in traffic past others. In fact, in Lymm (Christie and Prudhoe, 1980) and rural Hertfordshire (Prudhoe and Christie, 1981), significantly more households experienced an increase than a decrease in HCV flow, partly because the alternative routes were several kilometres longer. In both cases, though, the relative increase in households' exposure to lorry nuisance along the alternative route was less than the reduction in exposure enjoyed by households along the restricted route. A simple index was used to measure the net change in exposure to lorry nuisance. This was calculated by multiplying the number of dwellings by the increase or decrease in the amount of passing HCV traffic. In both Lymm and rural Hertfordshire, this indicated that, on balance, the routeing schemes had an adverse effect. This assessment failed, however, to take account of the fact that the HCV traffic was diverted onto better and busier roads where the environmental impact of each additional vehicle was less noticeable. In their rural Hertfordshire study, Prudhoe and Christie attached a weighting to the nuisance index to allow for this incremental effect and, as a result, calculated that this routeing scheme yielded a net environmental benefit. Such analysis offered little consolation to those living along roads that became designated lorry routes. Buchan (1978, p.9) argues that attempts by local authorities to plan lorry networks were frustrated by the lack of a 'well-defined scale' against which the relative suitability of roads for heavy lorry traffic could be judged. But regardless of how 'suitable' planners considered a road to be, local people generally resisted any attempts to channel more lorries past their homes.

Local authorities also had the difficult task of balancing any environmental gains against the economic cost of forcing heavy lorries to make detours. Christie, Hornzee and Zammit (1978) estimated that lorry controls in the Windsor area increased average journey length in one direction by 5.6 km, raising total vehicle operating costs by £410,000 per annum. This represented roughly £380 per annum for each resident in dwellings experiencing a reduction in heavy lorry traffic. In other places, such as Hatfield and Basingstoke, where the availability of good alternative routes permitted short diversions, large environmental benefits were obtained at little extra cost. On the basis of 23 lorry routeing schemes, Christie *et al.* (1982) estimated that lorry controls 'introduced solely for amenity reasons' increased road-freight operators' costs nationally by £25 million. It should be noted, though, that these estimates are based on flow data that Christie *et al.* admit are 'of very limited accuracy' (p.6) and on questionable assumptions about the variability of vehicle operating costs.

Area bans and bypasses

Since the late 1970s, several local authorities have placed greater emphasis on zonal restrictions as a means of excluding heavy lorries from areas of high amenity whose entire road networks are unsuited to this type of traffic. These area bans differ in their geographical extent, time periods and vehicle size limits. Their main purpose is to divert *through traffic*, though they can also be used to control the nature and amount of *access traffic*.

The removal of through traffic has been advocated by many politicians and planners as the most effective way of easing the burden of heavy lorry traffic. In 1982, the Secretary of State for Transport stated that 'we need to get lorries away from people' and claimed that this could be achieved by a 'vigorous bypass programme' (quoted by the Civic Trust 1983, p.8). At that time, however, most settlements lacked an adequate bypass. The Civic Trust found that of 1,251 towns and villages in England and Wales with populations of between 500 and 150,000, lying along routes intensively used by heavy lorries, only 321 (26%) had a complete bypass. A further 545 were scheduled to obtain one by 1992-3 but that would still leave 356 settlements 'unbypassed'. The government has since expanded its road development programme and given greater priority to bypass construction, but it is likely that many communities will still have to wait another 10-20 years for a bypass. The so-called 'bypass solution' is also deficient in other respects. In the first place, it is very expensive. The Civic Trust, for example, estimated that bypassing all the settlements in its 1983 survey without a bypass would cost £7.13 billion (at 1983 prices). In some cases, too, local topography prevents the construction of a bypass to required design and cost standards. Moreover, bypass construction itself can cause a loss of amenity and is often opposed by the same environmental groups that complain about the intrusion of heavy lorries in urban areas. There are also doubts about the effectiveness with which bypasses can 'get lorries away from people'. This largely depends on two factors: the ratio of through to access traffic and the propensity of lorry traffic to use bypass routes.

Research by Mackie and Urquhart (1974) established that there was quite a strong relationship ($r = 0.63$) between the population of an urban area and the proportion of lorries over 1.5 ton ULW passing through. In towns with a population of less than 20,000, through traffic accounted for roughly three-quarters of total HCV traffic. Such places could derive great environmental benefit from a bypass. Larger towns generated a much higher proportion of lorry traffic with an origin and/or destination within the urban area. On average, around 70% of the HCV traffic in towns with a population in excess of 100,000 fell into this 'access' category and could not, therefore, be diverted onto a bypass.

Representatives of the road transport industry have consistently argued that, where suitable bypass roads exist, lorries use them. Although bypasses generally increase journey length, they permit higher speeds, lower fuel consumption and easier driving. This was demonstrated by a comparison, made by the Freight Transport Association in 1987, of heavy lorry journeys around the M25 London orbital motorway and through the metropolitan area. The circumferential route was 10 km longer but reduced travel time from 120 minutes to 81 and the number of gear changes from 241 to 31. Once relieved of much of their through traffic, however, cross-town routes can appear not only more direct but also relatively congestion free, and hence lure a residual amount of through traffic. For this reason it is often necessary to compel through traffic to use a bypass by the imposition of 'no entry except for access' restrictions.

Enforcing these restrictions can prove problematical, though, as it is difficult to differentiate through from access traffic in all but very small settlements. One way of doing so is to issue permits to vehicles with a genuine need to enter the restricted area. This can create a great deal of bureaucracy and be difficult to operate effectively. For example, when planning its night ban on lorries of over 16.5 tonnes GVW, the GLC anticipated that, under its exemption policy for access traffic, around 25,000 such vehicles could be eligible for a permit, representing roughly a quarter of all British registered vehicles in this size class. The enforcement of area bans is much easier where vehicles are restricted on the basis of size rather than destination. Bans of this type apply to access as well as through traffic.

Peripheral transhipment

In the early 1970s, the idea of banning all heavy lorries from towns or their central areas gained wide currency. Collections and deliveries would then only be made by smaller, less environmentally offensive vehicles. It was anticipated that this would create a need for transhipment facilities on the periphery of the restricted areas, where loads could be transferred between vehicles of differing size. Studies were undertaken to test the feasibility of peripheral transhipment in Hammersmith (Metra Ltd, 1974), Camberley (CIDP Ltd, 1975), Chichester (Lichfield and Assocs, 1975), Bradford (Wytconsult, 1975), Swindon (Battilana and Hawthorne, 1976) and Barnsley (Urquhart, 1976). The results of these studies cannot be directly compared as they employed different cost functions and made varying assumptions about vehicle size restrictions, operating practices and the types of product likely to require transhipment. They, nevertheless, indicated that channelling goods through a peripheral transhipment depot would cost between £5 and £10 per ton. Calculations by Battilana and Hawthorne (1976) and Hewitt and Owen (1976) suggested that this cost would be translated into an increase of 1-2% in retail prices. These cost estimates were very sensitive to changes in the underlying assumptions (Urquhart, 1976). Most studies, for example, based their calculation of depot throughput on the assumption that all firms affected by the ban would actually use it. As it was doubtful that use of a peripheral transhipment service would be made mandatory, the level of usage was almost certainly overestimated. Indeed, of 93 firms surveyed by Smith (1976), only 15 indicated that they would be prepared to use such a service. If participation rates were accordingly revised downwards, the loss of scale economies in depot construction and operation would increase the cost per ton. The feasibility studies also tended to underestimate the cost of handling and securing goods at the transhipment depot (Smith, 1976). Using more realistic cost data provided by SPD Ltd, Wytconsult (1975) calculated that the annual cost of a transhipment depot for Chichester would be £800,000, or £16 per ton, rather than the original study estimate of £330,000, or £6 per ton. Plowden (1985), on the other hand, contends that some of the feasibility studies set vehicle size restrictions too low and, consequently, exaggerated urban delivery and collection costs. He admits that it is 'unclear what the maximum capacity of an urban lorry might be', but believes that it should be 'substantially greater than that of the lorries envisaged' (p.190), which in most cases was 3 tons ULW.

The vehicle size limit is a critical factor in determining the trade-off between the economic costs and environmental benefits of peripheral transhipment. The feasibility studies were preoccupied with the cost side of this trade-off and made only a very superficial assessment of the environmental effects. Bryant (1975) examined these effects in greater depth in the case of Chichester and concluded that, to achieve a substantial improvement in environmental quality, it would be necessary to deny vehicles of over 1.5 ton ULW access to the town and to channel all types of supplies through the transhipment depot. This would have been a very expensive option. Bryant, like other researchers in this field, measures environmental impact simply in terms of changes in the amount and composition of lorry traffic in and around the restricted area. No attempts have been made to measure or cost the external effects of these changes in traffic levels. Subjective judgements have, nevertheless, been made of the cost-effectiveness of peripheral transhipment as a means of ameliorating the urban environment. The consulting firms, Metra Ltd (1974) and CIDP Ltd (1975), for example, were quite confident that the amenity gains would justify the extra expense, whereas Urquhart (1976), the Lorries and the Environment Committee (1976) and Armitage (1980) were much more pessimistic.

In assessing the repercussions of peripheral transhipment, one must be clear about the precise nature of the operation. Much confusion has undoubtedly arisen over the use of such a vague term as transhipment which simply means the transfer of freight between vehicles. In this context, it involves either the disaggregation of loads for delivery within the restricted area or aggregation of loads originating there. In the case of deliveries, it is important to distinguish 'pure' break-bulk from break-bulk/consolidation operations. The former occurs where the entire contents of a large lorry are destined for the same point in the restricted area. The single direct movement of this vehicle would then be replaced by several shuttle movements from the transhipment depot by smaller lorries. Vehicle kilometres would then increase by the ratio of the carrying capacities of the large and small lorries. The second situation arises where trunk movements into the transhipment depot are of mixed loads destined for numerous points within the urban area. The break-bulk operation would then be combined with the consolidation of orders destined for the same customer. Under these circumstances, the multiple-drop deliveries of large lorries can be replaced by direct single-drop deliveries by smaller vehicles. While this might still result in a net increase in vehicle kilometres, the increase in traffic would be much less than in the case of the pure break-bulk operation and the cost penalty much lower. The feasibility studies assume that most of the transhipment would be of this break-bulk/consolidation type. As the economic benefits of the consolidation part of the operation increase with the maximum permitted size of the delivery vehicle, they might eventually offset the additional cost of the transhipment operation, though this would require the use of much larger vehicles than contemplated by the feasibility studies.

Low vehicle size limits constrain the opportunities for consolidation and inflate the net cost of the transhipment operation. They also result in a few large lorries being replaced by many small ones. Table 7.2 showed how, in the case of a shop delivery system, reducing the maximum vehicle weight increases the number of vehicles required and the distance they travel (Margason and Corcoran, 1978). As discussed earlier, the trade-off between lorry numbers and sizes poses a serious dilemma for environmentalists.

The concept of peripheral transhipment, as originally envisaged, had other serious shortcomings. Areas in the vicinity of the transhipment depot could be blighted by the concentration of lorry traffic on surrounding roads. There would be a general increase in lorry traffic around the urban periphery as lorries approaching the town from different directions circumnavigated the restricted area to gain access to the transhipment point. Only large towns would be likely to generate enough traffic to justify the establishment of more than one transhipment depot. Fears were also expressed by consignors that these depots would be publicly owned and operated as monopoly concerns by local authorities that had little management experience in this field. Costs might, therefore, be high and service levels well below those to which firms were accustomed. Smith reported a general feeling in the business community that planning authorities had little understanding of the complexity of physical distribution and little appreciation of the disruption peripheral transhipment could cause.

In fact, many firms already operated transhipment systems either for their own exclusive use or on a third-party basis for others. Wytconsult (1975) argued that existing depots could be used more effectively to disaggregate and consolidate loads and, thereby, reduce the environmental impact of lorries in urban areas. The use of existing distribution depots for this purpose would remove the need for an extra transhipment point (Plowden, 1985). The feasibility studies assumed that a peripheral transhipment depot would act as an additional node in the distribution channel and hence increase handling charges. Breaking bulk into smaller vehicles at depots where goods are being stored and handled anyway, eliminates additional terminal costs and delays.

Reliance on existing facilities, however, meant relaxing the assumption that each town should have its own dedicated transhipment depot and delivery system. Most firms with decentralised stockholding systems serve whole regions or subregions from a single depot, and even satellite transhipment depots usually have hinterlands containing many towns and villages. Breaking bulk at these premises would result in small vehicles travelling much longer distances to customers in restricted areas and considerably increase delivery costs. Battilana (1976) examined the effects of firms using small vehicles of 3 ton ULW to deliver supplies to shops in Swindon within their existing distribution systems. He found that this would increase vehicle numbers by 44%, total vehicle kilometres by 63%, vehicle kilometres in urban areas by 36% and fuel consumption by 24%. The Wood Committee (1983), however, in its study of the effects of a heavy lorry ban in London, calculated that the replacement of heavy lorries by vehicles with a maximum weight of 16.26 tonnes would increase delivery costs by only 1%. On the basis of this estimate, they concluded that there would be little demand for special transhipment facilities on the urban periphery. They also argued that when set against such a small cost increment, the environmental improvements likely to accrue from the lorry ban would be relatively inexpensive. The Wood Committee's calculations rest, though, on the dubious assumption that light vehicles would have much higher load factors than the heavy ones they replaced (Cooper and Doganis, 1985)

Where a factory or depot is a long distance from customers in a restricted area, it might be more economical for them to adopt a system of 'direct distribution' employing demountables. This system, which was described more fully in Chapter 4, has much lower terminal costs than conventional transhipment operations, as it requires only an area of hard-standing on which demountable bodies can be parked or transferred between vehicle chasses. The unit of transhipment is the demountable body, rather than the pallet or the case, removing the need for costly depot facilities and minimising the risk of theft and damage. Cooper (1983b) contends that, for many firms, a system of direct distribution employing demountables would be cheaper than using a peripheral transhipment depot or running small vehicles over long distances from their existing premises.

Wider repercussions of lorry controls

Most restrictions on the movement of lorry traffic are likely to increase distribution costs. It is generally assumed that these higher costs can be passed on to the consumer in higher prices, and that the resulting price increases will be so marginal that the aggregate level of consumer demand and pattern of expenditure will be unaffected. In theory, therefore, the public should pay a little more to reduce its exposure to lorry traffic and firms' profitability should remain intact. The reality is neither so simple nor so equitable. In marketing channels dominated by a few large retailers, small suppliers may lack the bargaining power to make the necessary price adjustments and hence suffer a loss of profitability. In extreme cases, firms might stop distributing their goods in restricted areas, reducing the degree of consumer choice. The high cost of servicing branch stores within these areas can also encourage retailers to decentralise their operations and run counter to the efforts of planning authorities to preserve the viability of town centre retailing. On the other hand, the removal of heavy lorry traffic can improve the quality of the retail environment and increase its attractiveness to shoppers. A supplier 'trapped' within a restricted area would incur higher transport costs on both inward and outward freight movements and be placed at a disadvantage relative to competitors not similarly constrained. A lorry ban could, therefore, promote the decentralisation of manufacturing and wholesaling from inner urban areas, where unemployment rates are already high. This was a major concern of many contributors to the Wood Inquiry into the banning of heavy lorries in London. The Wood Committee (1983), however, dismissed the 'apocalyptic view' that 'industry would flee the capital'. It argued that transport cost increases resulting from the ban would be too small to have much effect on an economy the size of London's. This somewhat complacent opinion probably underestimates, *inter alia*, the psychological impact of a lorry ban on industrial decision-making behaviour, especially in the case of firms which, for other reasons, are on the verge of relocating or even closing down.

Lorry bans also raise questions about social equity. Sharp and Jennings (1976), for example, assert that the higher cost of distributing goods in a restricted area should be reflected in higher prices within that locality. This would be extremely difficult to implement, though, and much less fair than it at first seems. As most manufacturers employ a system of uniform pricing, there is little relationship between prices and distribution costs anywhere in the country. Furthermore, the imposition of surcharges in areas gaining relief from heavy lorry traffic would merely convert an environmental disadvantage into an economic penalty for the small but significant minority of people seriously troubled by freight traffic.

Chapter ten

Future developments in physical distribution

The revolution in physical distribution management, which began in the late 1950s in the US and slightly later in the UK, is by no means over. Its basic principles of functional integration, cost trade-off and enhanced customer service are still diffusing through industry and commerce. Even among firms at the vanguard of recent developments in physical distribution, the pressure for change remains strong. Management strategies are continually evolving and new technology currently creating major opportunities for cutting costs and upgrading services. Distribution operations must also be regularly adapted to numerous external circumstances over which firms have little or no control, such as government regulations, interest rates, vehicle taxation, fuel prices, road conditions and planning policies. In the US, for example, firms have been modifying their distribution systems to take advantage of the new competitive environment created by the deregulation of road- and rail-freight rates in 1980.

  With so many factors inducing change and firms reacting to these pressures in different ways, forecasting future trends in physical distribution is a daunting task. Two methods of forecasting have been employed in this context. The simpler has involved extrapolating past trends into the future, on the assumption that the various conditions underlying these trends will continue to prevail. Recent experience has shown, however, that extrapolatory forecasts can easily be invalidated by short-term variations in key variables. For example, the sharp increase in interest rates in the early 1980s, accompanied in the UK by the withdrawal of tax relief on stock appreciation, dramatically reversed the previous upward trend in stock levels. Extrapolatory forecasting also lacks credibility when applied to processes that clearly cannot continue indefinitely. The spatial concentration of inventory, for example, must cease when all stock is centralised in a single location. Adams (1981, p.151) demonstrates the absurdity of assuming that road freight will continue to grow 'in perpetuity' by

257

projecting an official, extrapolatory forecast of lorry traffic forward to the year 2205 and estimating that, by then, everyone would have to be a lorry driver!

The second type of forecast is based on an understanding of the factors causing change and a reasoned assessment of how they are likely to vary in the future. This causal approach requires detailed analysis of past trends and relies heavily on the judgement of experts. There have been several attempts by individual authors to predict the future trend in distribution costs by this means (Morrell, 1979; Warner, 1987). Other forecasts have been compiled on the basis of consultation with panels of experts. Some have employed the Delphi technique of circulating questionnaires to respondents several times and allowing them to alter their predictions in the light of other panel members' opinions (Walters, 1976; Gattorna, 1977; McDermott and Stock, 1980; Cranfield School of Management, 1984). Although Delphi forecasts are more credible than the simple projection of past trends, their validity can be undermined by the divergence of expert opinion.

This chapter will focus on some of the major trends in physical distribution, rather than attempt to build up a comprehensive scenario of distribution in the future. Although the developments are considered separately, they are closely inter-related and several mutually reinforcing.

Functional integration

Giving a single department control over the transport, storage and handling of finished goods is only the first stage in a larger process of functional integration (Ballou, 1978). A.T. Kearney have identified two further stages of integration (Bowersox and Daugherty, 1987) (Table 10.1). In proceeding to the second stage, firms link the outward distribution of finished goods with the flow of supplies into the factory and give distribution managers greater say in determining customer service levels. Full integration is achieved with the absorption of other related functions, such as the storage and handling of raw and semi-finished materials, sales forecasting and production planning. This third stage is also characterised by the merging of domestic and international distribution operations. Between 1981 and 1985, the number of American manufacturers at the second and third stages rose from 45 to 58% (Table 10.1), revealing a pronounced trend towards more integrated logistical management. No comparable data are available for the UK, though anecdotal evidence suggests that British manufacturing is following a similar course, though with a time-lag of several years. Once the full supply chain is under unified control, the

Table 10.1   Stages in the integration of logistical activities

	% of firms at each stage	
	1981	*1985*
Stage 1	54	42
Outward deliveries		
Intracompany movement		
Storage of finished goods at depots		
Logistics system planning		
Logistics control and management		
Stage 2	30	38
Customer service		
Order processing		
Management of finished goods inventory		
Storage of finished goods at factory site		
Inbound transport		
Stage 3	16	20
Sales forecasting		
Production planning		
Procurement		
Management of raw material and work in progress stocks		
Logistics engineering		
International logistics		

Source: Bowersox and Daugherty, 1987.

principles of logistics requirements planning (LRP) can be applied to minimise total inventory and lead times, and to maximise the utilisation of logistical resources.

As Bowersox and Daugherty note, little is known about the way in which the organisation of logistics actually evolves. More research is required to establish the optimum sequence in which logistics-related activities should be combined and to explain why, in some firms, the process of integration is obstructed. Managerial inertia, inadequate strategic planning, poor communication and a lack of data can all prove major inhibiting factors. An increasing number of firms are relying on the expertise of outside consultants to help them reorganise their logistical management.

Growing concern for customer service

Although the distribution literature has emphasised the importance of customer service for over 20 years, many firms have only recently begun to appreciate its full potential, often while formulating, for the first time, explicit marketing and distribution strategies. As Westwood (1981, p.80) explains, 'The starting point for any distribution

259

reappraisal by a company must be service level'. Several factors have helped to press this message home. Industrial and trade customers are now demanding shorter and more reliable lead times to enable them to reduce stock levels. It has become increasingly common for vendors to appraise suppliers' delivery performance and to take it into account in trade negotiations. Research by Sterling and Lambert (1987) has shown that the quality of the physical distribution service can be an important source of competitive advantage, particularly in trades where products are becoming more homogeneous and price differentials narrowing (Christopher, 1986).

An increasing number of firms are also abandoning the long-accepted principle that all customers should receive a uniform standard of service. Efforts are now being made to tailor the quality of service to the particular wishes of individual customers, in recognition of the fact that some will be prepared to accept a lower-quality service in return for larger discounts, while others will pay more for a superior service. In developing a variable service policy, firms must explore individual customer preferences, as done by Gilmour (1977) in the case of the Australian scientific instrument industry. On the basis of such *customer service audits*, markets can be segmented and different customer groups offered service 'packages' that match their specific needs and expectations. By then varying prices in line with the costs of servicing particular accounts, suppliers not only ensure greater fairness, but can also capture sales from competitors whose customer service is less flexible. The adoption of a variable service policy, nevertheless, complicates the management task and can make it more difficult to operate distribution facilities efficiently. Clarkson and Macleod (1987) argue that the logistical relationship between supplier and customer is essentially strategic and should be compatible with the wider objectives of their respective businesses.

Inventory reduction

We are at present in an era of inventory reduction whose origins can be traced back to the development of computer-based MRP systems in the 1960s. In its early stages, attention focused on ways of minimising stocks of industrial inputs before and during the production process. In some sectors, particularly the motor assembly and electrical engineering industries, the application of the just-in-time (JIT) principle has virtually eliminated stocks of component parts at the point of production (Hall, 1983). The downward pressure on finished goods inventory has so far been less intense, though it is steadily increasing. With the extension of MRP into DRP and LRP, manufacturers will increasingly subject all types of inventory to the same strict discipline. Distributors, too, have been tightening their stock control to release working capital, improve cash flow and reduce storage requirements in warehouses and shops. Between the last quarter of 1979 and the second quarter of 1983 the ratio of retailers' stocks to sales declined by 12% and since then has remained fairly stable (Central Statistical Office, 1987b). Most large retailers believe that there is considerable scope for further stock reduction (Simpkin *et al.*, 1987). Cecil-Wright (1987) contends that shortening product life cycles and the new opportunities created by EPOS and EDI systems 'combine to make the distributive trades a very exciting field for the application of JIT'. Rushton (1984, p.10) believes that we are witnessing the development of a 'flow society' in which 'stocks and buffers are being reduced, or even eliminated, in favour of continuous flows from producer to consumer'.

Over the past decade, financial conditions have been unusually conducive to a decline in inventory levels. In the UK, the sharp rise in real interest rates and withdrawal of tax relief on stock appreciation in the early 1980s induced widespread destocking. It was also demonstrated in 1980-1, particularly in the US (Beman, 1981), that firms with low inventories are better able to withstand the rigours of economic recession. Inventory reduction has not simply been a temporary response to adverse economic circumstances, however. Inventory management has undergone a fundamental change and there is unlikely to be a reversion to previous practices. On the contrary, the development of more flexible systems of manufacturing and future improvements in the collection of sales data, transmission of orders, demand forecasting and delivery reliability should enable firms to cut stocks even further.

The suppression of inventory levels is naturally affecting other aspects of the logistical system. It is promoting the growth of express freight services and increasing the volume of goods moved in small consignments (Moskall, 1984; Anderson and Quinn, 1986). Manufacturers are forming closer relationships with smaller numbers of suppliers and carriers to secure the inward flow of supplies against disruption. In order to keep supply lines short, many American manufacturers are strengthening ties with local suppliers and some have encouraged distant suppliers to relocate their operations nearer the assembly plant (Estall, 1985). Mayer (1984), nevertheless, cautions firms against becoming obsessive in their drive to reduce stocks and allowing the trade-off between inventory and other logistical costs to become unbalanced.

Externalisation of the distribution function

Physical distribution is increasingly becoming a specialist service that manufacturers and retailers purchase from outside agencies rather than organise themselves. Contract distribution is now a major growth industry in the UK and predicted to be one of the main sources of new employment over the next few years (Rajan and Pearson, 1986). Participants in a Delphi forecasting exercise in 1983 unanimously agreed that the swing from own-account to dedicated contract distribution would continue, with the latter increasing by between 8 and 25% by 2003 (Cranfield School of Management, 1984). Since 1983, however, the change-over to contract services has gathered momentum, partly as a result of the phasing out of capital allowances between 1984 and 1987, and is now likely to exceed the Cranfield prediction by a considerable margin. Allowance must also be made for the increased use of contractors on a common-user basis.

Contract distribution is likely to become more attractive for several reasons. First, concentration in the distribution industry is creating large organisations capable of offering a wider range of services, greater geographical coverage and the option of buying out own-account operations. Second, as physical distribution becomes more capital intensive, a declining number of manufacturers and retailers appear willing to divert the necessary resources into this ancillary activity to keep up with new technology. Advances in information technology are meanwhile making it possible for them to exert similar control over the day-to-day running of a contract distribution service as over an own-account system (Quarmby, 1985). Many retailers now accept that they should 'concentrate their efforts on moving data, not lorries' (Rudd, 1987). Third, contractors are putting greater effort into marketing their services and tailoring them to clients' wishes (Marr, 1984).

Distribution contractors have considerable scope for expanding their sphere of operations. Some, such as the National Freight Consortium, have already diversified into consultancy and are helping clients plan their distribution systems. They could also have an important role to play in the development of electronic data interchange (EDI), acting as computerised clearing houses for the exchange of orders and invoices between retailers and their suppliers. Lowfield Distribution has already moved in this direction by joining Tradanet. Cooper *et al.* (1987) envisage the development of integrated contract distribution systems on an international scale, though within Europe this will have to await the deregulation of international haulage and relaxation of customs control. It has also been suggested that contractors may soon be prepared to assume ownership of the goods they handle, relieving clients of the need to invest capital in inventory and perhaps achieving tighter stock control (*Motor Transport*, 1 August 1987, p.4). Such a move would blur the distinction between contractors and wholesalers, though, unlike the latter, contractors would not buy and sell goods on their own account and would, therefore, avoid the associated trading risks.

Technological development

The application of currently available technology promises to transform many aspects of physical distribution. Over the next few years, advances in information technology and materials handling are likely to have the greatest impact.

Information technology

Sweeping improvements are currently being made to the way distribution data are collected, communicated and processed.

1. *Data collection.* Distribution operations have been notoriously difficult to monitor and control because they involve the movement of large numbers of separate units at different levels of aggregation, ranging from individual products through cases and pallet loads to vehicles. For example, a hypermarket can sell several million items a week, while a large grocery distribution centre might have around 1 million cases in stock and a weekly throughput of 300-400,000 cases. The laser scanning of bar codes on cases and products now greatly facilitates their monitoring and sorting at various points in the distributive channel, feeding information directly into a computer. The installation of scanning equipment at EPOS terminals in shops allows retailers to monitor sales continuously and thereby improve sales forecasting and stock management. In 1985, only around 1% of the packaged goods sold in the UK were handled by EPOS terminals, though this proportion is forecast to rise to 50% by 1990 and 70% by 1995 (Wolfe, 1987). A range of decision support systems (DSS) are now available to convert raw data captured by EPOS systems into the sort of information management required to regulate the physical flow of goods through the distribution channel. To exploit fully the benefits of EPOS, though, many retailers and suppliers still need to increase the responsiveness of their physical distribution operations to short-term fluctuations in sales.

   Within warehouses, electronic equipment is gradually reducing the need for conventional clerical work. *Portable data entry terminals* (PDET) carried by warehouse operators or mounted on fork-lift trucks relay stock location data to and from a computer creating what De Groof (1985) calls a 'paperless warehouse environment'.

It will soon be possible to track vehicles as they travel across the road network using either ground-based systems of *automated vehicle identification* (AVI) or *radio-determination satellite services* (RDSS). The former use roadside sensors to identify passing vehicles and relay information about their location, weight and speed to a central computer (Davies, West and Schmitt, 1986). While such systems may assist vehicle fleet management, their main use is likely to be in the enforcement of weight and speed restrictions and in the calculation of road-user charges. Unlike ground-based AVI, satellite-based systems can track vehicles continuously, provide navigational guidance and transmit messages between vehicles and a control centre. They will offer a much more effective means of supervising a freight transport operation, but at considerably greater expense.

2. *Communication*. Rapid progress is being made in establishing computer links within and between firms, through which logistical data can be exchanged. A prerequisite for the establishment of electronic links between firms has been the acceptance of standard protocols, such as the British ANA's Tradacoms, which ensure that all intercompany communication adheres to a similar format. Rapid progress has been made in the development of international EDI standards.

The number of firms using EDI to send orders, invoices and other messages is approximately doubling each year (*Guardian*, 13 April 1987). At the end of 1987, around 420 firms were connected to the British Tradanet system, the vast majority of them in the clothing, building/DIY and grocery trades. It is forecast that by 1993 the 'Tradanet community' will embrace some 5,800 firms (ICL, 1987). Manufacturers and retailers are currently the main participants in EDI systems, though wholesalers are also increasingly using them to consolidate and expand their businesses (Sparks, 1987). The pharmaceutical wholesaler, Vestric, for example, increased its market share by supplying 2,000 retail customers with computer terminals and having them relay stock data and orders electronically to its own central computer (Economist Intelligence Unit, 1985). In addition to any marketing advantage it confers, EDI shortens order lead times, reduces paper work, improves the accuracy of order documentation, accelerates cash flow and generally helps firms to manage their stockholding and delivery operations more efficiently.

3. *Data processing*. Physical distribution is becoming ever more dependent on computers. As the hardware has become cheaper in real terms, less cumbersome and easier to use, the use of computers in distribution planning and management has become commonplace. There has meanwhile been a veritable explosion in distribution software, with the number of packages available in the UK increasing from 25 in 1975 to around 340 in 1987 (Willmott, 1987). The vast majority of these packages are concerned with order processing and stock control, reflecting the dominant uses of computers generally within distribution. There has, nevertheless, been an increasing demand for software to support decision making in other areas, such as vehicle scheduling, vehicle fleet management and warehouse location. Most of the currently available software focuses on particular aspects of a distribution system, analysing and optimising them in isolation. A new generation of computer packages has recently been developed, however, which can simulate an entire logistical system and take full account of functional interdependence. Unlike many earlier attempts to model logistical systems, these simulations can be continuously updated, drawing information about sales, stock levels, vehicle capacity and so on from existing on-line computer systems. The use of these packages, in what Slater (1986b) calls 'computer aided logistics management' (CALM), helps firms both to design wide-ranging strategies and to assess the repercussions of smaller-scale changes, such as the closure of a depot or the raising of minimum order size. These packages are already becoming essential planning tools for firms integrating the management of logistical functions.

Computers are also helping manufacturers assess the profitability of selling goods through particular intermediaries and making it possible to calculate the overall profitability of distributing and selling particular products. *Customer profitability analysis* (CPA) (Anandarajan and Christopher, 1987) and the determination of *direct product profitability* (DPP) (IGD, 1987) require the collection and processing of large amounts of distribution data specific to individual customers and products. As manufacturers often deal with hundreds of customers and distributors typically handle thousands of products, the resulting computing requirements are enormous. The idea of DPP was originally canvassed by McKinsey and Co. in the mid-1960s, but firms have only recently acquired the necessary data management systems to put it into practice. The analysis of profitability at a disaggregate level helps firms strengthen their bargaining position *vis-à-vis* customers and suppliers, optimise their product mix and detect weaknesses in their marketing and distribution operations.

Willmott (1987, p.35) contends that distribution software 'has a long way to go before reaching maturity'. The development of fifth-generation computers will permit the introduction of expert systems into distribution management that will be much simpler to use than existing software, yet yield much better results.

To exploit the technical innovations listed above, firms are having to overhaul the management of information. Many are now treating the collection, transmission and analysis of logistical data as an integrated system and placing it under tight central control. Ideally, manufacturers should integrate the information subsystems dealing with procurement, production control and physical distribution (Skjøtt-Larsen, 1977). Christopher (1986, p.101) exhorts firms to undertake an 'audit of information needs' at different levels in the management hierarchy and to weigh up the costs and benefits of handling particular types of information. It has become easier to justify expenditure on the logistical information system (LIS) as the real cost of the relevant equipment and software has declined and the potential benefits, particularly in the areas of inventory control, warehouse management, order processing, vehicle scheduling and customer service, have become more widely recognised. This has led Schary (1984, p.316) to conclude that, 'The information system has probably the greatest potential of any area within logistics'.

Transport

The performance of road and rail vehicles is constantly being improved, with particular emphasis currently being placed on reducing fuel consumption and maintenance requirements. The internal compartmentalisation of lorries is enabling firms, particularly the grocery multiples, to improve space utilisation and to combine the delivery of products with differing temperature and/or handling needs (IGD, 1986a). Recent developments in the field of inter and intramodal interchange are having a significant impact on physical distribution. The UK has so far lagged behind other European countries in exploiting the benefits of *intermodalism*. The introduction of TrailerTrain, two new piggyback systems and road-rail demountable services creates major new opportunities for co-ordinating road and rail operations. Within the road transport sector, demountables will be increasingly used to enhance the flexibility of deliveries and reduce the need for conventional depots.

Warehousing

Warehousing operations are becoming more mechanised with the installation of equipment such as stacker cranes, conveyor belts and automated guided vehicles. In addition to cutting labour costs and facilitating internal stock movement, some of the new equipment allows firms to achieve more efficient use of warehouse space (Ackerman and La Londe, 1980). The new generation of deep-reach and swing-reach trucks, for example, requires narrower aisles than conventional fork-lift trucks and permits the stacking of goods to greater heights (Prabhu and Baker, 1986). As rising land prices and building costs are forcing firms to increase cube utilisation and stacking height, the use of these devices is likely to become more widespread. There has as yet, however, been comparatively little development of high-bay, fully automated warehouses in the UK. In 1982, there was estimated to be around 175 warehouses with *automated storage/retrieval systems* (AS/RS) in the UK, by comparison with over 700 in West Germany and around 3,000 in Japan (Williams, 1982). Many firms regard AS/RS as being too expensive, too inflexible, unsuited to their particular product range and order-picking requirements and incompatible with their existing depots. Some have undoubtedly been discouraged by the failure of early automated warehouses, such as that set up by the Co-operative Wholesale Society at Birtley, to live up to expectation (McKinnon, 1983). In some trades, automated systems have difficulty coping with the present multiplicity of pack sizes, though this problem could be eased with greater standardisation of packaging (Robson, 1985). As Hollander (1980, p.65) observes, 'There is a correct degree of mechanisation to give the right trade-off between investment and return, between flexibility and operating cost. Many over-automated warehouses owned by suppliers and retailers have got this balance wrong'. Although major technical improvements are being made to AS/RS, it is likely that, for the foreseeable future, most firms will prefer to mechanise their warehouses incrementally with cheaper, more flexible equipment (Anon, 1986).

Spatial reorganisation

Arguably the dominant spatial process to affect physical distribution in recent years has been the concentration of inventory in fewer locations. Delphi forecasts have suggested that this process will continue in the UK (Cranfield School of Management, 1984) and the US (McDermott and Stock, 1980) for many years. In the UK, some firms are still readjusting their stockholding systems to the new pattern of accessibility that has developed around the motorway network. The concentration of retail sales in fewer, larger outlets, the increasing consolidation of shop deliveries, the recent spate of company mergers and the transition from own-account to contract distribution are all creating conditions conducive to further inventory centralisation. The liberalisation of freight movement within Europe may also promote the concentration of stock at an international level, making it easier for multinational firms to serve several countries from a single warehouse. With the completion of the Channel Tunnel some foreign manufacturers may close stockholding depots in the UK and supply British customers from a central facility on the European mainland.

The pressure to centralise inventory may, nevertheless, ease as improvements in communications allow firms to centralise the control of inventory, even though it remains physically dispersed (Sussams, 1986). Some large firms would also find it inefficient to concentrate all their stocks at a single location as diseconomies of scale set in once a warehouse exceeds a certain size (Cecil-Wright, 1986). Centralisation increases the vulnerability of a distribution system to industrial action or even bad weather and this may deter some firms from pursuing a policy of stock concentration to its logical conclusion.

Several external factors may constrain the future concentration of stockholding. Competition for sites around what are widely recognised to be strategic locations for distribution are already inflating land values and thus reducing the net benefits of centralising inventory in these areas. In some areas, planning policies may increasingly discriminate against large warehouses and prevent firms from centralising stock in what they deem to be optimal locations.

The centralisation of stockholding may also, in the longer term, be inhibited by substantial increases in the cost of transport. The most likely source of such increases will be the inflation of fuel prices. Fuel, however, accounts for only 10-20% of total lorry operating costs, and its rate of consumption in road transport could be significantly reduced by various energy conservation measures (Cooke, 1981). Schutt (1982) has attempted to assess the effect on the American logistical system of fuel price increases of between two- and twenty-fold. He concludes that sharp increases in fuel prices 'may help to moderate the trend over the last few decades in many firms towards fewer and fewer warehouses', but that 'this economic change is not strong enough to quickly make obsolete good present warehouse configurations in logistics systems that primarily use truck and rail'. He contends that only systems heavily dependent on air freight would require major structural change.

Direct distribution to the home

Over the past 30 years, retailers have been able to shed logistical responsibilities onto consumers. With the introduction of self-service, customers were given the job of picking their own orders. The concentration of retail capacity in fewer, larger outlets has effectively increased their involvement in freight transport by lengthening the last link in the distributive channel from shop to home. Retailers and their suppliers have, as a result, been able to rationalise their transport operations, reducing the number of delivery points and replacing multiple rounds with direct consolidated deliveries. According to recent predictions, these trends may soon be reversed with the development of new types of 'non-store' retailing, which will make it easier for people to 'shop' in the comfort of their homes.

'Armchair' or 'remote' shopping has, of course, existed for many years in the form of mail-order and telephone sales, but its popularity may now increase with the use of new telecommunications systems for direct marketing. The main innovation is videotex, which permits the direct transmission of product information onto domestic television screens (Davies and Edyvean, 1984). By pressing buttons on a key pad, home-based shoppers can find out what merchandise is available, what it costs and when it can be delivered. At present this information is presented only as text, though it will soon be possible for videotex transmissions to incorporate pictures. Consumers wishing to make a purchase from home can do so in one of two ways. Those using teletext services must place their orders separately by telephone or post. Viewdata systems, such as the British Prestel system, on the other hand, are interactive, allowing customers to order goods and arrange for payment directly from their key pad.

Expert opinion is divided on the likelihood of teleshopping catching on. Rosenberg and Hirschman (1980, p.12) see it as a 'virtual certainty that the era of widespread telecommunication shopping is approaching'. Spencer (1980) too believes that, in the longer term, it will render supermarkets and hypermarkets obsolete. Quelch and Takeuchi (1981, p.84), however, doubt that new communication systems 'will accelerate the growth of non-store marketing' or 'soon bring about the predicted revolution in retailing'. Guy (1985) sees only a limited role for teleshopping, while the Economist Intelligence Unit (1984) is distinctly sceptical about its short-term prospects in the UK. A study by the Yankee Group in the US has indicated that teleshopping agencies will have difficulty overcoming people's social and psychological commitment to more traditional forms of shopping (*Financial Times*, 28 February 1985). Market research conducted in the UK by the Henley Centre for Forecasting suggested that only 18% of consumers would be likely to shop for groceries from the home, 16% for clothes and shoes and 12-14% for electrical goods (ICL, 1985).

The recent experience of teleshopping schemes in Britain has certainly not been encouraging. Club 403 in the West Midlands, which was launched in 1983 with financial support from the Department of Trade and Industry and offered the most comprehensive service, has recently withdrawn its grocery range. Telecard Supershop, a teleshopping service for grocery products covering six inner London boroughs closed down after only 18 months. In contrast to these commercial ventures, the 'communal' teleshopping experiment organised jointly by Tesco, the University of Newcastle upon Tyne and the district council, has the essentially social objective of catering for the needs of elderly and disadvantaged citizens who find it difficult, if not impossible, to shop at a superstore or in the town centre (Davies, 1985). Users of this service can place orders through Prestel terminals in local libraries or day centres, and have the goods delivered directly to their homes at no extra cost. Although the scheme is generally considered to have been successful, there are no plans to extend it into other areas.

The development of teleshopping is clearly being constrained in the UK by the relatively small numbers of households with teletext televisions and even smaller minority subscribing to Prestel. By mid-1987, Prestel had a total of only around 70,000 subscribers and many of these were business users. In few areas is there a sufficient density of households with videotex to make teleshopping viable (Bennison, 1985). Prestel-based shopping services have, therefore, tended to become simply an adjunct to traditional mail order, in some cases helping mail-order firms to improve communications with their local agents.

Interest in teleshopping has been stimulated by advances in telecommunications. Many of its proponents have been so mesmerised by these advances that they have overlooked the fact that physically distributing merchandise to peoples' homes remains both difficult and costly. Hiller (1983, p.15) observes that the delivery systems mail-order firms currently use:

> are simply not structured for the huge traffic increases that
> large-scale teleshopping would generate. It would require not
> only the total restructuring of existing routes and systems, but an
> investment of billions of dollars in equipment and personnel -
> resources that we are simply unable to spare either now or in the
> foreseeable future.

Given the problem of organising home delivery, American retailers tend to regard teleshopping 'not as a new form of distribution system...but as a new form of precisely targeted advertising' (Howard, 1985, p.143).

The future potential of teleshopping will largely depend on its ability to capture sales of convenience products, such as groceries, alcoholic drink, toiletries and home cleansing products, which most people at present buy in supermarkets, superstores and hypermarkets. These products account for around 40% of average household expenditure on material goods, but represent a much larger proportion of the weight of purchases transported to the home. Many consumers regard shopping for these products as a tedious and time-consuming chore and would welcome the opportunity to order them directly from home. As most of these products are packaged and standardised, they require little or no inspection prior to purchase. Ironically, these products, which consumers would most like to obtain by teleshopping, are among the most difficult to distribute directly to the home. Each of these product categories contains an enormous number of separate lines, while the typical customer order would probably have to comprise upwards of 30-40 items to make home delivery economical. Assembling orders of this size for thousands or tens of thousands of individual customers would either be highly labour intensive or require a heavy investment in automated order picking systems. Automating the operation would cause problems, though, as grocery and related products vary so much in their dimensions and handling characteristics. As these products tend to be fairly bulky, the average household consignment would be too big for distribution through conventional mail-order channels. New delivery systems would, therefore, have to be developed, using small vans capable of nego-tiating residential streets. Since most convenience goods are sold on a relatively small gross margin, they would be less able to bear the high cost of direct distribution than more expensive comparison goods.

Bartlett (1981), nevertheless, suggests that distributing groceries directly to the home can be roughly three times as profitable as distribution through a conventional supermarket. He calculates that the additional cost of delivery to the home is significantly less than the cost of operating a retail outlet. This cost comparison is suspect on two counts, however. First, it almost certainly underestimates the cost of order picking goods for direct delivery, and, second, it is based on the unrealistic assumption that home deliveries would be made directly from the same warehouse that supplied the supermarket. In practice, the distribution of small consignments to private homes would probably require the insertion of an additional break-bulk point. Home distribution would have to be organised on a smaller spatial scale than the system of supermarket supply because of the greater number of delivery points and more limited vehicle range. If proper allowance were made for order picking and the creation of a second tier of local depots, teleshopping would lose its apparent cost advantage.

It might be possible to organise the direct distribution of convenience goods more economically. By narrowing the range of products available, distributors could ease the burdens of order picking and data processing, but at the expense of customer choice. Consumers could be given financial incentives to adhere to a more efficient pattern of ordering. The main objectives here would be to minimise fluctuations in total demand, maximise the size of individual orders and maximise drop density by concentrating demand in certain areas on particular days. To achieve the last of these objectives, home distributors could adopt nominated-day delivery schemes, similar to those employed by suppliers further back along the distributive channel (see Chapter 7). Avon Cosmetics has successfully used such a scheme in the distribution of orders to the homes of local agents throughout the UK. Restrictions on the ability to purchase what you like when you like would, however, reduce the convenience of teleshopping and hence its appeal to many potential customers.

Distribution costs could also be substantially reduced by delivering orders in consolidated loads to local collection points rather than directly to customers' homes. In addition, this could speed up deliveries and avoid the problem of goods arriving at customers' homes when there was no one there to receive them. It has been suggested that small neighbourhood shops might assume the role of collection points. There has already been a move in this direction with the decision by the Next chain in the UK to use newsagent shops as collection points in its mail-order system. Many prospective teleshoppers would resent having to collect their purchases and not consider this form of distribution sufficiently advantageous to merit a switch from conventional retailing. Redmond (1987), nevertheless, sees considerable potential for this type of shopping in the grocery trade. He advocates the transformation of superstores into warehouses and the return of responsibility for order picking to the retailer. By ordering the weekly groceries from home and collecting them from these warehouses already assembled, the customer would avoid the tedium of 'ferreting among the shelves' (p.41).

Another economy measure, which can enhance the quality of customer service, is the sharing of facilities with conventional retailing and wholesaling operations. This spreads overheads and minimises the risks of investing in new supply systems. All the teleshopping schemes so far established in the UK have relied heavily on existing retail and mail-order systems. Many retailers and mail-order houses have seen teleshopping as supplementing rather than undermining their traditional business.

Table 10.2 Mail-order share of retail sales in selected products, 1984

	% of retail sales
Household textiles, soft furnishings	15.9
Women's, girls', children's and infants' clothing	12.8
Toys, games, cycles, sports and camping equipment	10.4
Men's and boys' clothing	9.5
Footwear	9.2

Source: Business Statistics Office, 1986.

It is easier for comparison and speciality goods like clothing, footwear, jewelry and small household appliances to be distributed to the home. They are less bulky and bought in quantities that permit their delivery by post or parcel carrier. Orders of such products contain relatively few separate items and are of sufficient value to withstand higher delivery costs. People, however, derive more pleasure from shopping for these products in the conventional manner and attach more importance to inspecting them and trying them on before deciding to buy. The fact that existing mail-order services have, nevertheless, been able to secure a significant proportion of total retail sales of these products (Table 10.2), indicates that home-based comparison shopping is widely accepted and indeed enjoyed.

If the direct distribution of comparison goods were significantly boosted by the advent of teleshopping, the delivery systems currently used by mail-order firms could probably cope. The increased throughput and drop density would, in fact, make them more cost-effective. It is likely, though, that several logistical difficulties would arise as teleshopping increased its market share. First, there would be a growth in the volume of goods flowing back through the distributive system. Like existing mail-order firms, 'tele-retailers' would have to give customers the opportunity of returning goods within a trial period. Teleshopping would, therefore, generate a much greater return flow than conventional retailing. As Densmore and Grabner (1972) have pointed out, the reverse movement of merchandise can seriously impair the efficiency of a distribution system. Second, in contrast to the present situation where users of mail-order catalogues tend to buy from a single firm, teleshopping will make it easier for consumers to purchase goods from many different suppliers. If each of these suppliers organised home deliveries independently, there would be a 'multitude of uncoordinated movements' in residential areas (Guy, 1982). This would create a need for local 'community depots' where orders destined for the same household could be consolidated (Foster, 1981). These depots would be too small and dispersed to support stockholding and order picking functions, but they could also serve as break-bulk points for convenience goods despatched from more distant warehouses. Third, the intrusion of increasing numbers of delivery vehicles into residential areas would reduce environmental quality and the level of road safety. Some relief would be offered by the consolidation of deliveries at community depots and by the use of electrically powered vehicles, but many local amenity groups would still resist a sharp increase in direct distribution to the home.

In the much longer term, vehicular deliveries to people's homes could be replaced by the movement of goods in pneumatic capsules through underground pipelines (James, 1980). Such a system would have low operating costs, low energy consumption and, once constructed, be totally unobtrusive. Several pneumatic capsule pipelines are already in existence, carrying mail bags, for example. Experimental projects in the UK, the US and the Soviet Union have indicated that they could have much wider application (Burns, 1985). Their main disadvantages are the high capital cost of laying the pipeline and the environmental disruption this causes. Both factors will naturally discourage their installation in existing urban areas, but present less of an obstacle in new settlements being developed on greenfield sites. Plans were, in fact, drawn up in the early 1970s for an underground delivery system below the new Czechoslovakian town of Etarea on the outskirts of Prague (Čělechovsky, 1972). Incoming retail supplies were to be collected at a large 'central storage complex' and from there distributed by underground trains to 14 district centres. Consumers could either travel to their local centre to obtain goods or have them delivered to their homes along pneumatic pipelines. The system was also designed to handle the return flow of household refuse.

Pneumatic pipelines offer the very distant prospect of physical distribution systems being not only conceptually and managerially integrated, but also mechanically integrated. Merchandise could then be retrieved from a warehouse shelf, loaded into a capsule and blown through a pipeline to a customer's home in a single, fully automated operation. Such a system was envisaged by E.M. Forster (1949) in his short story *'The Machine Stops'*. He portrayed it as part of a nightmare vision of the future. The more technocratically inclined may consider it to be utopian. For the present, however, those responsible for the planning and management of physical distribution must contend with the problems posed by more humble technology.

Bibliography

Ackerman,K.B. and La Londe,B.J.(1980) 'Making Warehousing More Efficient', *Harvard Business Review*, March/April, pp.94-102

Adams,J.G.U.(1981) *Transport Planning: Vision and Practice*, Routledge and Kegan Paul, London

Alderson,W.(1950) 'Marketing Efficiency and the Principle of Postponement', *Cost and Profit Outlook*, 3

—— (1954) 'Factors Governing the Development of Marketing Channels' in R.M.Clewett (ed.), *Marketing Channels for Manufactured Products*, Irwin, Homewood, pp.5-34

Alexander,M.(1969) 'Introduction' in J.Schorr, M.Alexander and R.J.Franco (eds), *Logistics in Marketing*, Pitman, New York, pp.3-16

Allcock,R.E.(1980) 'Containers Trail Behind', *Transport*, 1, 5, 61-3

American Marketing Association (1967) *A New Approach to Physical Distribution*, New York

Anandarajan,A. and Christopher,M.C.(1987) 'A Mission Approach to Customer Profitability Analysis', *International Journal of Physical Distribution and Materials Management*, 17, 7, 55-68

Anderson,D.L.(1986) *Logistics Data Interchange: An Emerging Competitive Weapon for Shippers*, Temple, Barker and Sloane, Lexington

—— and Quinn,R.J.(1986) 'The Role of Transportation in Long Supply Line Just-in-Time Logistics Channels', *Journal of Business Logistics*, 7, 1, 68-88

Anon (1986) 'Automated Warehousing: Opting for the Evolutionary Approach', *Retail and Distribution Management*, 14, 4, 49-53

Armitage,A.(1980) *Report of the Inquiry into Lorries, People and the Environment*, HMSO, London

Artle,R. and Berglund,S.(1959) 'A Note on Manufacturers' Choice of Distribution Channels', *Management Science*, 5, pp.460-71

Aspinwall,L.V.(1958) 'The Characteristics of Goods and Parallel Systems Theories' in E.J.Kelly and W.Lazer (eds), *Managerial Marketing: Perspectives and Viewpoints*, Irwin, Homewood, pp.434-50

Association of Metropolitan Authorities (1980) *Road and Rail Freight: A Study Group Report*, London

Atkins,R.J. and Shriver,R.H. (1968) 'A New Approach to Facility Location', *Harvard Business Review*, May/June, pp.70-9

Attwood,P.R.(1971) *Planning a Distribution System,* Gower, London

Baker, M.J. (1985) *Marketing Strategy and Management*, Macmillan, London

Ballou,R.H.(1968) 'Dynamic Warehouse Location Analysis', *Journal of Marketing Research*, 5, pp.271-6

—— (1973) 'Improved Stock Location in the Physical Distribution Channel', *International Journal of Physical Distribution*, 3, 5, 332-40

—— (1978) *Basic Business Logistics*, Prentice-Hall, Englewood Cliffs

Barber,N.C.F.(1976) 'The Martian Viewpoint: A Dispassionate Look at PDM Today', *Retail and Distribution Management*, 4, 4, 53-5

—— and Payne,L.S.(1976) *'The Distribution Company's Role in Retailing'*, paper presented to the CPDM National Conference, London

Barrett,R.S. and Wilkinson,A.E.(1977) 'Drop Size Pricing as a Method of Cost Allocation' in M.C.Christopher and D.Ray (eds), *Costing in Distribution: Problems and Procedures*, MCB Publications, Bradford

Bartels,R.(1976) 'Marketing and Distribution are Separate', *International Journal of Physical Distribution*, 7, 1, 22-9

Bartlett,R.L.(1981) 'Electronic Home Shopping', *Progressive Grocer*, 60, 9, 84-8

Battilana,J.A.(1976) *The Cost of Using Light Vehicles for Town Centre Deliveries and Collections*, Lab. Report no.710, TRRL, Crowthorne

—— and Hawthorne,I.H.(1976) *Design and Cost of a Transhipment Depot to Serve Swindon Town Centre*, Lab. Report no.741, TRRL, Crowthorne

Baugham,C.J.(1979) *Public Attitudes to Alternative Sizes of Lorry - A Study in a Residential Area*, Suppl. Report no.509, TRRL, Crowthorne

——, Hedges,B. and Field,J.(1983) *A National Survey of Lorry Nuisance*, Suppl. Report no.774, TRRL, Crowthorne

Baumol,W.J. and Vinod,H.D.(1970) 'An Inventory-Theoretic Model of Freight Transport Demand', *Management Science*, 16, pp.413-21

Baxter,J.(1981) 'Local Optima Avoidance in Depot Location', *Journal of the Operational Research Society*, 32, pp.815-19

Bayliss,B.T.(1973) *Demand for Freight Transport*, Round Table no.20, European Council of Ministers, Paris

—— and Edwards,S.L.(1970) *Industrial Demand for Transport*, HMSO, London

Beasley,J.E.(1982) 'Computer-Based Road Maps', *International Journal of Physical Distribution and Materials Management*, 12, 4, 52-6

Beattie,D.W.(1973) 'Improving the Structure of a Distribution System', *Operational Research Quarterly*, 24, 3, 353-63

Beckman,T.(1949) 'A Critical Appraisal of Current Wholesaling', *Journal of Marketing*, 14, pp.307-16

Beman,L.(1981) 'A Big Pay-off from Inventory Controls', *Fortune*, 27 July, pp.76-80

Benheddi,A. and Pitfield,D.E.(1980) 'Industrial Heterogeneity and Spatial Hierarchy in Multi-regional Freight Generation Models', *Environment and Planning* A, 12, 787-97

Bennison,D.(1985) 'Domestic Viewdata Services in Britain: Past Experience, Present Status and Future Potential', *Environment and Planning* B, 12, 2, 151-64

Bevington,T.(1979) 'Small Distribution Warehouses: Are They the Right Answer?', *Retail and Distribution Management*, 7, 2, 65-9

Bloom,G.F.(1983) 'Industry Co-operation: Key to Productivity in Physical Distribution', *International Journal of Physical Distribution and Materials Management*, 13, 7, 5-16

Botham,R.(1980) 'Regional Development Effects of Road Investment', *Transportation Planning and Technology*, 5, pp.97-108

Bott,K. and Ballou,R.H.(1986) 'Research Perspectives in Vehicle Routeing and Scheduling', *Transportation Research A*, 20, 3, 239-43

Bowersox,D.J.(1969) 'Locational Analysis' in J.Schorr, M.Alexander and R.J. Franco (eds), *Logistics in Marketing*, Pitman, New York, pp.45-59

—— (1972) 'Planning Physical Distribution Operations with Dynamic Simulation', *Journal of Marketing*, 36, pp.17-25

—— (1978) *Logistical Management*, 2nd edn, Macmillan, New York

—— (1983) 'Emerging from the Recession: The Role of Logistical Management', *Journal of Business Logistics*, 4, 1, 21-34

—— , Smykay,E.W. and La Londe,B.J.(1968) *Physical Distribution Management: Logistics Problems of the Firm*, Macmillan, New York

—— and Daugherty,P.J.(1987) 'Emerging Patterns of Logistics Organisation', *Journal of Business Logistics*, 8, 1, 46-60

Braithwaite,D. and Dobbs,S.P.(1932) *The Distribution of Consumable Goods: An Economic Survey*, Routledge, London

Breyer,R.(1934) *The Marketing Institution*, McGraw-Hill, New York

British Railways Board (1963) *The Reshaping of British Railways* (The Beeching Report), HMSO, London

—— (1987) *Annual Report and Accounts 1986-7*, London

Brouwer,T.A.(1971) 'Evolution of the Physical Distribution Concept: A Case History', *International Journal of Physical Distribution Management*, 2, 1, 33-6

Bruning,E.R. and Lynagh,P.M.(1984) 'Carrier Evaluation in Physical Distribution Management', *Journal of Business Logistics*, 5, 2, 30-47

Bryant,P.W.(1975) *Chichester Town Centre Interchange Report: An Environmental Assessment*, West Sussex County Council Planning Dept, Chichester

Buchan,K.(1978) *The Development of Lorry Routeing in England and Wales*, Freight Transport Information Service, London

—— (1985)Paper presented to the Seminar '*Towards a Rational Approach to Freight Distribution in London*', London Centre for Transport Planning, London

Buchanan,C. and Partners (1986) *Warehouse Development Trends*, Department of the Environment, London

Buck,D.(1985) 'Using a Third Party to Solve Transport and Distribution Problems', *Logistics Today*, 4, 4, 11-19

Bucklin,L.P.(1960) 'The Economic Structure of Distribution Channels' in

M.L.Bell (ed.), *Marketing: A Maturing Discipline*, American Marketing Association, Chicago, pp.379-85

—— (1962) 'Retail Strategy and the Classification of Consumer Goods', *Journal of Marketing*, 27, pp.50-5

—— (1965) 'Postponement, Speculation and the Structure of Distribution Channels', *Journal of Marketing Research*, 2, pp.26-31

—— (1972) *Competition and Evolution in the Distributive Trades*, Prentice-Hall, Englewood Cliffs

Burns,A.(1985) Paper presented to the Seminar *'Towards a Rational Approach to Freight Distribution in London'*, London Centre for Transport Planning, London

Burns,L.D.,Hall.R.W.,Blumenfeld,D.E. and Daganzo,C.F.(1985) 'Distribution Strategies that Minimize Transportation and Inventory Costs', *Operations Research*, 33, 3, 469-90

Burt,M.E.(1972) *Roads and the Environment*, Lab. Report no.441, TRRL, Crowthorne

Business Statistics Office (1986) *Retailing 1984*, SDO 25, HMSO, London

Button,K. and Pearman,A.D.(1981) *The Economics of Urban Freight Transport*, Allen and Unwin, London

Buxton,G.(1975) *Effective Marketing Logistics*, Macmillan, London

Cadbury Bros. (1945) *Industrial Record: A Review of the Interwar Years*, Bourneville

Campbell,K.C.(1987) 'Department Store "Quickship" Eliminates Inventory/Improves Customer Service' in J.Williams (ed.), *Proceedings of the 7th International Logistics Congress*, IFS (Conferences) Ltd, Bedford

Cecil-Wright,J.(1986) 'How the Boardroom Can Influence Warehouse Cost', *Retail and Distribution Management*, 14, 3, 67-9

—— (1987) 'Distributing Just-in-Time', *Focus on Physical Distribution and Logistics Management*, 5, 6, 8-9

Čelechovsky,G.(1972) 'Goods Transport in Etarea', *Transportation*, 1, pp.151-73

Central Statistical Office (1977) *National Income and Expenditure 1976*, HMSO, London

—— (1987a) *United Kingdom National Accounts*, HMSO, London

—— (1987b) *Economic Trends*, September, HMSO, London

Centre for Physical Distribution Management (1983, 1984a) *Survey of Distribution Costs: Results of a Study into Current Distribution Costs and Trends in UK Industry*, British Institute of Management, Corby

—— (1984b) 'Survey of Current Practices: UK Exporters to Europe', *Focus on Physical Distribution Management*, 3, 6, 3-5

Centre for Transport Studies (1977) *Third Party Operations for United Biscuits*, Cranfield Institute of Technology, Cranfield

Chapman,J.H.(1980) 'Implications of New Delivery Restrictions' in *Restricting Retail Deliveries: The Lessons to be Learnt*, Unit for Retail Planning Information, Reading

Chentnik,C.G.(1974) 'Fixed Facility Location Techniques', *International Journal of Physical Distribution*, 4, 1, 16-25

Childerley,A.(1980) 'The Importance of Logistics to the UK Economy', *International Journal of Physical Distribution and Materials Management*, 10, 4, 185-92

Chisholm,M. and O'Sullivan,P.(1973) *Freight Flows and Spatial Aspects of the British Economy*, Cambridge University Press, Cambridge

Christensen,L.(1986) 'Argyll Upgrades its Distribution', *Motor Transport*, 6 November, p.8

Christie,A.W.,Bartlett,R.S. and Cundill,M.A.(1973) *Urban Freight Distribution: A Study of Operations in High Street, Putney*, Lab. Report no.589, TRRL, Crowthorne

—— ,Hornzee,R.S. and Zammit,T.(1978) *Effects of Lorry Controls in the Windsor Area*, Suppl. Report no.458, TRRL, Crowthorne

—— and Prudhoe,J.(1980) *Effects of Lorry Controls at Lymm, Cheshire*, Suppl.Report no.566, TRRL, Crowthorne

—— and Hornzee,R.S.(1982) *Dykes Act Lorry Controls: Their Use and Effects*, Lab. Report no.1058, TRRL, Crowthorne

Christofides,N. and Eilon,S.(1969) 'An Algorithm for the Vehicle Despatching Problem', *Operational Research Quarterly*, 20, 3, 309-18

Christopher,M.C.(1971) *Total Distribution: A Framework for Analysis, Costing and Control*, Gower, London

—— (1981) 'Logistics and the National Economy', *International Journal of Physical Distribution and Materials Management*, 11, 4, 1-29

—— (1986) *The Strategy of Distribution Management*, Heinemann, London

—— and Wills,G.S.C.(1974) 'Developing Customer Service Policies', *International Journal of Physical Distribution*, 4, 6, 321-52

—— Schary,P.B. and Skjøtt-Larsen,T.(1979) *Customer Service and Distribution Strategy*, Associated Business Press, London

CIDP Ltd (1975) *The Urban Transhipment Depot: Case Study*, Wokingham

Civic Trust (1979) *Heavy Lorries: Nine Years On*, London

—— (1983) *Bypasses and the Juggernaut: Fact and Fiction*, London

Clarke,C. and Wright,J.W.(1964) 'Scheduling of Vehicles from a Central Depot to a Number of Delivery Points', *Operations Research*, 12, pp.568-81

Clarkson,A.H. and MacLeod,A.M.(1987) 'The Strategic Nature of the Customer/Supplier Logistics Relationship' in J.Williams (ed.), *Proceedings of the 7th International Logistics Congress*, IFS (Conferences) Ltd, Bedford

Cleary, E.J. and Thomas, R.E. (1973) *The Economic Consequences of the Severn Bridge and Associated Motorways*, Bath University Press, Bath

Coates,B.E.,Johnson,R.J. and Knox,P.L.(1977) *The Geography of Inequality*, Oxford University Press, Oxford

Coley,R.(1977) 'Siting Depots', *Commerce International*, March, pp.18-19

Collins,M.F. and Pharoah,T.M.(1974) *Transport Organisation in a Great City: The Case of London*, Allen and Unwin, London

Connors,M.M.,Coray,C.,Cuccaro,C.J.,Green,W.K.,Low,D.W. and Markowitz,H.M.(1972) 'The Distribution System Simulator', *Management Science*, 18, 8, B425-53

Cook,R.L. and Burley,J.R.(1985) 'A Framework for Evaluating International Physical Distribution Strategies', *International Journal of Physical Distribution and Materials Management*, 15, 4, 26-38

Cook,W.R.(1967) 'Transport Decisions of Certain Firms in the Black Country', *Journal of Transport Economics and Policy*, 1, pp.325-42

Cooke,P.N.C. (1981) *Energy Saving in Distribution*, Gower, Aldershot

Cooper,J.C.(1978) *Carrying for Others*, Discussion Paper no.7, Transport Studies Group, Polytechnic of Central London, London

—— (1983a) 'The Use of Straight Line Distances in Solutions to the Vehicle Scheduling Problem', *Journal of the Operational Research Society*, 34, pp.419-24

—— (1983b) 'Complying with Area Lorry Bans: An Evaluation of Some Operating Alternatives', *Transportation Planning and Technology*, 8, pp.117-26

—— (1987) 'Physical Distribution in the UK', *International Journal of Physical Distribution and Materials Management*, 17, 4, 1-47

—— and Doganis,R.S.(1982) *The Economics of Demountables in Distribution*, Research Report no.7, Transport Studies Group, Polytechnic of Central London, London

—— (1985) *Area Lorry Bans and Goods Vehicle Operating Costs*, Research Report no.10, Transport Studies Group, Polytechnic of Central London, London

—— and Jessop,A.T.(1983) *Planning Multi-Drop Deliveries*, Discussion Paper no.12, Transport Studies Group, Polytechnic of Central London, London

—— ,Browne,M. and Gretton,D.(1987) *Freight Transport in the European Community: Making the Most of UK Opportunities*, Transport Studies Group, Polytechnic of Central London, London

Cooper,L.(1963) 'Location-Allocation Problems', *Operations Research*, 11, pp.331-43

—— (1976) 'An Efficient Heuristic Algorithm for the Transportation-Location Problem', *Journal of Regional Science*, 16, 3, 309-15

Cooper,M.(1984) 'Cost and Delivery Time Implications of Freight Consolidation and Warehousing Strategies', *International Journal of Physical Distribution and Materials Management*, 14, 6, 47-67

Copeland,M.T.(1924) *Principles of Marketing*, McGraw-Hill, New York

Corcoran,P.J.,Hitchcock,A.J. and McMahon,C.M.(1980) *Developments in Freight Transport*, Suppl. Report no.580, TRRL, Crowthorne

Corley,T.A.B.(1972) *Quaker Enterprise in Biscuits: Huntley and Palmers of Reading*, Hutchison, London

Cranfield School of Management (1984) *Distribution in the Year 2003: Summary of Delphi Forecasts*, Cranfield Institute of Technology, Cranfield

Crawford, A.(1972) 'Problems of Distribution Cost Allocation' in *Strategy and Analysis in Distribution: The Universities Symposium*, CPDM, London

Cundill,M.A. and Hull,P.M.(1979) *Reducing Empty Travel by Goods*

Vehicles, Lab. Report no.876, TRRL, Crowthorne

—— and Shane,B.A.(1980) *Trends in Road Goods Transport, 1962-77*, Suppl. Report no.572, TRRL, Crowthorne

Cunningham,M.T. and Kettlewood,K.(1976) 'Source Loyalty in the Freight Transport Market', *European Journal of Marketing*, 10, 1, 60-78

Czinkota,M.R.(1982) 'Logistics - The Critical Ingredient in International Marketing' in M.G.Harvey and R.F.Lusch (eds), *Marketing Channels: Domestic and International Perspectives*, University of Oklahoma, Norman, OK, pp.24-9

Daganzo,C.F.(1984) 'The Distance Traveled to Visit N Points with a Maximum of C Stops per Vehicle: An Analytical Model and an Application', *Transportation Science*, 18, 4, 331-50

Dantzig,G.B. and Ramser,J.H.(1959) 'The Truck Dispatching Problem', *Management Science*, 6, pp.80-91

Das, C.(1974) 'Choice of Transport Service: An Inventory-Theoretic Approach', *Logistics and Transportation Review*, 10, 2, 181-7

—— (1978) 'A Re-appraisal of the Square Root Law', *International Journal of Physical Distribution*, 8, 6, 331-6

Davies,G.(1984) *Managing Export Distribution*, Heinemann, London

Davies,K. and Sparks,L.(1986) *Mergers, Takeovers and Acquisitions in the Retail Sector*, Working Paper 8604, Institute of Retail Studies, University of Stirling, Stirling

Davies,P.,West,P.O. and Schmitt,L.A.(1986) 'Automatic Vehicle Identification for Transportation Monitoring and Control' in *Research for Tomorrow's Transport Requirements: Proceedings of the World Conference on Transport Research*, Vancouver, May 1986, Center for Transportation Studies, Vancouver, pp.207-24

Davies,R.L.(1985) 'The Gateshead Shopping and Information Service', *Environment and Planning* B, 12, 2, 209-20

—— and Kirby,D.A.(1983) 'Current Trends in UK Distribution Research', *International Journal of Physical Distribution and Materials Management*, 13, 5/6, 68-92

—— and Edyvean,D.J.(1984) 'The Development of Tele-shopping', *The Planner*, 70, 8, 8-10

Davis,G.M. and Brown,S.W.(1972) 'Physical Distribution and Market Structure', *Logistics and Transportation Review*, 8, 1, 88-9

Dawson,J.A.(1973) 'Marketing' in J.A.Dawson and J.C.Doornkamp (eds), *Evaluating the Human Environment*, Edward Arnold, London, pp.134-58

—— (1979) *The Marketing Environment*, Croom Helm, London

—— (1980) *Retail Geography*, Croom Helm, London

—— (1982) *Commercial Distribution in Europe*, Croom Helm, London

—— and Kirby,D.A.(1979) *Small Scale Retailing in the UK*, Saxon House, Farnborough

De Groof,D.(1985) 'The Paperless Warehouse Concept - Fords Europe: A Case Study', *Focus on Physical Distribution Management*, 4, 6, 10-13

Densmore,M.L. and Grabner,J.R.(1972) 'The Effect of Returned Goods on Distribution Performance', *International Journal of Physical Distribution*, 3, 135-43

Department of the Environment (1986) *Commercial and Industrial Floorspace Statistics*, 1981-5, HMSO, London

Department of Industry (1982) *Materials Handling: The Systems Approach*, HMSO, London

Department of Transport (1976) *Transport Policy: A Consultation Document*, vol.2, HMSO, London

—— (1979) *Lorries, People and the Environment: Background Paper*, London

—— (1983) *Railway Finances: Report of a Committee Chaired by Sir David Serpell*, HMSO, London

—— (1985) *The Transport of Goods by Road in Great Britain*, London

—— (1986a) *Transport Statistics: Great Britain, 1975-85*, HMSO, London

—— (1986b) *Road Accidents: Great Britain, 1986*, HMSO, London

—— (1987) *Transport Statistics: Great Britain, 1976-86*, HMSO, London

Dommermuth,W.P. and Cundiff,E.W.(1967) 'Shopping Goods, Shopping Centres and Selling Strategies', *Journal of Marketing*, 31, pp.32-6

Drucker,P.F.(1962) 'The Economy's Dark Continent', *Fortune*, April, 103, 265-70

Dupuit,J.(1844) 'On the Measurement of the Utility of Public Works', *Annales des Ponts et Chaussées*, 2nd series, 8. Reprinted in D.Munby (ed.), *Transport*, Penguin, Harmondsworth, pp.19-57

Economist Intelligence Unit (1980) 'Cash and Carry Wholesaling', *Retail Business*, no.274, London

—— (1984) 'Shopping from Home', *Retail Business*, no.319, London, pp.15-18

—— (1985) 'Distribution Technology', *Retail Business*, no.334, London, pp.17-18

Edwards,R.(1982) *Developments in the Organisation and Location of Intermediate Distribution in Britain*, Unpublished PhD Thesis, University of Newcastle upon Tyne

Efroymson,M.A. and Ray,T.L.(1966) 'A Branch and Bound Method for Plant Location', *Operations Research*, 14, 3, 361-8

Eilon,S., Watson-Gandy,C.D.T. and Christofides,N.(1971) *Distribution Management: Mathematical Modelling and Practical Analysis*, Griffin, London

Elliott,N.R. and Fullerton,B. (1977) 'Transport' in J.W.House (ed.), *The UK Space*, 2nd edn, Weidenfeld and Nicolson, London, pp.360-443

Estall,R.C.(1985) 'Stock Control in Manufacturing: The Just-in-Time System and its Locational Implications', *Area*, 17, 2, 129-33

Euromonitor (1986) *The Small Electrical Appliance Report*, Euromonitor Publications, London

Feldman,E.,Lehrer,F.A. and Ray,T.L.(1966) 'Warehouse Location under Conditions of Economies of Scale', *Management Science*, 12, 9, 670-84

Firth,K.(1976) *The Distribution Services Industry - Operator and User Attitudes*, National Materials Handling Centre, Cranfield

Fisk,G.(1967) *Marketing Systems*, Harper and Row, New York

Ford,R.(1980) 'Wagonload Strategy for the 1980s', *Modern Railways*, August, pp.345-8

Forrester,J.W.(1961) *Industrial Dynamics*, MIT Press, Cambridge, MA

Forster,E.M.(1949) 'The Machine Stops' in *Collected Short Stories of E.M.Forster*, Sidgwick and Jackson, London, pp.115-58

Foster,A.(1981) 'Push-Button Shopping: When Will It Happen?', *Retail and Distribution Management*, 9, 1, 29-32

Foster Committee (1978) *Road Haulage Operators' Licensing: Report of an Independent Committee of Inquiry*, HMSO, London

Foulkes,M.(1979) 'Urban Distribution Problems and Opportunities in the UK', *Retail and Distribution Management*, 7, 5, 61-7

Fowkes,A.E.,Nash,C.A.,Tweddle,G. and Whiteing,A.E.(1987) 'Forecasting Freight Modal Choice', *Focus on Physical Distribution and Logistics Management*, 6, 7, 20-8

Freight (1985), An FTA Guide to Rail Freight Services, December

Fulop,C.(1962) *Buying by Voluntary Chains and other Associations of Retailers and Wholesalers*, Allen and Unwin, London

—— (1964) *Competition for Consumers: A Study of Changing Channels of Distribution*, Allen and Unwin, London

Garratt,M.(1981) 'Unitisation: The Era of Rapid Growth is Over?', *Transport*, 2, 3, 58-9

—— (1984) 'Ferry Operators in Better Shape to Combat Fixed Link Competition', *Transport*, 5, 3, 27-30

Gaskell,T.J.(1967) 'Bases for Vehicle Fleet Scheduling', *Operational Research Quarterly*, 18, 3, 281-95

Gattorna,J.(1977) *Innovative Developments in Distribution: The UK Grocery Trade*, MCB Publications, Bradford

—— (1978) 'Channels of Distribution', *European Journal of Marketing*, 12, 7, 467-512

—— (1983) 'The Total Distribution Concept and its Practical Implications' in J.Gattorna (ed.), *Handbook of Physical Distribution Management*, 3rd edn, Gower, Aldershot, pp.5-13

Gill,L.E.(1979) 'Delivery Terms - Important Element of Physical Distribution', *Journal of Business Logistics*, 1, 2, 60-82

Gillett,B. and Miller,L.(1974) 'A Heuristic Algorithm for the Vehicle Despatch Problem', *Operations Research*, 22, pp.340-9

Gilmour,P.(1977) 'Customer Service: Differentiating by Market Segment', *International Journal of Physical Distribution and Materials Management*, 7, 3, 141-8

GLC (1975) *A Note on Retail Distribution and Options for Reducing Vehicle Mileage*, Background Paper no.9, London Freight Conference, London

Goertz,J.(1976) 'Unitisation in Distribution' in P. van Buijtenen (ed.), *Business Logistics*, Martinus Nijhoff, The Hague, pp.200-17

Gray,R.(1981) 'Modal Choice for Urgent Consignments between Britain and Western Europe', *International Journal of Physical Distribution and Materials Management*, 11, 5/6, 52-63

—— (1982) 'Behavioural Approaches to Freight Transport Modal Split', *Transport Reviews*, 2, 2, 161-84

Guirdham,M.(1972) *Marketing: The Management of Distribution Channels*, Pergamon, Oxford

Guy,C.M.(1982) *Push Button Shopping and Retail Development*, Papers in Planning Research no.49, Dept of Town Planning, UWIST, Cardiff

—— (1985) 'Some Speculations on the Retailing and Planning Implications of Push Button Shopping in Britain', *Environment and Planning* B, 12, 2, 193-203

Hall,P.(ed.) (1966) *Von Thünen's Isolated State*, Pergamon, Oxford

Hall,R.W.(1983) *Zero Inventories*, Dow-Jones/Irwin, Homewood, IL

Hallett,S. and Gray,R.(1987) 'The Operating Costs of Heavy Lorries', *Management Research News*, 10, 3, 14-16

Hammond,R.J.(1951) 'Food vol.1: The Growth of Policy' in K.Hancock (ed.), *The History of the Second World War: UK Civil Series*, HMSO, London

Harris,D.G.(1987) 'Sub-contracting Distribution', *Management Research News*, 10, 3, 12-13

Hasell,B.B. and Christie,A.W.(1978) *The Greenwich-Lewisham Freight Study*, Suppl. Report no.407, TRRL, Crowthorne

Hawes,A.C.(1979) 'The Mechanics of Distribution at BhS', *Retail and Distribution Management*, 7, pp.55-60

Hay,A.(1977) *Linear Programming: Elementary Geographical Applications of the Transportation Problem*, CATMOG no.11, Geo-Abstracts, Norwich

—— (1979) 'The Geographical Explanation of Commodity Flow', *Progress in Human Geography*, 3, 1, 1-12

Hayter,D.M.(1980) *British-European International Road Haulage: An Operations and Costing Model for Driver-Accompanied Services*, PSERC Working Paper N4/80, University of Leicester

—— and Wingfield,M.(1981) *The Economics of Unit Transport Mode Competition on British-European Trade Routes*, Paper presented to the PTRC Annual Conference, University of Warwick

Heckert,J.B. and Miner,R.B.(1953) *Distribution Costs*, Ronald Press, New York

Hemingway,R.(1979) *Distribution Case Studies: Manufacturers*, Institute of Grocery Distribution, Letchmore Heath

Heskett,J.L.(1962) 'Ferment in Marketing's Oldest Area', *Journal of Marketing*, 26, 40-5

—— (1966) 'A Missing Link in Physical Distribution System Design', *Journal of Marketing*, 30, pp.37-41

—— ,Glaskowsky,N.A. and Ivie,R.M.(1973) *Business Logistics*, 2nd edn, Ronald Press, New York

Hewitt,J. and Owen,D. (1976) *Transhipment: A Study of a Major Town*, Paper presented to the Seminar on Transport Policy and Finance, PTRC, London

Highsted,J.(1980) *A Survey of Britain's Freight Forwarding Industry, with Special Reference to Leicestershire and Nottinghamshire*, PSERC Working Paper no. N2/80, University of Leicester, Leicester

—— (1981) *International Rail Freight Transport between Britain and Europe*, PSERC Working Paper no. N2/81, University of Leicester, Leicester

Hill,L.(1978) 'Will Patman be the Answer?', *The Grocer*, 18 March

Hill,S.R.(1966) *The Distributive System*, Pergamon, Oxford

Hiller,T.R.(1983) 'Going Shopping in the 1990s: Retailing Enters the Future', *The Futurist*, December, pp.13-19

Hitchcock,F.L.(1941) 'The Distribution of a Product from Several Sources to Numerous Localities', *Journal of Mathematics and Statistics*, 20, pp.224-30

Hodgkin,K.E. and Starkie,D.N.M.(1979) 'Values of Time in Long Distance Freight Transport', *Logistics and Transportation Review*, 14, 2, 117-26

Hollander,S.(1980) 'Retailers and Suppliers: Higher Productivity through Rational Co-operation', *Retail and Distribution Management*, 8, 4, 61-9

Holton,R.H.(1958) 'The Distinction between Convenience Goods, Shopping Goods and Specialty Goods', *Journal of Marketing*, 23, pp.53-6

House,R.G. and Karrenbauer,J.J.(1978) 'Logistics System Modelling', *International Journal of Physical Distribution and Materials Management*, 8, 4, 189-99

Howard,E.B.(1985) 'Teleshopping in North America', *Environment and Planning* B, 12, 2, 141-50

Howard,K.(1984) 'Inventory Management in Practice', *International Journal of Physical Distribution and Materials Management*, 14, 2, 1-36

ICL (1985) *Retailing Tomorrow: The Impact of Technology on Retailing*, ICL (UK) Ltd Slough

—— (1987) *Retailing Today: Retailers' Experience of Information Technology*, ICL (UK) Ltd., Slough

Ikeda,M.(1974) 'The Progress of PD in Japan', *Transportation and Distribution Management*, 14, 1, 41-4

Industrial and Commercial Techniques Ltd (1966) *Survey of British Industrial Distribution Practices and Costs*, London

Institute of Grocery Distribution (1982) *Grocery Distribution 1982*, IGD, Letchmore Heath

—— (1984) *The Federation of Wholesale Distributors' Trade Statistics*, IGD, Letchmore Heath

—— (1986a) *Retailer Distribution Profiles*, IGD, Letchmore Heath

—— (1986b) *Specialist Distribution Profiles*, IGD, Letchmore Heath

—— (1987) 'Direct Product Profitability', *Distribution and Technology*, April, IGD, pp.1-6

Institute of Physical Distribution Management (1986) *Survey of Distribution Costs: A Study into Current Distribution Cost Trends in UK Industry 1985*, IPDM, Corby

Jackson,G.C.(1985) 'A Survey of Freight Consolidation Practices', *Journal of Business Logistics*, 6, 1, 13-34

Jackson,P. and Brackenbridge,W.(1971) *Air Cargo Distribution*, Gower, London

James,J.G.(1980) *Pipelines Considered as a Mode of Transport: A Review of Current and Possible Future Uses*, Suppl. Report no.592, TRRL, Crowthorne

Jefferys,J.B.(1950) *The Distribution of Consumer Goods*, Cambridge University Press, Cambridge

—— (1954) *Retail Trading in Great Britain: 1850-1950*, Cambridge University Press, Cambridge

Jobson,R.(1976) 'The Case for Own Account' in *Distribution: Is There a Better Way?*, National Materials Handling Centre, Cranfield

Johnson,F. and Wilding,P.(1986) *Monitoring 38 tonne Goods Vehicles*, Statistics Bulletin (86)5, Department of Transport, London

Johnson,J.C. and Wood,D.F.(1982) *Contemporary Physical Distribution and Logistics*, Penn Well, Tulsa

Jones,A.B.(1986) *Financing the Acquisition of Commercial Vehicles*, Ernst and Whinney, London

Jones,B.A.(1982) *The Story of Halfords*, Halfords, Redditch

Jones,F.G.(1976) 'Local Delivery Systems: Vehicle Scheduling by Computer', *Retail and Distribution Management*, 4, pp.49-51

Jones,P.N. and North,J.(1982) 'Unit Loads through British Ports: A Further Revolution', *Geography*, 67, 1, 29-40

Joyce,D.(1982) 'A New Trunking System - Virtue Out of Necessity', *Focus on Physical Distribution Management*, 1, 2, 10-16

Kaminski,P.F. and Rink,D.R.(1984) 'PLC: The Missing Link between Physical Distribution and Marketing Planning', *International Journal of Physical Distribution and Materials Management*, 16, 5, 46-63

Kearney,A.T.Ltd (1978) *Measuring Productivity in Physical Distribution*, National Council of Physical Distribution Management, Chicago

—— (1980) *Improving Productivity in Physical Distribution*, CPDM, London

—— (1981) *Unlocking the Hidden Treasure: Logistics Productivity in Europe*, London

Keegan,W.J.(1980) *Multi-national Marketing Management*, Prentice-Hall, Englewood Cliffs

Khumawala,B.M.(1972) 'An Efficient Branch and Bound Algorithm for the Warehouse Location Problem', *Management Science*, 18, 12, B718-31

—— and Whybark,P.C.(1971) 'A Comparison of Recent Warehouse Location Techniques', *Logistics Review*, 7, 31, 3-19

—— (1973) 'Update on Warehouse Location Techniques', *Logistics and Transportation Review*, 9, 3, 195-206

Kirby,D.A.(1974) 'Shopkeepers Go Shopping', *Geographical Magazine*, 46, 10, 526-8

—— (1975) 'The Small Shop in Britain', *Town and Country Planning*, 43, 11, 496-500

Kirkwood,D.A.(1984) 'The Supermarket Challenge', *Focus on Physical Distribution Management*, 3, 4, 8-12

Kotler,P.(1967) *Marketing Management*, 2nd edn, Prentice-Hall, Englewood Cliffs

Kryter,K.D.(1970) *The Effects of Noise on Man*, Academic Press, New York

Kuehn,A.A. and Hamburger,M.J.(1963) 'A Heuristic Program for Locating Warehouses', *Management Science*, 9, 4, 643-68

Kuhn,H.W. and Kuenne,R.E.(1962) 'An Efficient Algorithm for the Numerical Solution of the Generalised Weber Problem in Spatial Economics', *Journal of Regional Science*, 4, 2, 21-33

La Londe,B.J.(1974) 'Strategies for Organizing Physical Distribution', *Transportation and Distribution Management*, January/February

—— and Dawson,L.M.(1969) 'Pioneers in Distribution', *Transportation and Distribution Management*, June, pp.55-60

—— and Zinszer,P.A.(1976) *Customer Service: Meaning and Measurement*, National Council of Physical Distribution Management, Chicago

—— and Lambert,D.M.(1977) 'A Methodology for Calculating Inventory Carrying Costs', *International Journal of Physical Distribution*, 7, 4, 193-231

Lambert,D.M.(1975) *The Development of Inventory Costing Methodology*, National Council of Physical Distribution Management, Chicago

—— ,Bennion,M.L. and Taylor,J.C.(1983) 'Solving the Small Order Problem', *International Journal of Physical Distribution and Materials Management*, 13, 1, 33-46

Lawrence,R.M. and Pengilly,P.J.(1969) 'The Number and Location of Depots Required for Handling Products for Distribution to Retail Stores in the South East of England', *Operational Research Quarterly*, 20, 1, 23-32

Lewis,H.T., Culliton,J.W. with Steele,J.D.(1956) *The Role of Air Freight in Physical Distribution*, Division of Research, Graduate School of Business Administration, Harvard University, Boston

Lichfield,N. and Assocs (1975) *Chichester Central Area Servicing Scheme: Local Interchange Depot Study*, Final Report, London

—— and Partners, Goldstein Leigh Assocs (1981) *Property Market Effects of the M25*, London

Lin,S.(1965) 'Computer Solutions of the Travelling Salesman Problem', *Bell Systems Technical Journal*, 44, pp.2245-69

Loasby,B.J.(1973) *The Swindon Project*, Pitman, London

Lorries and the Environment Committee (1976) *Report on Transhipment*, London

—— (1979) *Improved Goods Delivery*, London

Lösch, A.(1954) *The Economics of Location*, Yale University Press, New Haven

Lynagh,P.M. and Poist,R.F.(1984) 'Managing Physical Distribution/Marketing Interface Activities: Cooperation or Conflict', *Transportation Journal*, 23, 3, 36-43

McBeath,J.(1985) 'Maximising Own Account Operations', *Logistics Today*, 4, 4, 8-10

McCammon,B.C. and Bates,A.D.(1965) 'The Emergence and Growth of Contractually Integrated Channels in the American Economy' in P.D.Bennett (ed.), *Economic Growth, Competition and World Markets*, American Marketing Association, Chicago, pp.496-515

McClelland,W.G.(1960) 'The Least Cost Level of Stocks and the Rate of Interest', *Journal of Industrial Economics*, 8, pp.151-71

—— (1966) *Costs and Competition in Retailing*, Macmillan, London

McConkey,R.C.(1979) 'The True Cost of Small Drops', *Retail and Distribution Management*, 7, 2, 53-8

McDermott,D.R.(1975) 'An Alternative Framework for Urban Goods Distribution: Consolidation', *Transportation Journal*, 15, 1, 29-39

—— (1980) 'Urban Goods Movement: State of the Art and Future Possibilities', *Transportation Journal*, 20, 2, 34-40

287

—— and Stock,J.R.(1980) 'An Application of the Project Delphi Forecasting Method to Logistics Management', *Journal of Business Logistics*, 2, 1, 1-17

McGinnis,M.A.(1979) 'Shipper Attitudes toward Freight Transportation Choice: A Factor-Analytic Study', *International Journal of Physical Distribution and Materials Management*, 10, 1, 25-34

—— and Corsi,T.M.(1979) 'Are the Modes Really Competitive', *Distribution Worldwide*, September, 39-41

McGoldrick,P.J. and Douglas,R.A.(1983) 'Factors Influencing the Choice of Supplier by Grocery Distributors', *European Journal of Marketing*, 17, 5, 13-27

McKibbin,B.N.(1982) 'CPDM National Survey of Distribution Costs', *Focus on Physical Distribution Management*, 1, 1, 16-18

—— (1983) 'Towards an Integrated Distribution Policy for the House of Fraser', *Focus on Physical Distribution Management*, 2, 1, 26-31

Mackie,P.J. and Urquhart,G.B.(1974) *Through and Access Commercial Traffic in Towns*, Suppl. Report 117 uc, TRRL, Crowthorne

—— and Harding,S.B.(1982) 'The Case for Heavier Goods Vehicles - Some New Evidence', *Traffic Engineering and Control*, 23, 11, 544-6

McKinnon,A.C.(1981a) 'Transport Geography and Physical Distribution' in J. Whitelegg (ed.), *The Spirit and Purpose of Transport Geography*, Transport Geography Study Group, Lancaster, pp.115-34

—— (1981b) *The Historical Development of Food Manufacturers' Distribution Systems*, Occasional Paper no.7, Dept of Geography, University of Leicester

—— (1982) 'Distribution by Rail in the United Kingdom', Geography, 67, 1, 51-4

—— (1983) 'The Development of Warehousing in England', *Geoforum*, 14, 4, 389-99

—— (1984) *The Spatial Organisation of Physical Distribution in the Food Industry*, Unpublished PhD thesis, University of London

—— (1985) 'The Distribution Systems of Supermarket Chains', *Service Industries Journal*, 5, 2, 226-38

—— (1986a) 'Multiple Retailers' Distribution Strategies: Effects on Patterns of Land Use and Traffic Flow', *The Planner*, 72, 7, 16-20

—— (1986b) 'The Effect of the Centralisation of Inventory on the Movement of Freight by Road in the UK ' in *Research for Tomorrow's Transport Requirements: Proceedings of the World Conference on Transport Research*, May 1986, Center for Transportation Studies, Vancouver, pp.646-64

—— (1986c) 'Distributing Imported Goods To British Consumers', *Retail and Distribution Management*, 14, 5, 86-91

—— (1986d) 'The Physical Distribution Strategies of Multiple Retailers', *International Journal of Retailing*, 1, 2, 49-63

—— (1987) 'Recent Trends in Warehousing Development', *Management Research News*, 10, 3, 8-11

—— (1988) 'Physical Distribution Services' in J.N.Marshall *et al.*, *Services and Uneven Development*, Oxford University Press, Oxford

—— and Pratt,A.C.(1984) 'A Nation of Regional Distribution Centres', *Town and Country Planning*, 53, 7/8, 210-1

—— (1985) *Jobs in Store: An Examination of the Employment Potential of Warehousing*, Occasional Paper no.11, Dept of Geography, University of Leicester

McVey,P.(1960) 'Are Channels of Distribution What the Textbooks Say?', *Journal of Marketing*, 24, pp.61-5

Madigan,M.(1980) 'Small Food Firms Fight for Survival', *Retail and Distribution Management*, 8, 5, 59-65

Magee,J.F.(1960) 'The Logistics of Distribution', *Harvard Business Review*, 38, 4, 89-101

—— (1968) *Industrial Logistics*, McGraw-Hill, New York

Magson,D.W.(1979) 'Stock Control When the Lead Time Cannot be Considered Constant', *Journal of the Operational Research Society*, 30, pp.317-22

Maister,D.H.(1976) 'Centralisation of Inventories and the "Square Root Law"', *International Journal of Physical Distribution*, 6, 3, 124-34

Mallen,B.E.(1970) 'Selecting Channels of Distribution: A Multi-Stage Process', *International Journal of Physical Distribution*, 1, 1, 50-6

—— (1973) 'Functional Spin-off: A Key to Anticipating Change in Distribution Structure', *Journal of Marketing*, 37, 3, 18-25

Malloy,B.(1987) 'The Evolution of PD Systems to Meet Market Demands in the Retail Sector', *Focus on Physical Distribution and Logistics Management*, 6, 4, pp.30-1,36

Maranzana,F.E.(1964) 'On the Location of Supply Points to Minimise Transport Costs', *Operational Research Quarterly*, 15, pp.261-70

Margason,G. and Corcoran,P.J.(1978) *Operational Evaluation of the Effects of Heavy Freight Vehicles*, Suppl. Report no.417, TRRL, Crowthorne

Marks, N.E. and Taylor, R.M. (1967) *Marketing Logistics*, Wiley, New York

Marr,N.E.(1984) 'Marketing Freight Transport: The Need for Customer-Orientation', *Service Industries Journal*, 4, 3, 125-32

Martin,A.J.(1983) *Distribution Resources Planning*, Oliver Wright/Prentice-Hall, Englewood Cliffs

Masters,J.M.(1980) 'The Effects of Freight Consolidation on Customer Service', *Journal of Business Logistics*, 2, 1, 55-74

Matz,A.,Curry,O.J. and Frank,G.W.(1967) *Cost Accounting*, South Western, Cincinnati

Mayer,R.R.(1984) 'A Critical Look at Kanban, Japan's Just-in-Time Inventory System', *Management Review*, December, pp.48-51

Mentzer,J.T. and Krishman,R.(1985) 'The Effect of the Assumption of Normality on Inventory Control/Customer Service', *Journal of Business Logistics*, 6,1, 101-20

Menzies,A.F.(1976) 'Manual Load Planning: A Description of Lyons Tea's Own System and Experience' in F.Wentworth (ed.), *Handbook of Physical Distribution Management*, Gower, London, pp.352-64

Mercer,A.(1970) 'Strategic Planning of Physical Distribution Systems', *International Journal of Physical Distribution*, 1, pp.20-5

—— ,Cantley,M. and Rand,G.(1978) *Operational Distribution Research: Innovative Case Studies*, Taylor and Francis, London

Merchant,J.R. and Calcis,C.J.(1974) 'Routeing in a National Distribution Network', *Operational Research Quarterly*, 25, 1, 27-39

Metra Ltd (1974) *Supplying Shopping Areas*, London

Meyer,C.F.(1974) 'A Long Range Selection and Timing Analysis System for Facility Location: Theory', *Operational Research Quarterly*, 25, pp.457

Miehle,W.(1958) 'Link-length Minimization in Networks', *Operations Research*, 6, 2, 232-43

Miklas,W.E.(1979) 'Measuring Customer Response to Stock-outs', *International Journal of Physical Distribution and Materials Management*, 9, 5, 211-42

Miklius,W. and Casavant,K.L.(1975) 'Estimated and Perceived Variability in Transit Time', *Transportation Journal*, 15, pp.47-51

MIL Research Ltd (1986) *The Commercial Vehicle Market: Who, What, Why and Where*, Business Press International, London

Millar,J.L.(1983) 'Distribution in Multiple Food Retailing' in *The Changing Distribution and Freight Transport System in Scotland*, Discussion Paper no.8, Centre for Urban and Regional Research, University of Glasgow, pp.15-19

Mintel (1977) *Food Manufacturers' Distribution Costs*, London

—— (1979) *Grocery Wholesalers*, London

Mole,R.H.(1975) 'An Appraisal of Warehouse Location Models', *International Journal of Physical Distribution*, 5, 1, 31-5

—— (1979) 'A Survey of Local Delivery Vehicle Routeing Methodology', *Journal of the Operational Research Society*, 30, 3, 245-52

—— and Jameson,S.R.(1976) 'A Sequential Route Building Algorithm Employing a Generalised Savings Criterion', *Operational Research Quarterly*, 27, 2, 503-11

Monopolies and Mergers Commission (1981) *Discounts to Retailers*, HMSO, London

Morgan,F.W. and Wagner,W.B.(1978) 'The Back-order: Role and Relevance in Distribution Service', *International Journal of Physical Distribution and Materials Management*, 8, 6, 298-307

Morrell,J.(1979) *The Future of Distribution Costs*, Transfleet Lecture, CPDM, London

Moskal,B.S.(1984) 'Delivering Just-in-Time', *Industry Week*, 1 October, 44-8

Mossman,F.H. and Morton,N.(1965) *Logistics of Distribution Systems*, Allyn and Bacon, Boston

Murphy,G.(1978) *Transport and Distribution*, Gower, London

Nash,C.(1976) *Public versus Private Transport*, Macmillan, London

National Audit Office (1987) *Department of Transport: Regulation of Heavy Lorries*, HMSO, London

National Computing Centre (1968) *Computers in Distribution*, London

NEDO (1967) *Planning Warehouse Locations*, HMSO, London

—— (1971) *Channels and Costs of Distribution in the North East Region*, EDC for the Distributive Trades, HMSO, London

—— (1976) *Industrial Strategies in the Distributive Trades*, EDC for the Distributive Trades, London

—— (1977) *Trading with Europe - Through Transport and the Total Export Concept*, International Freight Movement EDC, London

—— (1985) *Factors Affecting the Cost of Physical Distribution to the Retail Trade*, Unpublished report, EDC for the Distributive Trades, London

Nelson,P.M. and Underwood,M.C.P.(1982) *Operational Performance of the TRRL Quiet Heavy Vehicle*, Suppl. Report no.746, Crowthorne

Newson,P.L.(1978) *The Future Role of Depots in a Distribution Network*, Post Office, London

Newton,W.H.(1985) *Trends in Road Goods Transport, 1973-83*, Research Report 43, TRRL, Crowthorne

Nielsen Researcher (1975) 'Out-of-Stock - Who Loses?', issue no.3, London

—— (1979) Annual Review of Grocery Trading, London

Nilsson,J.(1977) 'Purchasing by Swedish Grocery Chains', *Industrial Marketing Research*, 6, 317-28

Nuttall,C.(1965) 'The Relationship between Sales and Distribution of Certain Confectionery Lines', *Journal of the Market Research Society*, 7, 4, 272-85

O'Brien,J.(1986) '1985 Survey of Distribution Costs', *Focus on Physical Distribution Management*, 5, 3, 16-19

—— (1987) '1986/7 Distribution Cost Survey', *Focus on Physical Distribution and Logistics Management*, 6, 5, 3-6

Oddy,D. and Miller,D.(1976) *The Making of the Modern British Diet*, Croom Helm, London

OECD (1982) *Impacts of Heavy Freight Vehicles*, Paris

Office of Fair Trading (1985) *Competition and Retailing*, London

Ogden,C.(1979) *Buildings for Industry: An Appraisal of the Performance and Supply of User-Ready Industrial Buildings in the Public and Private Sectors*, Centre for Advanced Land Use Studies, Reading

Orlicky,J.(1975) *Materials Requirements Planning*, McGraw-Hill, New York

Ozment,J. and Chard,D.N.(1986) 'Effects of Customer Service on Sales: An Analysis of Historical Data', *International Journal of Physical Distribution and Materials Management*, 16, 3, 14-28

Perl,J. and Daskin,M.S.(1984) 'A Unified Warehouse Location - Routeing Methodology', *Journal of Business Logistics*, 5, 1, 92-111

Perreault,W.D. and Russ,F.A.(1976) 'Physical Distribution Service in Industrial Purchase Decisions', *Journal of Marketing*, 40, pp.3-10

Peters,M.(1986) 'Information Technology in Delivery Control', *International Journal of Physical Distribution and Materials Management*, 16, 3, 45-56

Pettit,D.(1973) *Lorries and the World We Live In*, HMSO, London

Picard,J.(1982) 'Typology of Physical Distribution Systems in Multi-National Corporations', *International Journal of Physical Distribution and Materials Management*, 12, 6, 26-39

Pike,J.(1982) *Major Factors Influencing Modal Choice in the UK Freight Market*, Research Report no.52, Transport Operations Research Group, University of Newcastle upon Tyne

—— and Gandham,B.(1981) *Review of the Commodity Flow Studies (1975-79)*, Research Report no.36, Transport Operations Research Group, University of Newcastle upon Tyne

Pitfield,D.E. and Whiteing,A.E.(1985) 'Forecasting Rail Freight Flows' in K.J.Button and D.E.Pitfield (eds), *International Railway Economics*, Gower, Aldershot, pp.209-33

Plowden,S.(1985) *Transport Reform: Changing the Rules*, Paper no.642, Policy Studies Institute, London

Poist,R.F.(1974) 'The Total Cost vs. Total Profit Approach to Logistics Systems Design', *Transportation Journal*, 14, 1, 13-24

Powell,V.G.(1976) *Warehousing: Analysis for Effective Operations*, Business Books, London

Prabhu,V. and Baker,M.(1986) *Materials Management*, McGraw-Hill, London

Pratten,C.(1985) *Destocking in Recession*, Gower, Aldershot

Price Commission (1978a) *Tate and Lyle Refineries Ltd: Sugar and Syrup Products*, HMSO, London

—— (1978b) *Cadbury-Schweppes Foods Ltd: Grocery Products*, HMSO, London

—— (1978c) *CPC (UK) Ltd*, HMSO, London

Prudhoe,J. and Christie,A.W.(1981) *Effects of a Lorry Control Covering a Rural Area of Hertfordshire*, Suppl. Report no. 679, TRRL, Crowthorne

PSERC (1981) *Trade and Transport Policies and their Impact on the Resource Requirements of the Transport of Freight between the UK and North West Europe (Final Summary Report)*, University of Leicester, Leicester

Quandt,R.E. and Baumol,W.J.(1966) 'The Demand for Abstract Transport Modes: Theory and Measurement', *Journal of Regional Science*, 6, pp.13-26

Quarmby,D.A.(1985) 'Distribution, the Next Ten Years - The Market Place', *Focus on Physical Distribution Management*, 4, 6, 3-6

Quelch,J.A. and Takeuchi,H.(1981) 'Non-Store Marketing: Fast Track or Slow', *Harvard Business Review*, July/August, pp.75-84

Quinet,E.,Marche,R. and Reynaud,C.(1982) 'Trends in Transport Organisation' in *Assessment of Society's Transport Needs: Goods Transport, 9th International Symposium on Theory and Practice in Transport Economics*, European Council of Ministers of Transport, Paris, pp.41-8

Rabiega,W.A. and Lamoureux,L.F.Jr (1973) 'Wholesaling Hierarchies, A Florida Case Study', *Tijdschrift voor Economische en Sociale Geografie*, 64, 4, 226-36

Rajan,A. and Pearson,R.(1986) *UK Occupational and Employment Trends to 1990: An Employer-Based Study of the Trends and Their Underlying Causes*, Butterworths, London

Rand,G.K.(1976) 'Methodological Choices in Depot Location Studies', *Operational Research Quarterly*, 27, 1, 241-9

Ray,D.(1981) 'Assessing UK Manufacturing Industry's Inventory

Management Performance', *Focus on Physical Distribution Management*, no.27, 5-11

—— and Millman,S.(1979) 'Optimal Inventories via Customer Service Objectives', *International Journal of Physical Distribution and Materials Management*, 9, 7, 323-49

—— and Gattorna,J. (with Allen,M.)(1980) 'Handbook of Distribution Costing and Control', *International Journal of Physical Distribution and Materials Management*, 10, 5/6, 207-429

Reader,W.J.(1969) *Hard Roads and Highways: SPD 1918-68*, Batsford, London

Redmond,B.(1987) 'Should Superstores Become Warehouses', *Materials Handling News*, November, p.41

Rees,G.(1969) *A History of Marks and Spencer*, Pan, London

Revzan,D.A.(1966) *Marketing Significance of Geographical Variations in Wholesale/Retail Sales Ratios*, University of California, Berkeley

Rimmer,P.J. and Hicks,S.K.(1979) 'Urban Goods Movement: Process, Approach and Policy' in D.A.Henscher, and P.R.Stopher (eds), *Behavioural Travel Modelling*, Croom Helm, London, pp.525-52

Robinson,D.(1987) 'Year of Reckoning', *Transport*, 8, 4, 162-3

Robson,A.(1982) *An Introduction to Computerised Vehicle Scheduling*, Institute of Grocery Distribution, Letchmore Heath

—— (1985) 'Retail Grocery Distribution', *Focus on Physical Distribution Management*, 4, 1, 8-13

Rosenberg,L.J. and Hirschman,E.C.(1980) 'Retailing Without Stores', *Harvard Business Review*, July/August, pp.103-12

Rosenhead,J.,Elton,M. and Gupta,S.K.(1972) 'Robustness and Optimality as Criteria for Strategic Decisions', *Operational Research Quarterly*, 23, pp.413-31

Rosman,P.F.(1976) *Alternative Sizes of Lorry: Two Investigations of Public Preferences*, Suppl. Report no.210, TRRL, Crowthorne

Ross,R.E.(1972) 'Selection of the Overseas Distributor: An Empirical Framework', *International Journal of Physical Distribution*, 3, pp.83-90

—— (1983) 'Understanding the Japanese Distribution System: An Explanatory Framework', *European Journal of Marketing*, 17, 1, 5-13

Roudier,J.(1976) *Freight Collection and Delivery in Urban Areas*, Round Table no.31, European Conference of Ministers of Transport, Paris

Rowley,G.(1984) 'Data Bases and Their Integration for Retail Geography: A British Example', *Transactions of the Institute of British Geographers*, 9, pp.460-76

Rudd,T.(1987) 'Trends in Physical Distribution' in E.MacFadyen (ed.), *The Changing Face of British Retailing*, Newman, London

Runciman Committee (1958) *Report on Horticultural Marketing*, HMSO, London

Rushton,A.(1979) *Improving Goods Delivery*, National Materials Handling Centre, Cranfield

—— (1984) 'Future Trends in Distribution', *Logistics Today*, 3, 1, 10-13

St Seidenfus,H.(1985) 'Germany' in *Changes in Transport Users' Motivation for Modal Choice: Freight Transport*, Round Table no.69, European

Council of Ministers of Transport, Paris

Saleh,F. and La Londe,B.J.(1972) 'Industrial Buying Behaviour and the Motor Carrier Selection Decision', *Journal of Purchasing*, 8, pp.18-33

Saunders,L.(1978) *Brewing Study*, Unpublished report, GLC, London

Schary,P.B.(1970) 'The Dimensions of Physical Distribution', *Transportation Journal*, 10, 1, 5-16

—— (1984) *Logistics Decisions: Text and Cases*, Dryden Press, New York

—— and Becker,B.W.(1973) 'The Marketing/Logistics Interface', *International Journal of Physical Distribution*, 3, 4, 247-88

—— (1978) 'The Impact of Stock-out on Market Share', *Journal of Business Logistics*, 1, 1, 31-44

—— and Christopher,M.C. (1979) 'The Anatomy of a Stock-out', *Journal of Retailing*, 55, 2, 59-70

Schell,A.M. and Heuer,J.(1983) 'Creating a PD Strategy for a Rebounding Economy', *Canadian Transportation and Distribution Management*, November, pp.79-85

Schutt,J.H.(1982) 'The Effect of Fuel Price on Logistics System Design', *Journal of Business Logistics*, 3, 1, 17-44

Scott,C. and Cooper,J.C.(1985) 'Hub Operations in UK Parcels Distribution', *Logistics Today*, 4, 4, 4-10

Sharp,C.(1970) *The Allocation of Freight Traffic*, Ministry of Transport, London

—— (1971) 'The Optimum Allocation of Freight Traffic', *Journal of Transport Economics and Policy*, 5, pp.344-56

—— (1973) *Living with the Lorry*, University of Leicester, Leicester

—— (1977) 'The Use of Taxes to Reduce Pollution Caused by Goods Vehicles', *Symposium on Heavy Freight Vehicles and Their Effects*, OECD, Paris

—— and Jennings,T.(1976) *Transport and the Environment*, Leicester University Press, Leicester

Shimaguchi,M.(1978) *Marketing Channels in Japan*, UMI Research Press, Ann Arbor

Shipley,D.D.(1985) 'Reseller's Supplier Selection Criteria for Different Consumer Products', *European Journal of Marketing*, 19, 7, 26-36

Shycon,H.N. and Maffie,R.B.(1960) 'Simulation - Tool for Better Distribution', *Harvard Business Review*, 38, 6, 65-75

Simpkin,L.P.,Maier,J. and Lee,W.M.(1987) 'PDM and Inventory Management', *Retail and Distribution Management*, 15, 1, 57-9

Skjøtt-Larsen,T.(1977) 'Integrated Information Systems for Materials Management', *International Journal of Physical Distribution and Materials Management*, 8, 2, 89-99

Slater,A.(1979) 'Vehicle Load Planning', *International Journal of Physical Distribution Management*, 10, 2, 79-99

—— (1980) 'International Marketing: The Role of Physical Distribution Management', *International Journal of Physical Distribution and Materials Management*, 10, 4, 72-91

—— (1982) 'Choice of Transport Mode', *International Journal of Physical Distribution and Materials Management*, 12, 3

—— (1986a) *Handbook of Physical Distribution Software*, Kogan Page, London

—— (1986b) 'A CALM Approach to Distribution', *Focus on Physical Distribution Management*, 5, 4, 8-14

Sletmo,G.K. and Picard,J.(1985) 'International Distribution Policies and the Role of Air Freight', *Journal of Business Logistics*, 6, 1, 35-51

Slijper,M.T.(1977) *Distribution for Exporters*, Management Guide no.6, British Institute of Management Foundation, London

Smith,K.J.G.(1976) *Constraints Affecting the Use of a Public Transhipment Depot*, Research Report no.19, Transport Operations Research Group, University of Newcastle upon Tyne

—— (1977) *Some Implications of Replacing Large by Small Goods Vehicles in Urban Areas*, Transport Operations Research Group, University of Newcastle upon Tyne

—— (1979a) *Distribution in the Confectionery Industry*, Research Report no.31, Transport Operations Research Group, University of Newcastle upon Tyne

—— (1979b) *Distribution in the Record Industry*, Technical Report no.40, Transport Operations Research Group, University of Newcastle upon Tyne

Smykay,E.W.(1964/5) *Physical Distribution, Military Logistics and Marketing Management*, University of Houston Business Review, Winter

Sokel,S.(1987) 'The Return of the Shed', *Estates Gazette*, 17 January, pp.75-6

Soorikian,L.(1974) 'Planning and Control in International Physical Distribution', *Transportation and Distribution Management*, January/February, pp.35-7

Sparks,L.(1986) 'The Changing Structure of Distribution in Retail Companies: An Example from the Grocery Trade', *Transactions of the Institute of British Geographers*, 11, pp.147-54

—— (1987) 'Electronic Communications in Wholesale Distribution', *Focus on Physical Distribution and Logistics Management*, 6, 7, 10-16

Spencer,J.F.(1980) 'Curtains for the Supermarket', *Handling and Shipping Management*, June, pp.58-62

Stacey,N.A.H. and Wilson,A.(1958) *The Changing Pattern of Distribution*, Business Publications, London

Starkie,D.N.M.(1982) *The Motorway Age*, Pergamon, Oxford

Starr,M.K. and Miller,D.W.(1962) *Inventory Control: Theory and Practice*, Prentice-Hall, Englewood Cliffs

Stasch,S.F.(1968) 'Distribution Systems Analysis: Method and Problems', *Logistics Review*, 4, 17, 7-34

Steer, Davies and Gleave Ltd (1987) *Turning Trucks into Trains: The Environmental Benefits of the Channel Tunnel*, Transport 2000, London

Sterling,J.U. and Lambert,D.M.(1987) 'Establishing Customer Service Strategies within the Marketing Mix', *Journal of Business Logistics*, 8, 1, 1-30

Stern,L.W. and El-Ansary,A.I.(1982) *Marketing Channels*, Prentice-Hall, Englewood Cliffs

Stewart,W.(1965) 'Physical Distribution: Key to Improved Volume and Profits', *Journal of Marketing*, 29, pp.65-70

Stock,J.R. and Lambert,D.(1982) 'International Physical Distribution Management: A Marketing Perspective', *International Journal of Physical Distribution and Materials Management*, 12, 2, 1-39

Stoker,R.B.(1978) 'Incorporating Market Characteristics into Physical Distribution Models', *European Journal of Operational Research*, 2, pp.232-45

—— (1980) 'Determining the Optimal Number of Depots in a Physical Distribution System According to Market Characteristics', *European Journal of Operational Research*, 4, pp.107-17

Sussams,J.E.(1969) *Industrial Logistics*, Gower, London

—— (1971) *Efficient Road Transport Scheduling*, Gower, London

—— (1986) 'Buffer Stocks and the Square Root Law', *Focus on Physical Distribution and Logistics Management*, 5, 5, 8-10

Sweet,M.(1984) *Why Centralise? The Benefits and Opportunities of an Integrated Distribution System*, Working Paper 8404, Department of Business Studies, University of Stirling, Stirling

Taylor,A.J.(1982) 'Some Experience in Planning a Distribution System', *Journal of the Operational Research Society*, 33, pp.891-8

Terpstra,V.(1978) *International Marketing*, Dryden Press, Hinsdale, IL

Thomas,A.B.(1980) *Stock Control in Manufacturing Industries*, Gower, Aldershot

Thorpe,D.,Kirby,D.A. and Thompson,P.(1973) *Channels and Costs of Grocery Distribution*, Research Report no.8, Retail Outlets Research Unit, Manchester Business School, Manchester

—— and Shepherd,P.M.(1977) *Some Aspects of Economies of Scale in Food Retailing with Special Reference to Two Superstores*, Research Report no.26, Retail Outlets Research Unit, Manchester Business School, Manchester

Tookey,D.(1971) *Physical Distribution for Export*, Gower, London

Toyota Transport Environment Committee (1977) 'Urban Physical Distribution in Japan: A Survey', *The Wheel Extended* (Toyota Motor Sales Co.), 6, 4, 6-43

Turnbull,P.W.(1985) 'The Image and Reputation of British Suppliers in Western Europe', *European Journal of Marketing*, 19, 6, 39-52

Urquhart,G.B.(1976) *Transhipment of Goods Deliveries to Shops*, Unpublished PhD Thesis, University of Leeds

Van Auken,S.(1974) 'The Centroid Locational Model: A Study in Situational Dependency', *Logistics and Transportation Review*, 10, 2, 149-63

Van Rens,J.H.P.(1985) 'The Netherlands' in *Changes in Transport Users' Motivation for Modal Choice: Freight Transport*, Round Table no.69, European Council of Ministers of Transport, Paris

Vergin,R.C. and Rogers,J.B.(1967) 'An Algorithm and Computational Procedure for Locating Economic Facilities', *Management Science*, 13, 6, B240-54

Voss,C.A. and Robinson,S.J.(1987) 'Application of Just-in-Time Manufacturing Techniques in the United Kingdom', *International Journal of Operations and Production Management*, 7, 4, 46-52

Walker,G.(1986) 'Quoting Delivered Price - A Costly Blind Spot for UK Exporters', *Focus on Physical Distribution Management*, 5, 3, 10-12

Waller,A.G.(1983) 'Use and Location of Depots' in J.Gattorna (ed.), *Handbook of Physical Distribution Management*, Gower, Aldershot, pp.55-78

Walters,D.(1976) *Futures for Physical Distribution in the Food Industry*, Saxon House, Farnborough

Wardroper,J.(1981) *Juggernaut*, Temple Smith, London

Warman,J.(1971) *Warehouse Management*, Heinemann, London

Warner,B.(1987) 'Prospects for Freight Transport and Physical Distribution - Key Issues and Forecasts to 1990', *Focus on Physical Distribution and Logistics Management*, 6, 5, 21-34

Waters,C.D.J.(1984) 'Is UK Manufacturing Industry Really Overstocked?', *International Journal of Physical Distribution and Materials Management*, 14, 5, 5-10

—— (1987) 'Progress and Difficulties in Vehicle Routeing', *Management Research News*, 10, 3, 22-3

Watson-Gandy,C.D.T.(1972) 'A Note on the Centre of Gravity in Depot Location', *Management Science*, 18, 8, B478-81

Watts,D.(1977) 'The Impact of Warehouse Growth', *The Planner*, 63, pp.105-7

Watts,H.D.(1975) 'The Market Area of a Firm' in L.Collins and D.F.Walker (eds), *Locational Dynamics of Manufacturing Activity*, Wiley, London, pp.357-83

Webb,M.H.J.(1968) 'Cost Functions in the Location of Depots for Multiple-Delivery Journeys', *Operational Research Quarterly*, 19, 3, 311-20

—— (1972) 'Relative Performance of Some Sequential Methods of Planning Multiple-Delivery Journeys', *Operational Research Quarterly*, 23, 3, 361-72

Weber,A.(1909) *A Theory of the Locations of Industries*, University of Chicago Press, Chicago

Weigand,R.E.(1963) 'The Marketing Organisation: Channels and Firm Size', *Journal of Business*, 36, pp.228-36

Wentworth,F.(1976) 'The Total Distribution Concept' in F.Wentworth (ed.), *Handbook of Physical Distribution Management*, 2nd edn, Gower, London, pp.3-16

Westwood,J.B.(1975) 'Location Analysis: The Decision Making Process', *International Journal of Physical Distribution*, 5, 1, 22-30

—— (1981) *Integrated Distribution Management: The Formula for the Eighties*, Transfleet Lecture, Transfleet, Stirling

—— (1985) 'Small Firms will Fail', *Commercial Motor*, 5 October, p.4

Whitehead Consulting Group Ltd (1974) *A National Survey of Physical Distribution Management*, London

Willett,R.P. and Stephenson,P.R.(1969) 'Determinants of Buyer Response to Physical Distribution Service', *Journal of Marketing Research*, 6, pp.279-83

Williams,J.(1975) *Food Distribution Costs: Results of an Inter-firm Study of Wholesale Transportation and Warehousing Costs*, National Materials Handling Centre, Cranfield

—— (1982) 'Automated Storage and Retrieval Systems', *Logistics Today*, 1, 2, 4-6

Williams,R.(1981) 'An Automated or Conventional Warehouse?' in the *Proceedings of the 4th International Conference on Automation in Warehousing*, IFS (Conferences) Ltd, Bedford

Willis,R.(1977) *An Analytical Approach to Physical Distribution Management*, Kogan Page, London

Willmott,A.(1987) '1987 Distribution Software Study', *Focus on Physical Distribution and Logistics Management*, 6, 4, 33-6

Wilson,P.R.S.(1979) *The Scope for Consolidation and Other Strategies in the Retail Distribution of Specific Commodities*, Research Report no.30, Transport Operations Research Group, University of Newcastle upon Tyne

Wolfe,A.(1987) 'The Customer of Tomorrow', *Focus on Physical Distribution and Logistics Management*, 6, 1, 20-4

Wood Committee (1983) *Report of the Independent Panel of Inquiry into the Effects of Bans on Heavy Lorries in London*, GLC, London

Wood,W.G.,Suen,L. and Ebrahim,E.(1982) 'Urban Goods Movement Research: Canadian Experience in the Seventies', *Transportation Planning and Technology*, 7, pp.121-33

Wren,A. and Holliday,A.(1972) 'Computer Scheduling of Vehicles from One or More Depots to a Number of Delivery Points', *Operational Research Quarterly*, 23, 3, 333-44

Wytconsult (1975) *Retail Deliveries in Urban Areas and the Relevance of Transhipment*, Doc.602, Wakefield

Yamey,B.S.(1966) *Resale Price Maintenance*, Weidenfeld and Nicolson, London

Author Index

Subject Index